The

END

of the

RAINY

SEASON

The
END
of the
RAINY
SEASON

DISCOVERING MY FAMILY'S
HIDDEN PAST IN BRAZIL

MARIAN E. LINDBERG

SOFT SKULL PRESS | BERKELEY | AN IMPRINT OF COUNTERPOINT

Library of Congress Cataloging-in-Publication Data Is Available

ISBN 978-1-59376-602-3

Soft Skull Press
An Imprint of COUNTERPOINT
2560 Ninth Street, Suite 318
Berkeley, CA 94710
www.softskull.com

Designed by Elyse Strongin, Neuwirth & Associates, Inc.

Printed in the United States of America
Distributed by Publishers Group West

10 9 8 7 6 5 4 3 2 1

For JML

CONTENTS

PART ONE 1

Chapter 1: Ipanema   3

Chapter 2: Steamship to Paradise   7

Chapter 3: Amazon Jungle, Amazon Grave   15

Chapter 4: Don't Cross-Examine Me   21

Chapter 5: The Investigation Begins   29

Chapter 6: Negligence   39

Chapter 7: Scoring on Varick Street   45

Chapter 8: An Introduction to Otto Ulrich   51

Chapter 9: Treasure Maps   55

Chapter 10: A Hard Lead to Follow   65

Chapter 11: Love Lessons   69

Chapter 12: Man on a Mission   74

Chapter 13: That Other Hemisphere   81

Chapter 14: Growing Up   88

Chapter 15: The Groom's Change of Name   95

Chapter 16: What's Wild   101

Chapter 17: The Forest for the Trees   109

Chapter 18: Documents for Christmas—Holy S---!   117

Chapter 19: Fraud in Três Lagoas   123

Chapter 20: Two Chaps in Hats   130

Chapter 21: The Missing Father, One Way and Another   137

Chapter 22: Basket Case   142

PART TWO 153

Chapter 23: Boa Tarde, Brazil 155

Chapter 24: A Change in the Current 163

Chapter 25: The Top of the Heap 167

Chapter 26: Alternative Reality 177

Chapter 27: Green Gold 183

Chapter 28: Ringing in the Old 189

Chapter 29: Good Deeds in Nova Dantzig 193

Chapter 30: Once Upon a Jungle 201

Chapter 31: The Kindness of Strangers, Brazilian Style 205

Chapter 32: A Thin Skull on a Big Man 211

Chapter 33: Small World, Big Ideas 214

Chapter 34: Of Writers and Pilots 219

Chapter 35: A Balcony on the River 225

Chapter 36: Mato Grosso 231

Chapter 37: Howlers 238

Chapter 38: A Platform with the Locals 244

Chapter 39: And Then We Go On 252

Chapter 40: Rio 266

Chapter 41: On a Silver Tray 274

Chapter 42: Home 284

ACKNOWLEDGMENTS 295

PHOTOGRAPHS 297

For sight is the most piercing of our bodily senses,
though not by that is wisdom seen.

PLATO, *PHAEDRUS*

PART ONE

chapter one

IPANEMA

"*QUANDO?*" I ASK the nurse again. When will the only doctor who speaks English arrive?

"*Logo*," the pretty nurse repeats from her desk, but the word has lost all meaning. "Soon" would have been an hour ago. The nurse shifts her gaze and speaks to the woman standing next to me, another person with a problem, so I reassume my position leaning against the wall a few feet away. I'm staying close so that I can eavesdrop—not that I understand fast Portuguese.

My legs feel weak, but I have no choice except to stand. Other people—maybe sicker than me—fill every space on the cement benches lining the small waiting area. It's an oval room with peeling paint, more like the foyer of a decaying mansion than the hospital entrances I'm used to—except for the glass window above the nurse's desk, and her seemingly absolute power.

I feel like I could fall to the floor any minute, but before I faint I want someone to know the reasons why I have come to the Hospital

Espanhol in the Lapa section of Rio de Janeiro: welts on my neck, pus crusting in my ear, aches throughout my body, and a head full of exploding gunpowder. Earlier, in Ipanema, when I touched above my hairline, it seemed as though my very skull had changed shape. There were protrusions of different sizes, some hard, some spongy, like the cells underneath were evolving into something other than gray matter.

Ipanema Beach was to have been the easy finish of my journey through Brazil. Instead, it became the launching pad for a long, slow trip to the hospital.

At home on Long Island, my son used to fill our house with bossa nova when he played "The Girl from Ipanema" on the piano. It was a strange coincidence, his new teacher assigning Brazil's most famous song only a short time after I had wired money to a lawyer in São Paulo.

The teacher knew nothing of my investigation into the life of a relative in Brazil who I had grown up believing was a family hero. The teacher had chosen "Garota de Ipanema" out of the blue, from the thousands of jazz standards he might have suggested my son learn while home from boarding school after his freshman year.

Written in Rio in the early 1960s, "The Girl from Ipanema" is surely one of the finest come-hither compositions, turning the act of listening into a seduction. Whether you aspire to be the "tall and tan and young and lovely" girl walking to the sea or identify with the male singer who longs for the girl's attention, the song with its sighs, lightly tongued consonants, and sensual beat consecrates the exotic, the beautiful, and, most of all, the unattainable.

I was happy to have Tom Jobin's composition played daily in our living room in New York, a mile from the same sea but half a world away from Ipanema Beach. Brazil already commanded so much of my attention I hardly needed the song's charms, but I wasn't immune to them either. Sometimes, while my son practiced the melody and experimented with different chord voicings, I would pretend to dance the samba with our dog, a toy stretched between her mouth and my hand. I'd never been taught samba steps, much less the bossa nova, but the dog and I would slide back and forth on the wood floor, circling in the space by the piano, as I tried to keep our movements in time with the rhythm. It was a silly ritual my son would go along with only if no one was around, but that made it special.

I realize just how special as I lean against the wall of the Hospital Espanhol nearly 5,000 miles from that living room. What seems silly now is the very idea of having left home in pursuit of a dead man I never knew. The fear that's been building inside me has finally broken through, and what I crave most in the world is to hug my son and play tug-of-war with our dog.

These are the things that seem unattainable now.

"Why do you need to go to Brazil?" my son had asked numerous times. In his mind, Brazil was a place that swallowed people, because that's what happened when our namesake Walter Lindberg went to Brazil from New York City in 1929 and never returned. At least my father, eleven years old at the time, had another parent in his life. This wasn't true for my son. Without me, my fifteen-year-old boy would be an orphan.

Still, I had come to Brazil. Against my only child's wishes, knowing virtually no Portuguese, and with a physiological disorder that made me dependent on several medicines and sensitive to external change, I had visited town after town in northern Paraná and ventured into the Amazon and now I could hardly stand.

"*Quando?*" I ask again.

"*Logo.*"

Why had I done it? Why did the search for Walter Lindberg matter so much to me? Whenever a Brazilian asked me that question in the preceding weeks, I managed to give an answer that seemed to satisfy the questioner, but now no answer is good enough.

I only know that a story led me here, a story I could never forget, a story that seemed to explain essential truths in deceptively simple words, not unlike "The Girl from Ipanema."

Before leaving home, I had reviewed many documents. Various Brazilians, including my attorney, unearthed additional information, so I knew in advance of arriving in Brazil that none of the story's elements was as simple as my father had led me to believe. My first days in Brazil had only confirmed that I was heading into unfamiliar territory. Now I was surely there.

I didn't yet know how the story would end, but I had a very clear understanding of its beginning, a voyage taken by a large group of unfortunate people many years before me to parts unknown.

chapter two

STEAMSHIP TO PARADISE

COUNTLESS TIMES THE *Vestris* had steamed across New York Harbor bound for Barbados, Brazil, and Argentina, and every time she had returned. For the 128 passengers who boarded her on Saturday, November 10, 1928, the *Vestris* gave every appearance of offering safe and luxurious transport to exotic points south.

This well-tested steamship was no *Titanic*, foundering on her maiden voyage. Though both ships had been built in Belfast and launched in 1912, the SS *Vestris* had proved sturdy. She was a stalwart in the western Atlantic route, traveling north to south and south to north, except during World War I when the ship carried United States medical personnel to France.

The beauty of the ship's interior was obvious to any eye, and as to those places kept from the passengers' view, such as the engine rooms, the ship's brochure promised that the *Vestris* was "strongly built, provided with every safeguard," and subject to "the most rigid inspection."

It was a glorious afternoon when the vessel left its Hoboken pier, across the Hudson River from New York City. From the upper deck, Henrietta Cubbin bid a silent farewell to the grand city that had been her home for eight years. As she looked back at lower Manhattan in the late-afternoon light, she saw a skyline dominated by the Standard Oil Building on lower Broadway. The ambition was new, building so high into the sky, but the design on top was old—a pyramid inspired by the ancient Greek Tomb of Mausolus.

In two weeks the American passengers were due to observe Thanksgiving, and they, indeed, had much to be thankful for in November of 1928, especially those who lived in New York City, the world's center of architecture, finance, music, and the arts, alive with postwar prosperity—jobs and jazz, fashionable people and cabarets. "New York is on top in everything," an advertisement boasted in *The New Yorker*, then an upstart magazine promising readers entrée to the smart set. Though it would be less than a year before the United States stock market began a 90 percent slide, the aftershocks of which would ripple throughout the world, few on the *Vestris* had reason to harbor anything but optimism.

Around 6 PM, Miss Cubbin felt chilly and summoned a steward to arrange for a chair and blanket. If she tipped well enough, even a second-class passenger could sit outside in comfort and watch the stars. Miss Cubbin, a forty-four-year-old nurse in the Bronx, welcomed the unbounded sky and water. She craved something to distract her mind from the image it held of her mother, pale and sick, lying in bed in the family home in Barbados. There had been a cable telling Miss Cubbin to come quickly. She needed to stop counting the hours, for she could do nothing to hasten her arrival or extend her mother's life.

Inside the *Vestris*, some passengers unpacked in their cabins while others sprawled in the large, first-class lounge that might have been mistaken for an upscale furniture showroom holding a sale on overstocked merchandise: All the sofas and chairs—with rolled arms and ruffled skirts—were covered in the same fabric, a beige and brown floral pattern. There was one type of dark wood table, tall and rectangular, with which each sofa or set of chairs was paired. The furniture groupings were spaced far apart and placed at angles, offering privacy if not variety.

The moldings and friezes around the dazzling central skylight and the elegant mantel above the fireplace offered some diversion from the furniture's uniformity.

Later in the evening, the first-class passengers would be summoned to the dining salon with its carved alabaster walls and crystal chandeliers, after which many would continue their Saturday-night festivities in the mahogany-paneled smoking room with after-dinner drinks, cards, and conversation. Others would listen as the ship's pianist filled the music room with beautiful sounds.

So luxurious were the *Vestris*'s passenger quarters that wood panels adorned even the second-class dining and smoking rooms. According to the brochure issued by the ship's owner, there were "grand staircases and imposing entrance halls ... libraries ... children's nurseries, open-air cafes, gymnasiums" as well as electric lamps, "which not only supply illumination but avoid the creation of artificial heat." The brochure also boasted of the "perfect ventilation secured by modern appliances," which offered "a delightful uniformity of pure atmosphere ... all the way between New York and Argentina."

In first class, the passengers included a Japanese diplomat and his wife, and a top executive of the new Radio Corporation of America. Another was Fred Puppe, traveling to Argentina with his wife and seven-month-old child to take an executive position in Buenos Aires. Two prize-winning automobile racers were on board, en route to competitions in Argentina, accompanied by their wives, one of whom brought along her dog, Speedway Lady. The drivers' racecars sat in the hold far below the first-class rooms, in the ample cargo space adjacent to the crew's quarters above the engine rooms.

Though named after an Italian family of dancers, the *Vestris* was the opposite of lithe. She operated at a time when paying passengers and commercial cargo traveled together, so the passengers and their belongings, from jewelry to racecars, shared the ship with a significant number of large items being transported at the behest of corporations—trucks, Model Ts, tires, engine parts, log-cutting machines, and many other heavy contraptions useful for extracting, using, exporting, and turning a profit on the plentiful natural riches of South America. The ship carried perishable items, too, mostly a great deal of fruit. The cargo weighed over 7,000 tons, and the steel ship itself weighed nearly 10,500 tons gross, including some 1,400 tons of refrigeration equipment for carrying chilled meats.

Such a large ship required many hands to operate: The ship's crew outnumbered its passengers, 197 to 128, for a total of 325 persons on board.

While others dined, Henrietta Cubbin left her deck chair around 7:30 Saturday evening and walked downstairs to her starboard cabin. She felt queasy in her gut. In the cabin, she tried to unpack, but found her wardrobe trunk shaking about. It was difficult to extract her clothes, so she got into bed, though she was unable to fall asleep on account of the ship's rocking.

The wind blew all night from the northeast, and by 5 AM the ship listed two to four degrees to starboard. Fred Puppe noticed the angle around 6 AM when he awakened to feed the baby and found it difficult to move about. When no steward answered his call, he tried to prepare oatmeal on an electric stove in his stateroom, only to find that he could not: The pan bounced and slipped on the burner and wouldn't get hot.

Neither Fred Puppe nor Henrietta Cubbin knew that during the latter part of the night water had begun seeping into the ship from several sources—through an open space in the port half doors, the starboard booby hatch to the firemen's passage, and the starboard ash ejector discharge that led into the stokehold.

Miss Cubbin encountered water when she went into the ladies' lavatory Sunday morning. A steward told her she couldn't go into the bathroom because it was flooded, but she went in anyway, out of necessity, because she felt ill. Then she returned to her cabin and tried to rest, as water seeped under the door along the flooring.

At lunch on Sunday, passengers in the dining rooms had to hold their plates while they ate.

On Sunday afternoon, unbeknownst to the passengers, the captain made a grave miscalculation in an effort to restore the ship's equilibrium, ordering one of the starboard ballast tanks to be pumped out, and then another. As a federal judge would later put it, "the effect of pumping out these tanks was to increase the list instead of reducing it" by removing needed weight from the bottom of the ship and raising its center of gravity.

By Sunday evening, many passengers felt sick as sixty-mile-per-hour winds whipped the ocean and the ship rolled and listed. Seawater carried away the wooden doors of the starboard booby hatch, allowing larger quantities of water to rush into the starboard bunkers. Fred Puppe's wife and child were too ill to leave their room, but when he called the ship's doctor requesting food, the doctor told him it was impossible to cook in the kitchen any longer.

Around 7:30 PM on Sunday, the ship lurched to a list of ten to fifteen degrees.

With water sloshing around in her cabin, Miss Cubbin had even greater difficulty sleeping Sunday night, and when the lights went out she called for the head steward and asked to be moved into a first-class cabin. He told her first class was sold out. Could he at least store her trunk somewhere dry? He regretted that he could not.

Miss Cubbin had taken off her jewelry and put it in her purse under the pillow, but everything she'd brought with her was now immersed in two to three feet of water. She rang for help again and eventually a cabin boy came to her door. She told him she was nervous and afraid, but he told her not to worry because the next day the water would be calm, and they would bail out the cabin and see if they could find her things.

Unlike Miss Cubbin's cabin boy, the judge who later assessed the circumstances did not blame the ship's troubles on the weather. In Judge Henry W. Goddard's words, the storm was in fact "not exceptionally severe." But Miss Cubbin, soothed by the cabin boy's reassurances, crawled into another starboard cabin, finding that it, too, was flooded.

All through the night, despite the water on board and the tilt of the ship, no distress signal was sounded. That was the captain's decision.

The cabin boy was right that the winds abated after midnight, yet by 4 AM Monday, the ship's starboard list had increased to around twenty degrees, and the captain ordered the starboard boiler turned off due to high water. A bucket gang began bailing water from the cross alleyway. Upstairs, Miss Cubbin heard voices in the hall and called to them; a steward and another man helped her out of the flooded starboard cabin into a dry cabin on the port side. She felt weak and fell to the floor on the way; other than a slice of bread and cup of hot water, she had not eaten since arriving at the pier some thirty-six hours earlier.

The ornate dining rooms did the passengers little good on Monday morning. The tables and chairs had slid to the starboard side, and little food was available, only rolls and biscuits for those who hadn't lost their appetites to sickness or fear. The few passengers on the starboard side who remained in their cabins found themselves peering into the ocean out of the bottom part of their windows. The angle of the list was now thirty to forty degrees.

Most passengers congregated on the upper deck, holding onto the port rails so as not to slide off the starboard side. Some passengers, including Miss Cubbin, begged for sips of water. Others lay on their stomachs. Children whimpered. Given the dire circumstances, Fred Puppe was sure the captain had sent a distress signal, and he and others looked anxiously at the horizon, expecting to see rescue ships on their way. In fact, no SOS had been sent. Crew members continued to speak of a passing problem that would soon be corrected, telling passengers to remain calm.

One passenger, a former seaman, descended from the upper deck to fetch life preservers for several women, but he was stopped by a steward, who would not let him pass. "What are you trying to do, frighten them?" the steward asked.

Captain William J. Carey finally sent the SOS just before 10 AM on Monday, off the coast of Virginia. Shortly after that, the list became undeniably extreme. The captain took charge of loading the port lifeboats while the chief officer attended to preparing and getting out the starboard boats, a slippery and difficult process considering that the starboard deck was under water. Because of the severe list, and the late start in loading the lifeboats, some passengers remained on board until the end. For others, the lifeboats proved useless.

At 2:30 in the afternoon the gigantic *Vestris* capsized and sank about 200 miles off the Virginia Capes, her bottom rolling upward like a huge whale and all her tonnage, finery, and cargo crashing into the sea.

According to Judge Goddard, the captain was "the last one to leave the ship passing down her side into the sea just before she sank and was lost." Since he drowned, Captain Carey never learned that the latitude and longitude he'd given with the SOS had been incorrect by some thirty-seven miles. There had been six ships within a radius of one hundred miles and twenty-six within 200 miles, at least some of which could have reached the *Vestris* before she sank had the captain given the SOS several hours earlier and provided the correct compass bearings.

As it was, a total of 114 people lost their lives, sixty-nine passengers and fifty-five crew members.

I was only eight when Daddy first told me about the *Vestris*, so many people drowning in waters teeming with sharks. I listened to him say how lucky it was that Walter Lindberg had decided not to board the ship for what would become her last voyage, electing instead to stay in New York City for a few more days with his wife, my grandmother, and her son, the boy who grew up to be my father.

When Daddy first told me the story, and for a long time thereafter, I did not know or care about the ship's name. I did not know that the ship figured in a major admiralty law case with hundreds of claims, or that its sinking would lead to reforms such as mandatory inspection of lifeboats' ability to disengage from the master vessel and a redesign of life preservers to keep people from drowning facedown while unconscious.

I did, on the other hand, care very much about the sharks. I was a pretty good swimmer, so drowning seemed unlikely, but it was easy to imagine floating in the ocean with no land around and a shark rising up unseen and biting off your leg or arm, returning for seconds and thirds. There were still sharks in Long Island Sound when I was a girl, and sometimes we would drive to the beach at Centre Island only to find a sign—BEACH CLOSED: SHARKS. So sharks weren't only in my father's story. They lurked in the near coastal waters of my own beach. Years later, when the movie *Jaws* inspired a generation of regrettable and unscientifically-based shark-fearing and shark-slaughter, my own anxiety about sharks was already emotionally well-embedded.

But it wasn't only sharks that made the Walter Lindberg story compelling. Eventually, the man who had avoided an untimely death on the

Vestris made it to the Amazon, where the story continued with a possible betrayal, a map worth killing for, and cannibals.

There may not have been beach closures on Long Island due to cannibals, but I did know what betrayal felt like. In fact, it was a betrayal in my own backyard that earned me the right to hear the story of our elusive namesake Walter Lindberg in the first place.

chapter three

AMAZON JUNGLE, AMAZON GRAVE

I HAD NEVER thought our last name strange until a few elementary school classmates came to my birthday party and chased me from the yew hedge to the back-door steps shouting "limburger cheese, limburger cheese." That's what I was named after, they claimed, a really smelly cheese.

"Am not," I retorted, before seeking protection inside the house. In truth, I didn't know where our name came from. Other than Mommy and Daddy, I had never met another Lindberg.

I stood inside the door leading from the garage to the kitchen, listening for the sound of Daddy's car pulling in from the train station. I often did that as a girl, waiting for the life Daddy brought into our quiet house—at six-foot-three, a lot of life. He set his briefcase down and hugged me, and I told him what the mean girls had said. After dinner, in the safety of our wood-paneled den, he assured me that we weren't named after an odiferous dairy product. Quite to the contrary, the name "Lindberg" came directly from a hero.

I listened rapt in my PJs that first evening Daddy deemed me old enough to hear about Walter Lindberg's tragic death. Daddy took his usual position in the big chair next to the bar. I sat across from him on the maroon-patterned sofa. Mommy had her own chair, an upholstered rocker where she read at least two newspapers every evening, but her chair was empty the first time Daddy told me about Walter Lindberg. In classic early 1960s middle-class fashion, Mommy remained in the kitchen washing the dishes, a long process for her on account of the high standards of cleanliness set by the servants in the homes of her pre-marriage years.

I knew virtually nothing about Mommy's wealthy background as I sat in the den with Daddy. I knew only that it was more fun to be with him than helping Mommy clean up.

Daddy explained in his clear voice, commanding enough to run meetings at the Manhattan bank where he worked, though softened in my presence, that Walter grew up in Denmark and then went to Brazil to help build a railroad. That could have put Walter in any number of places where workers sweated and died from fever, infection, and other causes in the early 1900s as they laid tracks used by the rubber industry to transport latex out of the jungle.

Daddy said that Walter moved from Brazil to New York City, where he married Grandma and moved in with her and Daddy. After a while, however, Walter longed to get back to Brazil to explore little-known parts of the Amazon. Daddy told me about the Amazon and I under-stood it to be a special place, big enough, lush enough, and dangerous enough to hold infinite secrets, a mosaic of rivers and jungle spanning nine countries and billions of acres in which animals, plants, and insects abounded, native tribes sharpened spears, and natural riches awaited the brave.

Daddy left no doubt that Walter, a skilled engineer and mapmaker, was among the brave.

After planning the expedition and borrowing money to buy the nec-essary equipment, Walter did not leave New York with his partners. He planned to meet up with the ship that was carrying his partners and gear later in its voyage—in Virginia—after spending a few last days with Daddy and Grandma in New York.

Daddy said Walter and his partners intended to follow a map in their possession showing the location of gold and diamonds deep in the Amazon, and this was the best part of the story as far as I was concerned, a real treasure map in our very own family.

The expedition did not happen as planned on account of the *Vestris* sinking, and consequently Walter stayed on living with Daddy and Grandma. I imagined Grandma, Walter, and Daddy having a fine time in New York while the ship's passengers were flailing about in the ocean, Walter so relieved that his affection for his family had spared him the ordeal of a sinking ship. I knew nothing then of the pain of a lost dream.

"What about the other men, Daddy?" I asked.

At least some of the partners survived, he said, and they went back to Brazil with Walter after he'd saved up enough money to try again. Walter was determined to get to the Amazon and use the treasure map, and sometime after the *Vestris* sank, he did go.

This time, Daddy said, Walter made it into the jungle, but he died there. The explanation given by the men in Walter's party was that Walter had been killed by cannibals, but Daddy said he believed the men traveling with Walter had murdered him to get the treasure map. They were bad men, Daddy said, and greedy.

Even though Daddy said the cannibal account was probably a cover-up, I believed it for the simple reason that if Walter's body was never found, which it wasn't, his being eaten would account for that. Of course, that meant it wasn't really so spectacular to my child's mind that Walter had avoided getting eaten by sharks only to be eaten by humans.

Whatever or whoever killed Walter, the consequence for Grandma was the same: There was something called the "Dead Man's Law," Daddy said, which, in the absence of a dead body, required her to wait seven years before marrying again.

Grandma's next husband was a man free of wanderlust, an affable barber firmly rooted in northern New Jersey, Joseph Hess, whom I grew up calling Grandpa. I knew nothing at first to contradict that he was my actual grandfather. He acted like a grandpa, kneeling to hug me, making me laugh, and bringing me toys on the special occasions when he visited.

I don't remember my parents reading to me, though I am sure that they did. What I remember is Daddy telling me the story of Walter

Lindberg's disappearance. I would wait for him to get home, make his martini at the bar in the den, eat dinner with Mommy and me, and then we would sit in the den and I would ask him to tell me the story again. As I got older, probably to scare me away from teenage temptations, my father would add the detail that the ship's captain had been drunk.

After the first telling, the Walter Lindberg story was often on my mind. My bathroom was down the hall from my bedroom and sometimes, while sitting in a tub full of warm water, I would close my eyes and imagine the water heating up. I figured that cannibals put their prey in boiling water, and I was wondering what it would feel like to boil to death—or would it be better to die by freezing? (As much as I loved summertime heat, I always came out on the side of freezing. I knew how snow felt on the skin, so I figured with freezing you would get numb before any real pain came.)

Daddy shared the story of Walter Lindberg with me alone. He had chosen a time when Mommy was busy to tell it to me the first time, and if I happened to ask him to repeat the story while all three of us were seated in the den, Mommy would stand up from her rocking chair and leave the room. There was always water boiling or another chore that needed doing and she had to go. I noticed this, and found it curious. I didn't understand why she wouldn't stick around for what seemed like the most exciting thing about our family.

Aside from the Walter story, neither of my parents volunteered much information about the past. Most of the time, it seemed that they had taken an extra vow at the altar, to conceal their histories if they ever had a child. I wasn't born until eleven years after their marriage, and they were characteristically mum about why they waited so long.

I had to figure that out myself, the same way I learned most of what I knew or thought I knew about our family: through stealth, research, and careful observation.

There was an oddly shaped room over the garage that my parents did not use, and the room became my retreat as I entered adolescence, my place for listening to music, sewing clothes, and entertaining friends. By that point, I was calling my parents Mother and Dad. No one at the private school they'd sent me to starting in sixth grade called their parents

Mommy and Daddy, so I had asked if we could make an adjustment. Daddy had no problem shifting to Dad, but my mother forbade Mom. My options were Mother or Mama. I chose the former.

There was a door off my new retreat that opened into a long storage area lined with boxes on both sides of a central aisle. The roof was low and pitched, so that one had to stoop or crawl on hands and knees. I knew that some of the boxes contained Christmas decorations, old Halloween costumes, and my childhood school papers. In eighth grade, I started to look through the other boxes. In particular, I was searching for Dad's army uniform. Military-inspired clothes were becoming popular, and when I asked Dad if he had any items from World War II, he told me that whatever had been saved was in the storage area.

I found Dad's army memorabilia, and in the same box were Mother's private-school yearbooks. I hauled the box out of the closet and sat on the floor reviewing its contents. The yearbook from her senior year at Spence School revealed that Mother used to enjoy walking around the Central Park Reservoir and once dreamed of becoming a foreign correspondent, two facts that I might otherwise never have known.

There was also a newspaper clipping in the box, a column by Damon Runyon about Mother's long-deceased father, John William Ryan, a successful men's clothier with several stores in New York City. The headline called my grandfather a "pioneer" for having bought a house in Miami Beach in the early 1920s, and he looked big and imposing and extremely well dressed in the accompanying photo.

I was excited because I, too, aspired to be a journalist. I was already writing for the school newspaper, and I knew that Damon Runyon was a famous reporter. I couldn't believe he had written a column about my very own grandfather. I ran down to the kitchen, clipping in hand, prepared to grill Mother.

Yes, her family spent many winters in Miami Beach when she was growing up, Mother confirmed, removing her rubber dish-washing gloves to take the clipping from me, glance at it, and hand it back.

I never saw the column again.

Years later, Mother swore she had picked the column up from where I left it and put it in the back of a picture frame for safe-keeping, an odd choice, but one that might have withstood the test of time if she could remember which picture. She was quite sure, or so she claimed, that it had been my baby picture, the embarrassing one before my hair grew in, but when we looked the column wasn't there.

Over time, I opened every frame in Mother's possession and spent countless hours in libraries from New York to Miami searching through old newspapers. I wrote letters to several of Damon Runyon's copyright owners, scanned collections of his writing, and spoke to various Miami historians. I never found the column.

My experience with the Damon Runyon column was quite typical: me having an interest in some aspect of family history and trying to satisfy it through the acquisition of facts on my own, seeking a substitute for the adult conversations that never seemed to take place about where we'd come from and who we were.

When it came to family narratives, the only one that had actually been communicated to me was the story of Walter Lindberg.

chapter four

DON'T CROSS-EXAMINE ME

"MY GRANDFATHER DIED exploring the Amazon," I'd say at boarding school, holding out the story like a tray of hors d'oeuvres to any new person who wandered into my life and seemed worthy of a cordial welcome. If someone liked the story, I had supposed, then that someone would like me. Telling the story made me feel exotic, as though what Walter Lindberg did two generations earlier said something about me—that I was adventurous and brave like him.

In my adolescent retelling of the story, I omitted the technical truth that Walter wasn't my actual grandfather any more than the New Jersey barber Joe Hess. This was an easy finesse as my last name matched Walter's, but at some point in high school I did learn that Lindberg wasn't Dad's original surname. Even his first name had been different. Dad spent his early years as Melville Jean DePay, the son of a French Alsatian by the same name who had deserted a German naval ship while it was docked in New York. Although Dad's father and little brother, an infant, perished in the New York City influenza epidemic of 1919, Dad and his

Hungarian mother survived, somewhat miraculously as Eastern Europeans were among those most affected by the disease. It was a few years later that Grandma married Walter Lindberg. When Dad was starting school, Grandma enrolled him as Jean Melville Lindberg, changing his names around to mirror the new man in the house.

Dad had no memories of his Alsatian father, but he described Walter as very tall, skilled, and handsome. Dad said his stepfather exuded charisma. He "took over the room" when he entered—just as he'd taken over my imagination.

Dad seemed to feel about Walter the way a person feels about a genuine father. If anyone had ever accused me of misrepresenting my relation to Walter, that would have been my defense.

People liked the story the way I told it. They wanted to hear more. They asked me to repeat the story to others. They would refer back to it. Some friends called me adventurous, and traced it to my background. I began to fantasize about finding the route that Walter had taken through the Brazilian interior and following it myself.

I never imagined I would find Walter's remains, but when I started to learn about the Amazon getting cleared for cattle ranches and soybean farms, I felt personally affronted, as if thieves had dug up a family grave. I had no idea where Walter's flesh and bones had mixed with other detritus in the rainforest—the new name for tropical jungles beginning in the 1970s—so the whole Amazon seemed like a graveyard. Even if he'd been cannibalized, traces of him were somewhere. It upset me to think that Walter's final resting place either had been or would be disturbed so that a few more people in the world could fill their stomachs with hamburgers.

Yet in college, something new began to happen when I talked about Walter dying in Brazil. I was rising through the ranks of the college newspaper and sometimes, when I told the story, I'd hear myself adding a journalist's attribution phrase such as "according to my father." Thinking about the narrative on my own, I had begun to notice certain illogical aspects. If no one ever found Walter's body, and no one was ever charged with his murder, how did Dad or anyone else know how Walter had died?

I resolved this by telling myself that even though Dad said he did not know the identity of Walter's partners, Grandma may have known one or more of them, and may have heard an account of Walter's demise that she condensed for her son. But if Dad was convinced that turncoat partners had killed Walter, not cannibals, presumably he had gotten that belief from Grandma. Why hadn't I ever heard about a prosecution or at least a police investigation?

By the time I started formulating those questions, Grandma was speechless in a nursing home after suffering a stroke that robbed her of language, so there was no making up for all that I hadn't asked her earlier.

Mother was no help either. She could talk, of course, but declined to. I couldn't get any information about Walter from her, though I never thought she had much.

"Don't cross-examine me," Mother often said when I asked her anything at all, whether about the past or simply to follow up a statement she had made so that I could better understand her meaning. She referred to my questions as cross-examination even back when I disdained lawyers. The rebuke carried a certain irony, considering she was one of the biggest advocates of my becoming an attorney.

Dad wanted that, too. He believed I had a logical mind, like him. There was one anecdote he told of something I'd said as a girl, which he claimed illustrated my logical disposition. It had to do with him driving me to the beach when he was taking time off from work. "How do you like the vacation so far," he said he'd asked me, and I had replied, "What vacation? My days are all like this." Personally, I never thought the story proved great logic so much as flippancy, which morphed easily into the kind of bantering relationship I developed with my father as a young adult.

Senior year of college I slept through the law school entrance exam in defiance of my parents' hopes for my future and instead accepted a reporting job in Buffalo with *The Courier-Express*, the morning newspaper in blue-collar, white-winter western New York. Dad condensed the parental response to this development into one trenchant word conveyed over the phone: "Balls."

Journalism seemed like the perfect field for me. I got money rather than admonishment for asking questions, and there was no shortage of stories or information as at home. I immersed myself in other people's stories and the world around me, covering government, crime, disasters, and environmental degradation, all of which merged toward the end of the 1970s when decades of toxic waste dumping and other pollution were quite literally bubbling to the surface in some neighborhoods, as dogs died and children sickened. The worst site bore the most ironic of names: Love Canal.

Information was what I lived by, and the people I respected were the ones who possessed the most information and used it to solve problems, help people, or correct injustices.

So it was natural that when I finally thought about investigating the Walter Lindberg story in earnest, I approached it as a fact-gathering mission. By then I had left journalism for law school, lured by what I had come to perceive as lawyers' abilities—often even stronger than those of journalists—to get and hold information, and their power—often more decisively exercised than that of elected officials—to effect change.

Fortunately, the journalist's skill set—talking to all sorts of people, reviewing documents, and looking for answers beneath the surface— proved to be good training for a law career.

The first semester of law school I was back under my parents' roof on Long Island, not the house of my childhood, but a newer one. I commuted to Columbia by train, sometimes alongside Dad, who had an executive job in the tower atop Penn Station after retiring from the bank. On the train, I would sit next to him and read a legal decision or the newspaper, as he did. He'd taught me how to fold *The New York Times*, or in his case the *Wall Street Journal*, in quarters so it could be read easily on a train or standing up on the subway.

Working in Buffalo right up to the start of school, I hadn't had time to look for an affordable place to live—no simple matter in New York— and no dorm space was available because my parents' address, now offi- cially mine, was considered too close to the school.

Not since the summer after college, three years earlier, had I lived at home. The house was eerily quiet, my father either out or sitting in the den with the crossword puzzle or a televised golf match, Mother usually busy in the kitchen baking, cooking, or cleaning. Occasionally she com- plained to me that Dad didn't do enough around the house.

Even when my parents both sat in the den, there was little conver- sation unless I prompted it. At dinner, the only meal we ate together,

Mother would race through her food and I started to do so, too, eager to return upstairs to my law books. Better that than argue with Dad or bite my tongue at one of his conservative remarks, usually directed at Jimmy Carter, whose election I'd praised in a letter printed in *The New York Times* a few years earlier.

I'd left a boyfriend in Buffalo and a life full of breaking news, urgent deadlines, and mostly liberal friends. This new living situation was very different. My parents were distant from each other and from me. I felt alone.

When, a few weeks into law school, we first-year students learned how judges' opinions were organized and cross-referenced in books and computerized databases, and received training in online search language, I knew exactly how I wanted to use this newfound tool: to trace Walter Lindberg. He was the family hero, my old connection to my father. I thought it likely that a lawsuit had stemmed from the sinking of the ship, and perhaps any decision rendered might mention either Walter's partners or the equipment they lost.

During my years as a reporter, there had been no escaping the name that came from Walter. "Lindberg" was how I answered the phone. "Lindberg" was what an editor called to get my attention across the newsroom. I eliminated my first name from my byline and used initials: M.E. Lindberg. This was an old journalistic convention, designed to impart an aura of objectivity and omniscience, but being known primarily by my last name also suited a woman in a male-dominated field, concerned with the biases readers sometimes brought to articles that they knew to be written by women.

Though I was by no means famous, I sometimes had occasion to explain where the name came from. I even received a letter once asking if I was related to Captain Jean Lindberg from World War II, my father. In moments such as the one in which I read that letter, my surname seemed to serve its basic function, identifying its holder as part of a group, whether a white family in New York or a Bororo clan in the Amazon.

At other times, my surname proved a source of confusion. I first learned in Buffalo that many equate names including "-berg" with Jewish origins. Such was the case when I called a pizza parlor after coming home from an assignment, placed an order and gave my name, only to have the man on the other end of the phone inform me that I probably wanted the restaurant's other location, the one "near the university." He was referring to the State University of New York at Buffalo, apparently known to harbor a high percentage of people with "-berg" in their names.

Having learned that some people presumed I was Jewish, it was odd during my first week of law school to have a Jewish woman identify me as Scandinavian. She came from Minnesota, where many Swedes and Danes settled years ago, and she knew right away that Lindberg was Scandinavian. She even told me what it meant: "tree on a hill."

Other classmates asked if I was related to Charles Lindbergh, the man who made the first solo flight across the Atlantic in 1927.

Names are supposed to identify us, but as I embarked on a new chapter in my life, I was learning that my last name told the world very little that was true. I wasn't Jewish and I wasn't Scandinavian. I wasn't related to a long line of past Lindbergs in Minnesota, Denmark, or anyplace else. I had no relation, so far as I knew, to any famous aviator or to any living Lindberg in the whole world except my parents. The only true information conveyed by the name was my relationship to them, and thus it was as a kind of present to Dad that I first conceived of researching the heroic phantom of a man whose name we bore.

Giving presents was one thing my family excelled at. We put a lot of time into the birthday and holiday gifts we gave each other, and if the item was wearable, such as a sweater, tie, or piece of jewelry, it would be worn on the next special occasion, so that if my parents and I went out to dinner together to celebrate a birthday, we would usually all be dressed in what had come out of boxes the previous Christmas.

I believed that unearthing more information about a man who had obviously been important to my father would please him like a holiday gift. I also wanted to warm up the cold air in our house. I wanted to feel some of the connection I had felt as a girl, listening in the cozy den to my Daddy tell me about treasure maps, the Amazon, and cannibals.

One autumn weekend, I told Dad about my plan. I walked a few feet into the den, a bigger room than our old den, with wall-to-wall carpeting instead of plank wood floors, but housing the same bar and rows of old books, sets of Dickens and Sir Walter Scott, more than a dozen red-bounded volumes of piano music, Latin and other language dictionaries, and anthologies of the world's great literature and art, most of which had been passed down to Mother by her mother or acquired during Mother's schooling.

Dad was sitting footrest-up in his white leather recliner, sipping a cocktail, as the hushed voice of a golf sportscaster drifted from the television. I stopped next to the large color photograph of our prior house, the house where I'd grown up playing in the large yard, walking in the woods that surrounded the house, and listening to the story of Walter Lindberg. My parents had decided to leave that house after my freshman year of college. There was an energy crisis, and they said they should live closer to stores, the train station, and Dad's country club. I had cried in the car following the moving van. Mother apparently missed the house, too, which is why she had hung a photo of our old house in their new house. I later learned that the old house had been purchased with her inheritance. Dad wasn't making enough at the bank then to afford a two-story shingled house in a new subdivision with two-acre zoning. Now the plot was smaller, less than half an acre.

"What was the name of the ship that your stepfather almost took to Brazil, the one that sank?" I asked from across the room, not wanting to disturb Dad's late-Saturday-afternoon ritual, which usually followed his own round of golf at the club, plus a few rounds of gin rummy and gin drinks.

Dad shifted his eyes from the TV and looked in my direction. There was a slight pause, and then he said, "The *Vestris*. That was the name. V-E-S-T-R-I-S. Why?"

"I was thinking of doing some research," I answered. "They have these computerized legal databases you can search now. Maybe I'll find something."

"Oh" was all he said.

His eyes went back to the television, and I turned to head upstairs to my room. I had gotten the ship's name, but if I had wanted to restore a connection to my father, I had failed. It wasn't entirely his fault. How could he possibly have known how much the story meant to me? I hadn't told him that. All I'd done was ask him a question, which he answered.

His answer, however, was a strong sign that Dad didn't possess a yearning for more information about Walter. His indifference to further inquiry seemed to communicate that if I truly loved my father, then I should go on loving the story of Walter Lindberg as he told it. I loved both of them—Dad and the story—and so I took my cue from him. I dropped the matter. Our professor had warned us about using the library computer system for personal projects, and Dad gave me no reason to violate the rules.

I found myself staying later at school, spending nights with a class-mate, partying on weekends in Manhattan with my old college friends, but I also grew to appreciate the quiet of my parents' house. When I learned to pretend it was a library, I studied well there, discovering that I was more of an academic than I had ever realized. I had left jour-nalism wanting to grapple with issues at a deeper level than thirteen column inches of print allowed, and in law school that was happening. When grades were posted at the end of the first semester, I was pleased. Over winter break, searching for a place to live, I stumbled across a man on West 107th Street moving his belongings into a car and snagged his apartment, a small place I could afford on the second floor of a brownstone.

Much would happen in that apartment, much that was good. I would thrive in law school and begin a career in media and First Amendment law, using my new profession to help members of my old one. I would fall in love, and begin contemplating a family of my own, but a few years later I would lose that love, along with a great many aspects of life that I valued.

My hands-off attitude toward the Walter story would start to change, because it had to. A series of emotional and physical shocks occurred in rapid succession, and I could no longer regard misfortune as something that only happened to others.

When that time came, in my mid-thirties, the story of Walter Lind-berg began to seem like a smoking gun at a crime scene, not something worthy of my devotion. My father's fingerprints were all over the mess, and the mess was my life.

chapter five

THE INVESTIGATION BEGINS

DAD PLUNGED FACE forward into a thin layer of foam, smacking the water and sand like a felled tree. He had misjudged the wave completely. It wasn't coming in. It was going out. I stood behind him on the beach, not sure what to do. His movements were goofy and erratic, yet it didn't seem right to intervene. He was a grown man who had been to the shore plenty of times. Our family vacations almost always involved a beach somewhere on the East Coast, only there hadn't been a family vacation in a long time. Clearly, Dad's bodysurfing skills had suffered.

Earlier in the day, Dad had thrown himself under high, crashing waves, and when I expressed concern about his timing, he told me he was only demonstrating what he used to do in the army at Wrightsville Beach. Waves like this were child's play for him then, he said, but that was in the 1940s, when Dad was young, his body thin, and his back free of pain. Now, the vertigo he'd recently been treated for seemed to be playing tricks on him, making him dive at the wrong time into too little water. He moved himself into a sitting position, letting the water splash on his big belly and long legs, until he sank into the sand and the undertow nearly pulled off his swim trunks.

I watched, still as a piece of driftwood, realizing that I had no idea who this man was and whether he was having fun or trying to kill himself. Then I walked over and put my hand under his arm, coaxing him to stand.

This was the person I adored in childhood, but also the person who had caused me to suffer in the last few years in ways I could have never imagined. He was the person I blamed for setting in motion the series of traumatic events from which I was still reeling, but also the person who had saved my life in the midst of them.

I brought Dad to the towel where Mother was sitting, looking up at us from behind oversized sunglasses as she frowned at the wind. It was my parents' wedding anniversary, which was why I had invited them to the cottage I was renting during August in Bridgehampton, but now I wondered if I had let duty cloud my better judgment. Were they really the people I wanted to spend my weekend with?

Mother handed her husband of forty-six years a towel, and I turned to walk back to the house. I couldn't think of a single thing to say to either of them.

A simple "I felt dizzy" would have helped counteract the image in my mind of a man heedlessly out of sync with himself and the world around him, but Dad offered no such explanation, not even when I raised the subject at dinner. I thought I was being tactful, using a scene from *Tender Is the Night* as a way of discussing Dad's difficulty with the waves. I was in the midst of re-reading the book, and the parallel between Dad's awkwardness and Dick Diver's inability to perform a stunt he used to do—raising a man above his head while on a boat—seemed apt. Mother clamped the discussion shut, saying "don't rub our noses in our age," and that was that. I did not mention that Dick Diver wasn't even old when he tried his trick to impress Rosemary and failed. Age wasn't the point.

Empathy had been my point, empathy that might flow in both directions. I was trying to say to Dad that I knew how it felt not to be able to do what was once so easy for you. Even at less than half Dad's age, I had come to feel diminished every day, ever since a large tumor had been extracted from the base of my brain, where it had consumed my pituitary gland.

I had been trying hard not to complain since the surgery, straining to recover my equilibrium, and perhaps the analogy to Dick Diver was too muted a lament. Early in our relationship, my boyfriend of nearly eight years used to tease me and say I spoke like the aunts in *Remembrance of Things Past*, so subtly as to be easily misunderstood, and Michael might have repeated that observation had he heard me talk about a Fitzgerald character to two people who mainly read newspapers, stock quotes, and recipes. But Michael wasn't at the dinner table that night in Bridge-hampton. He and I had broken up five weeks earlier, ending our dis-cussions—more like a protracted negotiation—over whether to raise a family. It wasn't clear that I could conceive without a pituitary gland, but I had wanted very much to try, yet Dad's persistent interference with the relationship, his continuing lack of acceptance of Michael, the after-effects of my illness, and other circumstances had gotten in the way. Now Michael and I were through.

Renting the cottage, I had thought, would bring consolation and tran-quil days to write as sea sparrows chirped around me, but the day after my father's dive into the sand, my writing transformed into a rampage. Seeing my father's erratic behavior and then enduring an evening when no one would talk about it unlocked something inside me, as though I'd seen my own denial personified and could not abide it any longer.

For the first time, I truly felt the fear I'd suppressed before the oper-ation and all the sadness I'd tried to bury as I learned that removal of the tumor was not the end of a short-term problem, but the beginning of a life-long condition that left me dependent on my own constant vigilance, on self-regulating tricks to mitigate discomfort and prevent dehydration and electrolyte imbalances, and on numerous pharmaceuti-cals taken over the course of each day, which Michael poetically labeled my portable life-support system.

Sitting at the picnic table outside the cottage, journaling my hurtling thoughts as best I could, I felt like never before the horror and shame of another consequence of losing my pituitary gland—the post-operative hallucinations that had me walking around New York City believing I was on speaking terms with God and the Devil. Following the surgery, on my second day back in the law department of the media company where I worked, I'd heard church bells, walked out of the building, tossed my pocketbook into a cardboard box, and headed to St. Patrick's Cathedral, where, at first, I felt at one with the divine, but later grew troubled by the sounds of the angry mob sent by the Devil, waiting outside to get me. When I believed the mob had dispersed, I walked sixty blocks to my apartment on West End Avenue, a two-bedroom co-op I owned, the small law school rental apartment being a thing of the past. I stayed up most of the night pulling books off shelves, full of manic energy, following phrases from my favorite authors where they led me, falling asleep amid a mile of Penguin Classics. I spent the next day sometimes thinking I was an angel, and sometimes that I was Minnie Mouse in the Thanksgiving Day Parade. I also believed that a camera had been placed inside me and was broadcasting live from my private parts to the television audience.

There were actions, too, that the delusions had caused me to take—some of them unspeakably violent, some surprisingly generous—such as giving away all my jewelry to a church in which I'd never set foot, and handing out twenties to homeless men and women instead of the usual dollars or coins. My delusions, bizarre thoughts, and actions were etched into my memory as indelibly as the small white scar was into the skin of my right thigh.

I hadn't gone into the hospital for a head operation expecting to emerge with a scar on my thigh, but the surgeons needed a piece of fat to plug the hole in my head, and that oddness, not disclosed until a bespectacled orderly showed up with a razor the morning of the operation, was a harbinger of all the bizarre consequences to follow, ones that nearly killed not just me, but Mother, too.

Michael had brought me to the hospital for the operation, and later identified himself as my "future husband" to a nurse, but a few days after my discharge, as new voices started entering my head, I'd called Michael and told him to leave me alone.

When the delusions progressed, I called my parents and told them I wouldn't be coming to their house in two days for Thanksgiving because

I needed to stay in New York and help the homeless. Believing that something was wrong—and the help I might have offered the homeless in my state was truly questionable—my parents drove into the city the next day to bring me to their house, where at one point I put a Sharpie between my toes and scrawled "Are you my father?" with my foot up on the white Formica table in the kitchen. I had stopped talking by then, not trusting my mouth to say what I meant, not trusting my brain to know what I thought.

Dad didn't comment on the unusual choice of writing limb. He looked down at the piece of paper I ripped off the pad and handed him, then up at me, and with all of the earnestness he must have shown the shah of Iran or Jackie O back when they were clients of his, he answered, in an even voice, "Yes, that's right."

When I'd run out through the garage, trying to escape the voices, Dad managed to find me across Route 25A hiding behind bushes. There were other great saves he made that day, but there was also the crucifix. As I huddled in my old bed upstairs under a pink polka-dot comforter, Dad walked in and stretched out his hand toward me and I saw he was holding the small bronze crucifix that had belonged to Grandma. Even in my psychotic state, I remembered enough about my father to feel a surge of shock. Dad hadn't gone to church in years. He'd only taken me to church to please Grandma—or so I'd thought. Deep inside him lay a believer.

I pulled the comforter over my head and tried even harder to turn myself into a rock. Downstairs, Dad eventually called a doctor in New York City, the endocrinologist into whose care I'd been placed following the operation. Dad told her I was "depressed," and she advised him to take me to the nearest emergency room, a conclusion Dad had failed to reach on his own, resorting to a crucifix when what his daughter urgently needed was medical attention. Perhaps it was because of his strong will, his habit of being in charge. He'd led a cadre of men shooting at German planes in World War II, having risen from enlisted man to officer, and after the war he excelled in his army reserve duties. He was a commander, usually smart, logical, and quick, especially in a crisis, but nothing had prepared him for what he was experiencing after my operation, watching his only child lose her mind.

I endured a stomach pumping without a word, and eventually the emergency room doctor spoke to the endocrinologist by phone, realized I was in a post-operative free fall, and administered cortisone and fluids. After the IV drip, I started talking again, and was permitted to leave with my parents, but, like a river so swollen from rain it continues to rise even after the downpour has stopped, the delusions only worsened the next day until Dad brought me back to the hospital in the evening. There, my status changed. I became a resident of the psychiatric ward, not the place where a lawyer for a major television network, a former editor of the *Columbia Law Review*, a woman who had regularly argued in court on behalf of other people, including the incarcerated, ever expected to wind up.

Fortunately, it didn't take long for anti-psychotic medicines to bring the delusions under control. I got out of the ward after nine days, in time to use the moccasins I'd stitched in crafts therapy as Christmas presents. I returned to my office, no questions asked, where I tried to bury the bad memories in my job, working long hours advising journalists and broad-casters around the country about their problems, keeping the spotlight off of my own. From the mental ward I retracted my ban on Michael, and he visited me there—as did two good friends and Mother, who was first in line each morning despite what I'd tried to do to her. All I wanted was to show Michael, my parents, my friends and colleagues how sane I was.

At work, it seemed I could be practically all mind, but that was only a newer delusion that couldn't be blamed on endocrine irregularities. I wasn't all mind. I still had a body and a heart, and they appeared to be broken. That is what I had to admit to myself, sitting at the picnic table outside the cottage feeling upset, alone, and increasingly enraged.

With others, I often felt tongue-tied about the strange and internal physical things that were still going on, not wanting to sound whiny or unhinged, but now, as I wrote with the sound of waves in the distance more like static than white noise, my pent-up frustrations raced to the page.

From its large size, the surgeons estimated that the tumor had been growing for at least two years before its detection. The tumor changed my body, gradually, as it grew, and then the tumor's excision changed my body again. Distance glasses, which I learned I had only needed because of the increasing pressure the tumor put on the optic nerve, made my vision blur when I put them on after the operation. I never wore them again. The shape of my face changed over the course of the tumor's growth—evident from photos—and the shape changed yet again after the operation. The color of my skin changed, too. "That's completely the wrong shade for you," said the lady at the cosmetics counter when I showed her a tube of makeup that had been the right shade some weeks earlier.

After law school, when Michael and I lived together in Washington, he had commented on a diminution in my "playfulness." I wondered whether something like that, going back years, could be explained by hormonal changes caused by the tumor. I wondered, vainly, about the weight I'd lost, reducing me to a size 6. Was that the tumor's doing, and not the self-discipline for which I'd congratulated myself?

Was I me, or was I the tumor during the years when it was growing? And now that the tumor was gone, and my body was different yet again, who had I become? In my ruminations after my father's dive into the sand, I confronted that it wasn't only my parents whom I did not know.

In the mental hospital, I had asked the psychiatrist about the religious content of my delusions. He told me that was my brain's way of processing elemental fear, probably the earliest way I had been taught to do so. He said my body was coming apart through the shocks to the endocrine system, but my mind didn't understand. I'd never lost a pituitary gland before, but the nuns in my childhood catechism classes had taught me a way to process fear: God versus the Devil, and for a couple of days my mind had swung between the two, back and forth like a pendulum whose swings were getting faster and faster. Close the window shades in your apartment so that the Devil can't see in. No, that is just what the Devil wants you to do. Go open them now and take your jewelry to a church. Good. You are the best of people. No, you are the worst. And on and on.

If the psychiatrist's explanation was correct, then it wasn't only Dad who might run for a crucifix in times of unprecedented threat. This was shocking to me, a person who thought she was an agnostic, involved for years with a man who considered himself an atheist. The notion that a believer might lay within me was among the possibilities that galloped to the page during my afternoon of writing at the picnic table. Who was I, who were my parents, and why had they ceded my emotional upbringing to nuns and fiction writers?

All of the traumas before and since the surgery, right up to the previous day of watching my father act without tether to reality, now felt connected in my mind, and for reasons both rational and intuitive, they pointed me in the direction of Walter Lindberg.

The rational reason was an examination of my ancestry, what little I knew of it. If my parents were unwilling to discuss themselves, their own parents were a logical point of entry, and a common feature of my four biological grandparents was departure from their homes, two crossing an ocean, two crossing land to arrive at New York City. "Desertion/flight" was how I summarized it in my journal. Then there was Walter, Grandma's second husband: "leaves to lead expedition up the Amazon—never comes back" is what I wrote.

The intuitive reason was simply the belief that there was more to the Walter story than my father had ever let on. How could my father's story of a hero drive my mother out of the room? Why wasn't she sitting there rapt, like me? And why had I heard a more complete story about my step-grandfather than about any of my actual grandparents?

With or without a pituitary, I was still an investigator. I felt rootless, alone, overly sensitive to betrayal, unsure about my faith, emotionally distant from my parents, disconnected from my own body, horrified by my past actions, and angry about all I'd been through, yet I was still functioning as an attorney for other people during the week and a dutiful daughter on the weekends. What sort of splintered sense of self and capacity for denial created this disaster and how could I make it all stop?

I also knew that I didn't place much weight on information unless I'd found it myself.

On the morning of Dad's seventy-first birthday, three weeks after his strange behavior at the beach, I wrote out a question: "Is there a lack of trust in information that comes from others based on an early sense that others didn't really describe the world as I experienced it?"

I knew the answer was yes. I also knew the "others" were my parents and that Dad had offered me only one story to describe the world, my world, my family, to explain why it was that we were named after a heroic explorer, not a smelly cheese.

After eating dinner at my parents' house in honor of Dad's birthday, two months after my break-up with Michael, and one year and eight months after the tumor operation, with its detour through a mental ward on my way to a chronic health condition, I asked Dad to tell me everything he knew about Walter Lindberg.

That night, I recorded what he told me in my journal:

Walter was Danish, educated in Denmark and Germany. He was an engineer, draftsman, architect and explorer. Before he met Grandma he worked in the Amazon area building railroads. Then he came to the US and married Grandma when Dad was about five years old (around 1923). Dad liked Walter very much. He was the sort of man to whom other men looked up, Dad said, literally and figuratively. He was well over six feet tall and very imposing. In 1927 Walter got investors to give him money for an expedition up the Amazon to a point where very few people had been. He wanted to map the area and prospect for minerals and diamonds. All of the supplies were aboard a ship called *Vestris*, of the Lamport & Holt Company. The ship went down off of Virginia (supposedly a drunken captain). Walter had stayed behind; 300 lives were lost (the boat sank in shark-infested waters), but not all of Walter's crew. Walter helped the families of the dead and the survivors plus had many debts. They sued the steamship company but it didn't have the proper insurance and went bankrupt. Grandma and Dad were supposed to have gone to Europe to see her family while Walter was on the expedition, but this now was cancelled. Walter worked for two years to pay off the debts (designing the mobile home among other things) and in 1929 had put together another expedition party. This time he got to the Amazon but never came back. About a year after he left, his colleagues came back and said he'd been killed by cannibals in the Amazon.

I was no longer a child on this telling of the Walter story. I was a few months shy of thirty-five. This was how Dad told the story adult to adult, virtually the same way he had told it when I was a girl. He had lived his whole life with one unquestioned version of the story. He'd never updated it with ideas arising from his own reflection or research or any sort of annotation. It was like a passage from the Bible. You don't tinker with the Gospel, and clearly Dad hadn't tinkered with the Walter story. There were no parentheticals, no expressions of doubt, no sources referenced, and, perhaps most striking of all, no indication of his emotions.

The only new element on this telling—at least an aspect I didn't remember hearing previously—was the part about Walter inventing the mobile home. I doubted that was true. If Walter were the father of Winnebagos, I figured I'd have known about it.

It seemed like a good metaphor, though. My father, a mere boy when Walter went to Brazil, must have felt left behind, his home disappearing without a trace.

There was no Internet yet, so I couldn't Google "Walter Lindberg's mobile home," but I was finally ready to use what I did have: the legal database whose capabilities I'd resisted for almost a decade. I was alone, confused, and gushing anger. I wasn't going to continue laying mental flowers on a hero's Amazon grave without some proof.

The Monday morning after my father's birthday, the first thing I did in my office was log into Westlaw and tap V-E-S-T-R-I-S on the keyboard.

chapter six

NEGLIGENCE

FOR ALL THE years I had waited, the computer took only seconds to reveal that the *Vestris* had indeed figured in several legal decisions. I stared at the list of case names as though I had just hacked into long-hidden secrets. Two decisions dealt with procedural issues, but one from the Southern District of New York dated May 24, 1932, went on for pages and looked full of information. I took a copy home.

That night, not caring whether the shades were open or closed, I read the facts as found by a federal judge about a disaster I'd grown up with.

To my surprise, Judge Henry Goddard said nothing about intoxication. Nowhere did the judge state that excessive intake of alcohol caused or was alleged to have caused the captain's colossal error of judgment, failing to send the SOS until more than a day after the ship started taking in water, then transmitting the wrong location.

Nor did Judge Goddard give the sharks any ink. No gory details sullied his reserved prose. He alluded to the horror of the ship's final hours only indirectly, when he noted that witnesses' ability to observe and recollect details would reasonably have been "affected by the mental and physical strain which they underwent."

Metacentric height, depth of the saltwater draft, airtightness of the port half doors, weather conditions—these were the issues that mattered to the seasoned admiralty judge. Yet despite its cold tone and preoccupation with nautical details, the *Vestris* decision thrilled me. Even if there were discrepancies, such as Dad saying the deaths numbered 300 and Judge Goddard 114, the decision was the first proof that the story of Walter Lindberg intersected with something called truth. Like a photograph that proves you visited a place you can't remember, the decision in my hands confirmed that the story of Walter Lindberg wasn't all make-believe. There had been a ship named *Vestris* and it had gone down at sea with a terrible loss of life not attributable to extreme weather but to a confluence of bad decisions by human beings. Wasn't that just as Dad had told it?

Inside, I was like a jury deliberating my father's guilt or innocence. Was Dad fundamentally a bluffer and a blowhard, as my boyfriend had often been quite willing to perceive him? My anger at Dad unleashed since the break-up with Michael demanded that I consider the possibility.

Judge Goddard came across as a steady, though not compelling, witness in my father's defense. While the judge went on for pages discussing points that Dad had conveyed in a sentence or two, there was consistency. Even though there was no mention of sharks or alcohol, the decision confirmed something else Dad had told me: An astonishingly large number of the dead were women and children.

I read with sadness and a feminist's anger how the mariners' law of chivalry—women and children first—had the perverse result of killing most of the women and all of the children. The ship was listing so badly with the starboard rail underwater that it was difficult to guide people into the lifeboats on the starboard side without them slipping and falling. So the captain ordered the crew to take the women and children to the port lifeboats, which were easier to get into, hanging as they were fifty to sixty feet above the sea.

However, it's not just getting into a lifeboat that's important. The lifeboat must make contact with the water and move away from the sinking mother ship. Neither of those things happened to two of the port lifeboats crammed with women and children "with the lamentable result that . . . the women and children in them went down with the ship," as Judge Goddard wrote. "This accounts for the unusually large proportion of women and children who were lost."

A third port lifeboat full of women and children proved worthless for a different reason. As the crew lowered it, using oars as skids to try to hold the lifeboat away from the sloping side of the *Vestris*, a hole ruptured in the bow of the lifeboat. The hole was hastily patched with a piece of tin. When this lifeboat reached the ocean, water poured in through the poorly patched hole. The lifeboat capsized several times during which "many of her occupants were lost."

As Judge Goddard wrote in his understated way, "From what we now know, it seems to have been a mistake in judgment on the part of the captain who was in charge to have made use of this boat instead of trying to launch another to take its place."

The *Vestris* had sailed out of the Hudson River with fourteen lifeboats having a theoretical capacity of 800 people, yet they proved an illusory failsafe for the women and children who sat in the two lifeboats that went down with the ship and the third that capsized because of a hole in its bow. As maritime disasters go, the loss of 114 lives when the *Vestris* sank may be dwarfed by the *Titanic*'s horrific tally of more than 1,500 people drowned, but the message of the *Vestris* disaster was different in kind. To the extent that death was meted out on the *Titanic* due to gender, it was the men who suffered disproportionately. The women and children placed into lifeboats were rescued. Not so with the *Vestris*. On the *Vestris*, chivalry killed.

There was another striking thing about the makeup of the *Vestris* casualties. Of the 128 passengers, fifty-nine survived. Of the 199 ship personnel, 144 survived. That's a survival rate of 46 percent for the passengers and 72 percent for the crew. Most of the crew members used the starboard lifeboats, climbing out on the davits and dropping into the boats after they were launched or jumping into the sea and swimming to the boats. Those acrobatic means of entering the lifeboats may not have been the orderly way to treat paying passengers, but they turned out to be a way to survive. All of the starboard lifeboats made it to safety except for one, while all but one of the port lifeboats failed.

Though restrained and methodical, Judge Goddard ruled in favor of the passengers and cargo owners and against the ship's owners, which had sought to limit their liability on the grounds that severe weather and a burst pipe caused the sinking.

Rejecting those arguments, the judge found that the ship's owners bore responsibility for a number of reasons. In essence, for the passengers who boarded the *Vestris*, things weren't what they seemed that sunny afternoon in Hoboken. Notwithstanding the brochure's claims of "safeguards" and "the most rigid inspection," the owners allowed the ship to be overloaded despite clear maximum-load markings, a practice that was common with the *Vestris*, the judge found. That brought the various inadequately covered openings closer to the water, and deprived the ship of buoyancy that would have helped it survive the winds on the day after its departure, winds that, though not of hurricane force, were strong. Moreover, the ship's owners had failed to inform the captain that the ballast tanks should not be emptied. He didn't know that the ship's stability required them to be full.

The captain had a duty to exercise a "high degree of care" as a common carrier of passengers, and yet the captain did not sound the SOS in time for rescue ships to arrive, even though the *Vestris* was already listing twenty degrees, the engine room was awash in two feet of water on the starboard side, water had extinguished the fires of the starboard boiler, and the pumps were not working. When the order was finally given to abandon the ship, the crew did not put the passengers' safety first. All of this added up to negligence, and worse, a series of decisions made for expedience and short-term gain that cost many lives.

Judge Goddard did, however, discount one theory put forward against the ship company. He found no evidence to support the allegations that the captain hesitated to sound a distress signal because of a company policy discouraging calls for help and rewarding captains for resolving problems on their own. As the judge wrote, "Why Captain Carey neglected to summon aid sooner will probably never be known. Certainly he should have done so, and it can only be assumed that he failed to fully realize the great danger to his passengers and ship."

Was it denial, intoxication, or groundless optimism that led to Captain Carey's lack of full realization? The answer remains unknowable, though Judge Goddard seems to have thought it was his duty to write a complimentary epitaph for the man my father alleged was drunk. The judge referred to the captain's "many years experience at sea," and gave him the benefit of the doubt, even as to the botched launchings of the lifeboats. According to Judge Goddard, Captain Carey "was devoting all his efforts to saving the passengers before [the ship] sank, and he met this last crisis with the courage and the fidelity traditional [of] men of the sea."

What wasn't in the judge's decision was Walter Lindberg's name. I knew that Walter had not been on the ship, but I had hoped I might find some reference to him as the owner of equipment and/or partner of some passengers.

Even so, though I didn't have proof of the veracity of Dad's story insofar as Walter was concerned, I found enough correspondence between dates and facts about the *Vestris* that I let go of some of my doubts about the larger tale, and by extension its teller.

I looked forward to discussing the judge's opinion with Dad, going over every section, every detail.

The next time I visited my parents' house, I gave Dad the decision, which he put on the table next to his recliner to read later. I asked Dad where he got the information that the captain had been drunk, and he said he really didn't remember. He supposed that Walter had told him.

Some weeks later, Dad mentioned to me that he found the decision "very interesting." That was it.

I suppose I should not have been surprised that Dad and I didn't have much of a discussion about the decision. He read the ruling, and he told me he read it. What more was there to say? It's not like he was going to tell me how reading it made him feel, just as we would never discuss why he dove into a few inches of water at the beach or what went through his mind when he saved my life three times during my post-operative craziness. We lacked the words to talk about such things. We could only live them.

When he was in a good mood, Dad was quick to laugh or pat your back, but talking about emotions or showing sadness was not his style.

Only once did I see tears in his eyes—at Grandma's wake my sophomore year in college. More typical was his reaction when our family dog died: "When you have a pet, Marian, you have two choices—either the pet dies before you, or you die before the pet. Which would you rather have it be?"

You could apply that logic to any loss, and Dad did. I believe he told himself that as long as he was alive, there wasn't really anything worth crying about. He might have made an exception had Mother or I predeceased him, but I'll never know. Nor will I ever know for sure what I surmise, that the day Dad started talking himself out of crying over loss was the day his mother told him Walter Lindberg had died.

chapter seven

SCORING ON VARICK STREET

WITNESSES HAD TESTIFIED in Judge Goddard's courtroom, and I thought that if Walter's team was truly aboard the *Vestris*, the transcripts and other court records might contain information about the partners and lost equipment.

On a Friday afternoon in April, I took the subway downtown to the National Archives, where the *Vestris* court docket was housed. When I arrived, the clerk warned me that the docket was huge, even larger than the *Titanic's*. He wished me luck getting through all of the documents before closing time and wheeled out a cart stacked with three shelves of files. He mock-grimaced at its size.

The top shelf contained accordion files full of typed complaints from corporations and individuals seeking money from the steamship owners and insurance company. Over 600 plaintiffs had filed suit against Lamport & Holt and its subsidiary, Liverpool, Brazil & River Plate Steam Navigation Company, seeking compensation for lost lives, lost cargo, physical injuries, and "pain and suffering."

General Motors, having helped establish Brazilian dependency on the automobile, sought $244,978 in damages for its many cars and auto parts that sunk to the ocean floor. Fox Film Corporation requested compensation for "printed positive motion picture film" and two cases of advertising matter. Victor Talking Machine Company made a claim, as did the United States government, for $30,257 in lost mail, closer to $500,000 at today's dollar values. Clearly, the 1920s were the days before Federal Express.

Walter's wasn't among the plaintiffs' names, not as an individual suing for lost equipment, not as an employer suing for dead or injured workers.

Next, I waded through transcripts of testimony delivered at the hearing before Judge Goddard. Because the ship owners and insurance company were asking to be excused from liability on the ground that Mother Nature caused the ship's sinking, Judge Goddard held a hearing at which he heard arguments of counsel and testimony from survivors and various types of shipping experts.

I was a one-person audience for a blockbuster reality show from the late 1920s. First there had been the tightly packed facts and tempered words of Judge Goddard in his formal decision. Now I traveled back in time to read the gripping sworn accounts of *Vestris* survivors such as Henrietta Cubbin, the nurse trying to reach Barbados before her mother died. Miss Cubbin was one of the women placed in a port lifeboat that never made it down to the water because the ropes were not long enough to compensate for the ship's steep list. Miss Cubbin described her time hanging in the lifeboat as the *Vestris* was about to go under:

> Somebody said, "Loose the lifeboat from the *Vestris*; we cannot stay, we cannot wait, for she is going to sink." They searched for a hatchet and knives in the lifeboat and could not find any. They called to a sailor on the *Vestris* to pass down a hatchet, or something, to cut the rope and they said they could not find them. There was suddenly a commotion which I took to be the *Vestris* in her last plunge.

Miss Cubbin was knocked unconscious but, unlike many of the others, she was wearing a lifebelt and floated to the surface. Her luck continued.

When I came to the surface, the *Vestris* had disappeared. I saw crowds of people in the water and I did not know whether they were living or dead; and all the wreckage around there, there was everything. I tried to keep my head above water and away from this wreckage. I held on to a piece of wood; I held on to that for some time, it seemed to me for hours. Eventually I saw a lifeboat passing and I called to the men . . . "For God's sake save me." Some of the men said they could not stop. One of the men said, "It is a lady, let us save her." So they rowed near to me and I was so weak I could not get in. Two of the men leaned over the lifeboat and pulled me into the lifeboat.

Joseph Pollard, who had chosen the wrong ship on which to return home to the West Indies after twenty-three years in the United States, testified about a life's work lost on the *Vestris*. He had toiled as a cook ever since arriving in the United States in 1905, earning $25 to $30 per week, until his savings exceeded $12,000, about $156,000 today. In November 1928, when he boarded the *Vestris*, he was finally going home with his hard-earned cash, which he stashed in his cabin for safe-keeping. As he testified, "When the boat sank I could not go back for my money but was glad I could escape with my life. In that way I lost all my money."

Whole families were lost when the *Vestris* sank, and large parts of many others. There had been twenty-one children on board, all of whom were lost, including little Liesdale Puppe, who died along with her mother, Charlotte, leaving Fred Puppe to start his new job in Argentina all by himself.

Some women proved stronger than their husbands. When a rescue ship finally arrived, the wife of the Japanese diplomat was found delirious, but alive, one arm clinging to a piece of flotsam and the other clasping her dead husband, whom she refused to release.

The big clock in the research room counted down the time until the clerk would retrieve the book cart and the National Archives would close for the weekend. I wouldn't be able to resume searching the files on Monday, since I was expected back at the law firm where I was now working. How much time could I sink into seeking evidence for Dad's story? Walter's name was turning up nowhere.

As I neared the last few volumes on the bottom shelf, I was losing hope. I wondered if I had missed something. Soon there remained only one three-inch accordion folder on the right side of the lower shelf. I hesitated. What were the chances the last folder would be the one that mentioned Walter Lindberg? Anticipating disappointment, I slowed down my movements. The sense of urgency was waning; I was in no hurry to go home empty-handed.

The folder contained transcripts of testimony given months after the judge's decision, by a German couple seeking money for their losses. A special master had been appointed to hear the evidence.

The wife, Marie Ulrich, came across as a difficult witness. She did not speak English, and there was considerable back-and-forth among the lawyers as to whether the translator was getting the words right, especially since Marie Ulrich gave short answers and had trouble remembering events. The lawyers asked leading questions, inciting objections from the other side.

This sort of sparring among lawyers was all too familiar to me, but my interest picked up as soon as Mrs. Ulrich was asked her purpose for going south. Was it "because your husband was about to go on some tour of exploration in South America?"

This was the first time I'd seen "exploration" as a reason for a passenger's being on the *Vestris*, and it raised my hopes, especially when Mrs. Ulrich added that she and her husband planned to disembark in Brazil.

"And you were going to accompany him to South America and stay at Rio, or some place?"

"Yes."

My pulse quickened.

Marie Ulrich testified that she and her husband were together as the ship's list increased, when "going from the sun room my husband and I were both thrown against the iron pillars." She sustained injuries to her left ankle and right knee, the latter "all torn open and swollen."

Shortly after that accident she was placed into a lifeboat, crowded with nearly seventy other passengers, but her husband wasn't among them. He had remained on the *Vestris*.

I picked up the husband's transcript, a much thicker volume, and started reading the deposition testimony of Otto Willi Ulrich given on

December 29, 1932. Finally, I had found the man who would take me to Walter Lindberg.

Ulrich testified that he had watched the lifeboat containing his wife depart the *Vestris*. Soon afterward, the *Vestris* capsized, throwing him into the sea.

He was brought to the surface by "auto tires, tables and chairs" as waves tossed "heavy beams and boards" against his head. He grabbed a beam and clung to it.

Approached by a "negress" unable to swim, he gave the beam to her. She was pulled into a lifeboat, which promptly left, refusing to take him.

"And then what happened?" asked one of the lawyers.

"Then upon the request of the negress they afterwards took me into the boat."

Early the next morning, the steamer *American Shipper* found the lifeboat bearing Ulrich and the "negress" and took its dazed passengers to New York City. That's where Ulrich learned that his wife had survived and was recuperating in a navy hospital in Portsmouth, Virginia. He traveled there at once.

Obviously, Marie and Otto Ulrich were two very fortunate people, fortunate and strong. They were the only married couple I'd come across both of whom had survived.

There were many more pages in Otto Ulrich's transcript and the questioning turned to his background. I skimmed ahead and saw the words "maps" and "tributary." Then I saw the words "gold and amazonite." A flame of recognition ignited in me.

Prior to traveling on the *Vestris*, Ulrich had gone to Brazil in 1926. On that trip, he testified, his expedition party found one and half kilograms of gold along a remote Amazon tributary "in the form of grains the size of rice, in the sand of the river," but he'd been obliged to leave the gold behind. That was the agreement with the local surveyors and guides.

Ulrich had made "many charts and maps" showing the locations of the gold and gems, and his reason for boarding the *Vestris* was to return to those mineral-rich places and use his charts and maps to find gold and gems once more. This time he planned to keep what he found. No longer would he work as an orderly for St. Vincent's Hospital in New York City. He had expected to return from South America a rich man. Instead, he had returned with an injured wife and a litany of losses.

The lawyer questioning Ulrich wanted to know what Ulrich did with the charts and maps from the 1926 trip after bringing them to New York. Ulrich answered that he'd "handed these things to an engineer, in order that he should make fair copies of them."

"Who was that engineer?" the lawyer asked.

"The name of the engineer was Lindberg."

"What was his first name?"

"Walter."

It was then that I started to cry, sinking my face into my hands. There, in the silence of the archives, time stopped.

I looked around the room, past the tables of other researchers and out the window. To my astonishment, it was snowing. There were inches of white on roofs and window ledges. It was an April afternoon, officially springtime, and outside there was a blizzard going on that had entirely escaped my notice.

Oddly, Mother Nature did not send a heat wave to New York the day I found Walter Lindberg's name in the *Vestris* court file. That would have been consistent with a jungle story. Rather, she sent a frigid message from the north, from the opposite end of the world.

I took a deep breath and returned my gaze to the transcript. There was much to read and very little time. So what if it was snowing in April.

chapter eight

AN INTRODUCTION TO OTTO ULRICH

TO MY ASTONISHMENT, the ship's lawyers wanted to know the same thing I did: Where was Walter Lindberg?

The lawyers' curiosity about Walter arose from the fact that loss of property, not physical injury, formed the basis for most of Otto Ulrich's claim against the owners of the *Vestris*. Ulrich had boarded the ship with sixteen pieces of luggage, some containing expensive and rare goods, such as an Eastman Mirror Reflex camera, a Goerz portrait camera, riding equipment for eight horses, a Voigtländer camera, and four telephoto lenses.

Ulrich had brought along a sextant, which he described as an instrument "for measuring degrees of latitude and time," two tripods, and a medicine chest containing fifty grams of hexamethylene tetramine, at least twenty other chemicals, plus "knives, probes, saws, chisels, scalpels, tongs, needles, stitching silk, and catgut and numerous other instruments which I cannot enumerate now." There were "three or four hypodermics," a compass, and a radio.

"What was the idea of taking along that radio set?" one of the lawyers asked.

"In order to give the natives pleasure, a treat," answered Ulrich.

There was no question that Otto Ulrich planned to put the gear to good use, along with his maps and charts from the earlier expedition, searching for gold and amazonite with Walter, the Brazilian surveyors from the 1926 trip, and the group of "natives" who would be obliged to listen to the white men's radio set. Ulrich's legal problem was that he hadn't paid for the items in the sixteen trunks and bags, except for the few personal belongings he and his wife brought along. Throughout Ulrich's testimony, the answer was the same. The source of the expedition equipment Ulrich brought onto the *Vestris* was Walter Lindberg.

The lawyers questioned Ulrich exhaustively about who furnished the money for every item he had brought aboard.

"Lindberg furnished it," became his automatic response.

"The whole affair was financed, and I obtained money from Lindberg in order to make these purchases."

Yet Walter Lindberg was not the person seeking recompense. Otto Ulrich had filed the claim, thus Walter's absence from the lists of plaintiffs. The ship's lawyer was, to say the least, not satisfied with Ulrich's assertions of entitlement to compensation.

"What relation did you have to Lindberg at that time?"

"Lindberg was my partner."

"And the damages that you are claiming for the loss of property would go partly to Mr. Lindberg, if you recovered?"

"As far as I am posted," Ulrich replied, "I have to yield half of it."

The lawyer proceeded to ask Ulrich numerous questions about Walter's whereabouts and the efforts Ulrich had made to locate Walter, both before the judge's decision in May 1932 and since that time, right up to the beginning of Ulrich's deposition on December 29, 1932. From what I could gather, reading quickly, Ulrich testified that Walter had intended to meet Ulrich in Rio a couple of weeks after the *Vestris* arrived, and together they were going to lead a party into the Amazon. Instead, after the sinking radically altered their plans, Walter sailed to Brazil on his own a few months later, and Ulrich had not seen Walter since.

I looked at the clock. There were only minutes left. I hurried to the center of the room to photocopy the transcript.

Soon, I had in my hands a sheaf of papers that constituted my Holy Grail. Outside, the blizzard swirled. I remembered back to the time after my surgery when voices and hallucinations took hold of me. There were moments when I'd felt as if I were communicating directly with God, protected by a divine shield. The doctors called it organic brain syndrome, yet a similar sensation had overtaken me in the archives when I was completely in possession of my faculties. I felt as if I were in step with the universe. There were no strange voices this time—only the real words of Otto and Marie Ulrich, proof of which I held in my hands—but there was a strong sense of being in exactly the right place at the right time, an intimation, perhaps, of destiny.

As I made copies of as many pages as time allowed, I mulled over what I had read so far. I had already formed an opinion of Otto Willi Ulrich, and it wasn't favorable. "He was con man" is what I wrote at the end of my notes. Yet he was all I had to go on.

As a journalist, I'd learned to separate the information from the source. Sources who wanted to meet in parking lots at night or use aliases could be as valuable as any others, as long as the documents they handed over were genuine.

Many years after leaving my job with the newspaper, I was once again a reporter with a questionable source. I didn't like Otto Ulrich, but I needed him, and I intended to make full use of the information he'd left for me. I couldn't meet Otto Ulrich face to face, but I felt as though Ulrich was speaking to me nonetheless, across seven decades, his sworn words to my eyes in the last file of the records from the case about the ship whose name my father gave me. For whatever reason, Dad had asked no further questions, but that wasn't going to be true of me. I was going to cross-examine the hell out of Otto Ulrich. So what if the man was dead. I was alive, and accustomed to searching for information stored in dark places.

During my law school years, I had found four flapper dresses made of sequins and fine lace in a plastic bag in the basement of my parents' home. I brought the dresses upstairs to Mother, who reacted like a pet owner whose cat has just presented her with a dead mouse. She didn't want to touch the dresses, but she did explain that they had been made for her mother during a trip to Paris in the 1920s.

I tried on the dresses, and they fit me perfectly. That's how I wound up with four unique additions to my wardrobe and discovered that I had a similar body to my grandmother, Marion Kondolf Ryan, the woman whose first name I had been given, albeit with an alternate spelling.

The dresses were every bit the equal of those displayed in the Costume Institute of the Metropolitan Museum of Art, but as far as Mother was concerned, they belonged in a bag in a dark, moldy basement. Such was her attitude about the past.

I wore the below-the-knee, short-sleeved ivory lace dress with the multilayered hem in Paris with Michael. I wore the sleeveless dress with the diagonal hem and floral patterns made of black sequins and gold thread to a formal event in New York for which Michael rented a tuxedo. I wore the long black lace gown to the opening of the Philadelphia flower show with a friend from law school whose firm was a sponsor.

I thought the dresses deserved to be worn out in the open, even if some sequins fell off or a high heel snagged a section of lace, just as I longed to know about the past—at least I thought I did. I didn't yet realize how painful it would be to follow Otto Ulrich into the jungle in search of a dead man. I thought it could be like playing dress-up.

chapter nine

TREASURE MAPS

WHEN I WAS a girl, the only Amazon explorer I knew about was Walter Lindberg; he was famous in our house.

Later, I learned about truly famous explorers such as Candido Rondon, the Brazilian who identified the River of Doubt, Rio da Dúvida, in 1909—so named because it led to an unknown area about which nothing could be sure. Rondon returned to paddle down this tributary with Theodore Roosevelt and others in 1913, a trip that resulted in the collection of 2,000 bird species and 500 mammals for the American Museum of Natural History, and that revealed Roosevelt's famed courage and concern for others, as Roosevelt begged his comrades and twenty-four-year-old son Kermit to trek on and leave him to die from an infected leg laceration. The group did not leave and Roosevelt survived, though he said the trip took ten years off his life, and the River of Doubt, having had the doubts about it erased by the feat of its being navigated, became Rio Roosevelt by declaration of the Brazilian government.

I also learned about Hiram Bingham, the Yale historian who discovered Machu Picchu in 1911, and about Percy Harrison Fawcett, the British colonel who disappeared in 1925 in the Amazon trying to find vestiges of a lost city, causing the British Royal Geographic Society to send in a search party.

By the time I read Ulrich's transcript, I had stopped believing Walter belonged in the same group as Rondon, Bingham, and Fawcett, but I didn't really have a good explanation for his obscurity. Why wasn't Walter Lindberg famous outside our small family? Had he not known the right people? Had he not taken the time to promote his expedition to scientific societies and the press? Was he simply not a very good explorer? Was my father's account all exaggeration?

To my continuing amazement, Ulrich's testimony provided some answers.

Important Piece of Information Number One concerned the maps. The maps described by Ulrich, which roughly matched my father's description, could rightfully be called treasure maps. I delighted in this discovery the way you might if Tinker Bell flew in the window and invited you to Never Never Land on a night when you were home alone wishing for something different to do.

The maps Ulrich made on his 1926 expedition didn't show the location of gold and diamonds, as Dad had said, but rather gold and amazonite. Amazonite is a soft, opaque blue-green stone that various legends link to Brazil. Its name is traced either to the Amazonian women warriors or the mineral's location along the Amazon River. Though Brazil was once rich in diamonds, most of its known supplies had been depleted by the late 1920s.

Dad could have researched that issue himself and adjusted the story he told me, but he never demonstrated any interest in fact-checking. He seemed to like the story as he knew it.

Personally, I wasn't sorry to learn that the diamond part of the story appeared to be wrong. "Diamond" comes from a Greek word meaning "I subdue" for good reason, given the many people who have been subdued, and far worse, in the diamond trade. Diamonds may be dazzling, the world's hardest substance, the gem of kings, and a boon to industry, but I'd never heard about a civil war being fought over amazonite.

Important Piece of Information Number Two concerned the maps' origin. Ulrich, not Walter, had created the maps. What Walter did was to make "fair copies" of the maps, at Ulrich's request, for which Ulrich paid Walter $1,000 (equivalent today to over $13,000).

As Ulrich testified, "Lindberg took all the sheets and redrew them on a different scale."

"Then did he make one map?" asked one of the attorneys.

"He made four large maps."

"Just a minute. Does that mean four copies of one map or four sections?"

"That one map comprised four different sheets, sections, because otherwise it would have become too large. . . . The sheets were stitched together in the form of a book."

Walter hadn't been along on the 1926 journey through Brazil when Ulrich drafted the original maps. Walter didn't meet Ulrich until after that, in New York City. Ulrich went to Brazil in 1926 at the invitation of two men he had known in Germany before World War I, Alexander Alexandrovitch and Otto Herbinger, both of whom had moved to Brazil. Ulrich sailed from Germany to New York, left his wife with her brother in New Jersey, and took a steamboat to Brazil, where he and his former friends entered the interior in May, in the state of Mato Grosso, along with a local surveyor and "maybe altogether 30 natives." They traversed several hundred kilometers and emerged in October.

Though Ulrich first described the 1926 venture as "a scientific exploration expedition," a few answers later he made clear the pecuniary motive, saying, "The special purpose of the expedition was to explore an unknown river and an unknown territory, particularly in regard to minerals."

Ulrich described the route he took in 1926—the same one he planned to take with Walter in 1928. One of the attorneys asked if he had any records of the expedition left. He said that he did not. All of them, including the maps, were "on the bottom of the sea."

What was I to make of my father's insinuation that Walter had been subsequently murdered in Brazil because his team wanted the maps, when the maps, according to Ulrich, no longer existed?

Perhaps the route they depicted was stored in Walter's memory, I rationalized, or perhaps he had made a secret copy of the maps that would lead him to the "vast deposits" of gold and amazonite of which Ulrich spoke.

It was entirely possible that I was reading an account of the very route that Walter had taken after he made it down to Brazil on his own, assuming he truly did, the route I had often fantasized about trying to navigate myself.

"Follow your journey along and show us where you went on the 1926 expedition," prompted Ulrich's attorney.

"The expedition began at Rio de Janeiro, and from Rio de Janeiro to Sao Paulo, and from Sao Paulo north to Corumba on the river Paraguay."

"Then where did you go, from Corumba?"

"From Corumba to San Louis des Casaras."

"And where did you go into the jungle on this journey you have described, where you found the gold?"

"From San Louis des Casaras to Villa Matto Grosso."

"Then where did you go?"

"Along the Rio Guapore to Rio Madeira."

"Then did you travel on the Rio Madeira?"

"Along the Rio Madeira to the Rio Gy Parana."

"And from that . . . did you go on . . . the 'Juruena'?"

"[W]e went to the Rio Juruena."

"How long did it take you to go from the Gy Parana to the Rio Juruena?"

"Several months."

"What kind of land is that?"

"It is partly mountainous, partly open country, partly swampy and partly jungle."

I couldn't help but wonder whether a woman without a pituitary gland could survive such a journey.

Even aside from Walter and Ulrich, the place names resonated with mystery. The region between the rivers Ji-Paraná and Juruena (misspelled in the transcript, like many of the Brazilian locations) was where Rondon discovered the River of Doubt in 1909. Cáceres, where Ulrich said his party stopped, about halfway between São Paulo and the Rio Madeira, was the last outpost of civilization that both Roosevelt and Fawcett passed through on their trips into the interior. Ulrich won my grudging admiration for having made such a difficult journey, and I wondered how much Ulrich and Walter had been influenced by the great explorers of their day. Was 1920s Mato Grosso (then spelled Matto Grosso*) today's Mt. Everest peak—a remote destination that proved the mettle of those who reached it and returned?

Roosevelt wrote a memoir about his 900-mile odyssey, *Through the Brazilian Wilderness*, which Walter may have read, and Walter would certainly have been aware of the disappearance of Colonel Fawcett in 1925. Indeed, the extensive publicity about efforts to find traces of Fawcett's small party could have been a factor propelling Walter and Ulrich to plan their expedition in the first place. So many people trying to find Fawcett ended up disappearing themselves that the Brazilian government banned all such searches in 1934.

Important Piece of Information Number Three shed light on how Ulrich and Walter had met.

Ulrich said a man named Maas, either Otto or Max, introduced him to Walter in late 1927, after Ulrich returned to New York from Brazil to join his wife. She left her brother's house, and the Ulrichs moved into rooms in Manhattan, where Ulrich went to work at St. Vincent's.

Ulrich and Walter first met on East 86th Street, the heart of what was then a predominantly German neighborhood, where Maas lived and where Walter resided with my father and grandmother. Ulrich learned that Walter, like Ulrich, had spent time in Brazil, where he worked on a railroad.

It wasn't clear whether the introduction was a social one, with the map-copying assignment coming after Walter and Ulrich had established a rapport, or whether Maas had set up the meeting because Ulrich was looking for an engineer who could copy a map. Ulrich did say that when he came to New York from Brazil, the maps were in a trunk and stayed there until he hired Walter to copy them. Either Ulrich was actively seeking the right man for the job, or a synergy developed between Walter

---

* Author's Note: Throughout the book, quotations of documents are presented with the spelling, capitalization, and accents of words as they appear in the original, even if the original was mistaken or the usage is now considered archaic, as in the case of Matto Grosso. In text, the generally preferred contemporary spelling, capitalization, and accents are used.

and Ulrich that made Ulrich want to open the trunk and embrace the maps' possibilities. Surely, the maps would only have been worth paying $1,000 to copy if Ulrich was serious about using them.

Charging Ulrich would have been a strange decision if Walter were originally planning to accompany Ulrich to Brazil. Presumably, if Walter had that in mind from the outset, his copying would have been part of his investment in the joint venture. I imagined Walter in the midtown office described by Ulrich—never mentioned by my father—haggling with the map owner over the fee. I wondered how soon it was that an assignment to copy maps for a client morphed into a plan to leave New York with the client and put the maps to use in the wild. It seemed likely that as the two men came to know each other, and Walter spent time with the maps, the relationship changed and the idea of becoming "partners" emerged. That would explain why Ulrich made "frequent visits" to Walter's office as the men became more serious about their objective and Walter started to raise money and buy equipment.

Certainly, Walter must have trusted Ulrich. Walter must have believed that Ulrich had found over a kilo of gold in 1926 and that the maps would lead them both back to those gold-bearing places.

Import Piece of Information Number Four told me how it was that Ulrich and the equipment wound up on the *Vestris*.

Having heard from Dad that there was a great deal of equipment lost on the ship, and believing the best about my childhood hero, I inferred that the expedition had been well-planned and well-financed by generous third parties—patrons of the sciences, investors, perhaps members of the exclusive Explorers Club, whose focus was shifting at that time from the earth's icy crown and bottom to her dark and shrouded midriff.

What I found in Ulrich's testimony was more worthy of Groucho Marx.

There was a letter from Brazil. Come at once, it demanded. Unlike the letter received by Henrietta Cubbin, telling of an elderly woman lying on her deathbed in Barbados, the letter from Alexander Alexandrovitch to Otto Ulrich warned of a different sort of deadline imposed by nature: the onset of the rainy season.

Ulrich testified that he and Walter were originally planning to leave New York together "at the beginning of October" 1928 "but the expedition was not ready soon enough" so a December date was chosen instead. The two men expected to join Alexandrovitch and the other surveyor and head into the interior with their maps, equipment, horses, and local helpers. Ulrich, who had traveled with Alexandrovitch in 1926, had written to his former traveling mate informing him of the December arrival date.

Unacceptably late, Alexandrovitch wrote back at once. According to Ulrich, the letter instructed "that I should immediately come down" in order to "be there before the beginning of the rainy season." Alexandrovitch wrote that he and Severino Tovares Bezerro would not wait until December to begin the expedition. They would find other work.

It is astonishing that Ulrich and Walter didn't place more consideration on the infamous Amazonian summer, with daily downpours that swelled the rivers, quickened the rapids, and turned soil to mud. The ship's lawyers expressed their incredulity several times. In his memoir, Roosevelt blamed his party's late departure—December 9, 1913, the beginning of the wet season—for many of the difficulties the group encountered.

To say the would-be treasure hunters in New York responded with alacrity to the letter from Brazil is an understatement. They made a hasty decision that changed the course of their lives. Ulrich received Alexandrovitch's letter on Friday, November 9, 1928, before noon. Ulrich and Walter decided that Ulrich and his wife would sail the very next day. There was only one ship leaving New York for Brazil on Saturday, November 10—the *Vestris*.

In a frenzy, Ulrich and Walter purchased the remaining equipment they needed on Friday afternoon and prepared lists for the consular office of the items being taken abroad. Ulrich stayed up most of the night packing.

Ulrich finished packing the equipment into trunks around four on Saturday morning. A few hours later, he went to the bank and withdrew all of his money (about $650 or $700). He continued on to the shipping line office, where he bought two tickets shortly before 1 PM and had an incomplete discussion about baggage insurance. Then he went home to 73rd Street to pick up his wife and load the luggage into automobiles, assisted by a man named Carl Zimmerman.

With the ship scheduled to depart at three forty-five, one can only infer that gridlock had not yet come to Manhattan. As it was, Ulrich arrived at the pier "a few minutes before the *Vestris*'s departure." The crane used to load large cargo had stopped operating, so the sixteen pieces of luggage had to be carried on board by crew members.

Walter met Ulrich at the pier. Consistent with what Dad always told me, Ulrich confirmed that Walter did not sail on the *Vestris*. "Lindberg was not completely prepared," Ulrich explained. "I sailed first and Lindberg was to follow me."

Ulrich claimed that while he was busy showing travel documents to various officials, "the luggage was looked after by Lindberg, who had already negotiated with several officials regarding the insurance of the luggage."

"I move to strike that out," said one of the defense attorneys.

"Strike it out," ruled the special master. "The objection is sustained."

The defense lawyers were protecting their position that the items for which Ulrich was claiming compensation had not been insured.

Ulrich then testified that Walter gave him $1,600 in cash "intended for paying the insurance," which Ulrich put in his back pants pocket and tried to use during the trip to purchase insurance, but the proper officer could never be found. Whether Ulrich made those efforts or not, one can believe that as water began entering the vessel, requiring bailing and the management of increasingly alarmed passengers, processing insurance transactions dropped to the bottom of the crew's priorities.

Ulrich never did use the $1,600 or purchase insurance. Instead, Ulrich testified, he lost his pants when the *Vestris* went down along with the $1,600 they contained.

Ulrich didn't lose all his money, though. He said he had placed the $650 or $700 withdrawn from his own account in the breast pocket of his shirt. Though he lost his pants and Walter's $1,600 in cash, and never succeeded in buying insurance covering the expedition equipment, one thing Otto Ulrich said he didn't lose when the *Vestris* went down was his shirt.

Important Piece of Information Number Five and Earth-Shattering Revelation Number One offered a startling new reason why Walter did not sail on the *Vestris* with the Ulrichs.

One of the key parts of Dad's story—and, of course, one of the most flattering for him—was that Walter did not board the *Vestris* because he wanted to spend more time with Dad and Grandma before leaving. Dad said Walter was going to meet the *Vestris* in Virginia. By now I knew that the *Vestris* wasn't scheduled to stop in Virginia to pick up passengers— quite the opposite. It was in Virginia waters that the *Vestris* discharged its passengers in a most unplanned way, by sinking. This was another error in my father's tale, though it paled in comparison to what I was about to learn.

According to Ulrich, Walter intended to take a different boat, which departed two weeks after the *Vestris*. Walter must really have wanted some extra time in New York, because Ulrich could do little during his two weeks alone in Brazil, save for some administrative details. Ulrich, Alexandrovitch, and the whole expedition party would have to wait for Walter before setting out.

More than likely, Ulrich and the equipment were being sent down right away as a good faith offering to underscore Ulrich's and Walter's seriousness and try to restrain the men in Brazil from leading other fortune seekers into the interior.

Given the way things turned out, the men waiting in Rio had to find other work anyway. Ulrich never arrived in November, and Walter never arrived in December. Had Alexandrovitch not written—allowing the departure date for both Walter and Ulrich to remain in December—or had Walter and Ulrich responded to the letter in any way other than rushing to get Ulrich and the gear onto the *Vestris* on November 10, the story would have had a different ending. Maybe Ulrich would have found gold and amazonite, and Walter, too. Maybe Walter would have brought some treasure back to New York, and Dad wouldn't have finished grade school and high school as a poor city kid living on the income of his seamstress mother.

If he had to stay up most of the night packing, it didn't sound as though Ulrich was completely ready to go to Brazil himself, but for whatever reason—his devotion to the gold and gems of the Amazon or his lack of commitment to his life in New York—he was willing to disrupt his and his wife's existence to leave on a day's notice.

Walter wasn't willing to make such a quick break, but there was nothing in Ulrich's testimony about the reason being a sentimental attachment to Grandma and Dad. As the financier, Walter perhaps held the upper hand and could legitimately say "you go" to Ulrich on one day's notice without giving a reason. And maybe a man sending his partner off to Brazil in a hurry wouldn't stress his desire to remain behind to spend quality time with his family, but the transcript suggested that there was another, very different reason for Walter's staying behind.

Her name was Emmy Kern.

chapter ten

A HARD LEAD TO FOLLOW

HERS WAS THE last in a string of names.

"Did some of your friends carry some of your baggage on board?" one of the lawyers asked Ulrich.

"Only a small hand-baggage," he answered.

"And which friends of yours carried small hand-baggage on board?"

"Lindberg, Zimmermann and Miss Kern."

Emmy Kern was Walter's employee. Ulrich said he saw her "repeatedly" in Walter's office. In addition to helping Walter carry luggage onto the *Vestris*, she later spoke to Ulrich about correspondence from Walter in words that didn't exactly shed light on Walter's whereabouts but certainly cast a new light on Dad's story.

"When did you last see Lindberg?" one of the attorneys asked Ulrich.

"As far as I remember, it must have been March, 1929."

"Did you correspond with him after that?"

"Yes. He wrote me a letter."

"From where?"

"As far as I remember, from Barbados."

"Was he bound north or south, or was he sojourning, or don't you know?"

"He was on his trip to South America. . . ."

"Well, has he communicated with someone else . . . ?"

Ulrich answered yes, that Walter had written his former stenographer.

"Well, where is she, and what is her name, and what is her address?"

"Her name is Emmy Kern. At the time she was living in Brooklyn. I do not know where she is living now."

"Where did you communicate with her?"

"I met her two times, quite accidentally."

"Where?"

"As far as I remember, it was near 86th Street."

"Was it on the street?"

"Yes, a German movie theater, or whatever kind of theater it is."

"Did you inquire from her, either one of those times, where Lindberg was?"

"Yes, I asked her whether he had written and whether he was still in the interior."

The first time that they met at the theater, Emmy Kern told Ulrich that she had received a letter; the second time she said "that she was going to marry and that she was no more interested in Lindberg's letters."

"When was that?"

"As far as I remember, that was a year after Lindberg went, early 1930."

I put down the transcript and waited for my mind to adjust. The evidence was circumstantial, but it strongly suggested that Walter was having an affair with his stenographer. Emmy Kern, not Grandma, accompanied Walter to the *Vestris* to say good-bye to the Ulrichs and officially begin the ambitious venture that Walter had been planning for months. And if her interest in Walter were truly professional, why would Emmy Kern have stopped caring about his fate once she became engaged to marry someone else?

November 10, 1928 was a Saturday. My father was ten and presumably out of school for the weekend. Wouldn't he have liked to see the big ship at the pier, watch the activity before the *Vestris* set sail, hear the horn blow as the ship steamed off toward foreign lands? Wouldn't a stepfather with a strong relationship with his family have taken his wife and stepson to such an exciting occasion? There is no mention in Ulrich's testimony of Grandma or Dad at the pier. Indeed, my father is absent from the testimony altogether.

It appeared Walter hadn't stayed behind to be with Dad and Grandma, strolling through Central Park, drawing out their final good-byes. He had stayed behind to be with Emmy Kern.

But depart Walter did, a few months later. According to Ulrich, Walter sailed on the *Van Dyke* in March 1929, with stops in Barbados and Brazil. Was Walter running away from a double life? Had Emmy Kern given him an ultimatum—to leave his wife and stepson—that was easier to avoid than answer?

Dad's recitation to me on his seventy-first birthday had Walter working in New York for two years between the sinking of the *Vestris* and his departure for Brazil, paying off debts and inventing the mobile home, but that wasn't the case according to Ulrich. The *Vestris* sank on November 12, 1928, and Ulrich said Walter sailed on the *Van Dyke* four months later.

Ulrich claimed his wife's slow recovery from her *Vestris*-related injuries required him to stay in New York, and he gave that as the reason why he did not accompany Walter to Brazil in 1929, though he did go to the pier of the *Van Dyke* to see Walter off.

According to Ulrich, Walter sailed alone. He traveled lightly, without equipment or scientific instruments, lacking money to replace what had been lost.

Perhaps Walter intended to head toward the Rio Juruena, even without Ulrich and the maps, or perhaps he was open to whatever opportunities presented themselves. From the Ulrich transcript, it doesn't appear that anyone in particular was waiting for Walter in Brazil. What Ulrich recounted was simply an oral agreement he made with

Walter promising to try to raise funds, buy equipment, and come to Brazil later in 1929 if he could arrange it.

Ulrich testified, "He had nothing with him, because, according to our agreement, I was to follow him with those instruments which I had to procure first."

In essence, Walter left New York in March 1929 with nothing but his ticket to Brazil and the hope that Ulrich would join him and bring expedition equipment at a later date.

That's how eager Walter Lindberg was to get away from his home, to get away from my grandmother, and from the boy who thought his stepfather was some kind of great man.

chapter eleven

LOVE LESSONS

MOTHER PAID A rare visit to my apartment shortly after my discovery, and I deposited myself next to her on the sofa with the Ulrich transcript in my lap. I knew Mother didn't care about the story of Walter Lindberg, but I was going to make her care. Dad had been dead for over six years and she was now eighty-one, too slow on her feet to leave any room in a hurry no matter how much she didn't want to talk about something.

We'd just come from lunch at a restaurant. Mother had been nervous about taking the train into New York—which used to be simple for her—and I was proud of her for doing it. She still made an effort with her appearance when she came into New York—unlike the way she was now dressing at home in the same, worn clothes—except that even for a trip into Manhattan, at this point in her life she would wear her clunky Merrell's with tire treads for soles. She was afraid of falling, because that had happened a year earlier, resulting in a fractured hip. My drop-dead gorgeous mother had become a wrinkled woman with a hunched back due to osteoporosis, but on the day we discussed Otto Ulrich's testimony she looked elegant in her understated way, wearing a little makeup, the gold Tiffany seashell earrings I had given her for her eightieth birthday, and a pretty olive green sweater and pants. I could have overlooked the shoes, except that they were one of the few things Mother allowed me to tease her about, so I was secretly glad for them.

"Listen to this," I said, reading aloud the excerpts about Emmy Kern as Mother sat next to me.

To my surprise, Mother did listen. She paid attention, didn't interrupt, and didn't try to change the subject.

"Do you agree with my inferences?" I asked.

"Yes, I do," she said. "I think you're right." Then she said it was a good thing Dad wasn't around to know what I'd found.

Mother was better educated than her late husband, but she didn't always choose her words with precision, usually due to social anxiety. At my law school pre-graduation party, I introduced her to a professor, and Mother said to him "I see you have no hands" because he was carrying a drink in each hand. Michael, who met my parents for the first time that evening, chuckled for years over that remark. What Mother meant, of course, was that she could see it would be difficult for the professor to shake her hand, and she was assuring him in her "do-I-dare-to-eat-a-peach?" way that he should not go to the trouble of trying to hold both glasses in one hand, or finding a horizontal surface on which to place one of the drinks, in order to greet her with hand-to-hand contact.

I knew that Mother hadn't meant that it was good Dad was dead, just that it might have upset him to hear about his revered stepfather likely cheating on his mother.

My research project, begun as an offering of love for my father, had uncovered a dagger. But with Dad gone and Mother unperturbed, whose flesh could it pierce?

Grandma and Mother were very different people and had never been close. Though Mother acted dutifully toward Grandma, taking her into our house for a few months until Grandma suffered her stroke, there was a tremendous divide between their backgrounds and interests that never seemed bridged. Grandma was an uneducated former factory seamstress with an Eastern European accent who lived with a barber when Mother met her in the 1940s, Mother having grown up in a twelve-room apartment on Fifth Avenue, with multiple vacation homes, and attended some of the East Coast's finest schools, obtaining an undergraduate degree from Columbia University, a place few women attended in her days there.

When I was young and Dad drove us to Grandma's house in New Jersey for Thanksgiving, the differences between Mother and Grandma were obvious. In one photo of the guests sitting around a table practically as big as the entire house, Mother in her pillbox hat sticks out like a fashion model in the desert. Many of the people in the photo spent winter in the Cherokee Mobile Home Park in Fort Lauderdale, where evening pastimes included canasta and playing bingo for prizes such as rolls of paper towels. (I know, because I won a roll once when I spent a high school spring break in Grandma's trailer.)

In contrast, Mother's idea of a trip to Florida was a stay at The Breakers resort in Palm Beach, built by the railroad baron Henry Flagler, the sort of man Mother's father would have known at the Halcyon or Roney Plaza Hotel in Miami Beach in the 1920s when both men participated, in their own ways, in the transformation of south Florida from swampland to tropical Mecca.

Mother visited me once when I had a summer job in Washington during law school, and at dinner she broke the mold and told me a few things about her past. Mostly they had to do with her father, who apparently used to complement his well-dressed look with a glass of scotch on a fairly regular basis, sometimes becoming violent. The man harbored conflict even inside himself. Mother told me he disdained his Irish roots so much that he wouldn't allow any green in their homes, yet in the evening, after more drinks, what he asked his wife to play on the piano were Irish ballads. He died of liver disease at the end of Mother's freshman year of college, and that's why she left Vassar and transferred to Columbia. Mother indicated that this wasn't only to keep her newly widowed mother company, but that with her alcoholic father gone, her home had become a safer and more livable one.

By comparison, another disclosure by Mother that evening seemed benign. She told me that my father, during their courtship, misled her about Grandma and their family background. He was so handsome in his army uniform when the two met in Virginia Beach, my mother visiting the resort town with her mother after her father's death and her debutante tea party, my father on furlough from an army camp in the South. The uniform was a great equalizer and apparently, in hindsight, a good disguise. Jean Lindberg asked Patricia Ryan to play Ping-Pong. They talked and, after he returned to the South and she to New York, they wrote letters. That was how the relationship progressed, and I knew from letters Dad had written me in the past that he had an elegant way of expressing himself in fine, strong script.

Dad's puffery became immediately apparent to Mother when she met Grandma, an event Dad apparently deferred as long as possible, perhaps right up until the wartime wedding.

This information had new meaning as I reflected on Walter Lindberg and Emmy Kern. If Mother felt misled about Grandma and Dad's social status, if Grandma was a painful symbol of Dad's dissembling, should I have expected Mother to feel sad now, many years after Grandma's death, learning that Grandma may have been cheated on by Walter Lindberg?

It was I who felt stabbed by the dagger unsheathed from Otto Ulrich's transcript. It upset me to think that Walter was the man from whom Dad received his boyhood lessons about love. Dad truly loved Walter. I'd seen that demonstrated convincingly during Dad's narrations of the Walter Lindberg story, the way he would look straight ahead—never at me—as though he was seeing that tall and handsome Dane taking over the room.

What Otto Ulrich's testimony suggested was that it hadn't been a full, two-way kind of love between Dad and Walter, but more like the lopsided gush of a groupie. The record gave no indication that Walter much cared for Dad in return for all the admiration Dad tossed about. I wondered whether Walter had left Dad and Grandma emotionally well before he went to Brazil, if he'd ever really joined with them in spirit and affection at all.

I had started asking questions about the Walter story sparked by anger at my father over his interference with my relationship with Michael. I had been searching for answers. So it mattered to me to learn that my father's earliest exposure to love may have felt a lot like being robbed.

chapter twelve

MAN ON A MISSION

"CHAPEAU BAS," MICHAEL said upon entering my apartment at the end of our third and last year in law school. He bowed and gestured as though removing a hat and sweeping it toward the floor. "You got an E in Federal Courts."

"E" stood for "excellent," the top grade in a notoriously difficult course. I didn't let on how glad I was to hear this news, which Michael brought directly from the law school bulletin board nine blocks north. He knew my code, so he could check my grades along with his.

I acted restrained, but I had worked hard and wanted that E. So had Michael. In fact, he had requested a break in our seeing each other so that he could concentrate on studying. He was first in our class, the best student in a generation in the opinion of some of our professors, and even he thought the course was challenging.

Earlier in his career, the professor who taught the class had argued significant First Amendment cases, resulting in Supreme Court decisions that gave American journalists some of the strongest legal protections in the world. The professor was an icon for me. I wanted to excel in his course, and believing that I was working for something more than a grade on a transcript only added focus to my studying. My performance in the course had emerged as a test of my long-term suitability for Michael.

All of that desire to be worthy felt sweetly satisfied as Michael pretended to bow before me, his long black hair practically touching the floor. He and I were lovers, but we were also engaged in a kind of duel, intellectually and emotionally. It was sexy, it was intense, and it was like nothing I had ever experienced before.

"*Chapeau bas*," a phrase used to congratulate the winner of a competition, was an apt choice by Michael—but that was true for his word choices generally. Michael was the most articulate man I had ever met, and I quickly grew addicted to the way he could express his thoughts—and my own—with fitting, lucid language, whether the topic was politics, the movies, or a classmate's quirks.

Mutual friends had been trying to bring Michael and me together since the first year of law school, but it took five semesters for us to get into bed, and even then it wasn't clear whether a relationship had started. I was coy, for I was wary. I had never been with the likes of Michael, and he let me know that I was an atypical choice for him. We were very different, and once a relationship did start, it derived much of its power from those differences, he the brilliant academic, I the street-smart journalist; he the thinker, I the doer, who knew how to use tools and fix things. He was from the socio-economically mixed south shore of long Island, near the Queens border, I was from the "Gold Coast" on the north shore. He was cautious, I was a risk-taker. He was Jewish, I was not. We did have tennis in common, which meant that the tennis court became one more place where we competed while falling in love.

Eventually, Michael won my complete trust, combining intellect, judgment, integrity, a strong social conscience, and fun in a package I'd never before encountered and couldn't previously have conjured up if asked to describe my ideal man.

I was Michael's first non-Jewish girlfriend in many years, and he was concerned about his mother's reaction (his father was deceased). He and I were both relieved when I met his mother, a former public school math teacher, and we got along fine. She told me I could visit her any time. Not so with my parents. My father was the only person whose judgment I had ever trusted as much as Michael's, but this was no longer true. Four months into the relationship, my father told me it would "kill" my mother if I married a Jew, and he offered his own list of objections. I recorded this extremely poor judgment in my journal, labeled it bigotry, kept Michael and my parents separate, and made far fewer visits to Long Island. Michael had met my parents at the pre-graduation party. After a brief conversation, during which my parents seemed flustered, Michael had a fair idea of what he was up against.

In the fall after graduation, I moved to Washington for a prearranged clerkship with a federal judge. Michael stayed in New York, where he was already clerking for a prominent judge. We saw each other on weekends. One weekend Michael tossed out a reference to marriage as we were crossing Broadway carrying grocery bags. It was a spontaneous burst of affection that I didn't take too seriously, but seriously enough, like the time he and I sat at a bar downtown with a large mirror over the bottles and he started to analyze our facial features, which ones if passed on would make for the most handsome children. Like the reference to marriage, it was done with humor, and yet we both knew that two people wouldn't joke about something as serious as conceiving children unless there was a growing commitment underneath.

As Michael and I passed the one-and-a-half-year mark it was time, I thought, to end the lack of contact between Michael and my parents. Whatever objections Dad had raised early on, I felt that the longevity of the relationship and the depth of my happiness proved he had been wrong. I told my parents that I wished for them to get to know Michael, and they agreed to come into New York to have dinner with us.

Dad showed up at the restaurant alone, giving an excuse about Mother's absence.

First we sat at the bar. Dad and Michael could both be charming, and to my delight each chose to be charming to the other over a drink or two. I started to relax, feeling something wonderful and new, a fusing of separate selves, daughter to one man, lover to another.

It wasn't until dessert that my father revealed the true reason for Mother's absence. My father was on a mission, best accomplished alone.

"Mrs. Lindberg and I disapprove of this relationship," he began, and I realized to my shock that all of the charm up until then had been a ruse. There had never been an intention to honor our agreement, to try to get to know Michael. It was an ambush. Michael and I had wanted the meeting to be in our city, not my parents' suburb, but we'd forgotten that my father was a war veteran, accustomed to fighting and winning on foreign soil. My father fired words like rounds of ammunition in the name of what was best for me, because of course I couldn't be expected to know that, brainwashed as I was with the potent hormones of love.

My father referred to Michael's Jewishness and at one point Michael said "you wouldn't even know I was Jewish if you hadn't been told," and my father begged to differ. Michael baited him, "What is it, my nose?", and my father fell for the bait, saying yes and that wasn't the only thing. My father even went after Michael's intellect, dismissing academics as impractical fools—unlike men of industry and business like him. My father didn't understand that by now, I considered myself an academic, too, so he was disparaging his daughter along with her lover.

My father said he could tell I'd felt happy earlier in the evening. He didn't apologize for taking that away. It was more like he was accusing me of naiveté, from which it was his duty to rescue me with discipline and guile.

Why didn't I stand up and leave, Michael asked ever after. I wished that I had. Instead I sat through the back-and-forth between the two men I loved, tears in my eyes, clasping Michael's hand on top of the table, which was my way of choosing sides, admittedly insufficient in hindsight, but there had been wine, and I had been happy.

"Go out and be with your father," my mother often said on the weekends of my girlhood, when I'd had enough of practicing the piano or reading and wandered into the kitchen. I was always glad to obey her instruction, even if it just meant following Daddy around the yard while he sprayed weeds from a canister.

Daddy was the one who taught me carpentry, who discussed with me the merits of angel fish versus guppies, who helped me enter photo contests, and who took me to the 1964 World's Fair in Queens half a dozen times. (Yes, we saw telephones of the future with video images!) At the World's Fair, Daddy bought me a sequined Indonesian basket that became one of my most treasured possessions.

Dad was the one who wrote letters to me during my first year of boarding school about his business trips to Japan and the Middle East, and also about Mother's depression, how we had to be gentle with her, how she wasn't even interested in sending Christmas cards that year. Perhaps, he wrote, my visit home for the holidays would snap her out of it.

Dad was the one who got me tickets for Rolling Stones concerts and US Open tennis matches and took my side in college when a research paper I'd left for a teacher was said to be missing and the semester grade came home an F. A janitor found the paper, the grade was revised, and Dad lectured school administrators that they ought to have better procedures so as not to upset a student like that.

But my father was also the one who chased my friend Allen out of our yard with a metal flower pot in his hand—not giving me a chance to explain that Allen had gone up to my bedroom for the innocent purpose of looking at photos of a former classmate of mine whom he fancied, not for anything improper having to do with me.

For a long time after the bait-and-switch dinner, I had no contact with my father at all. I didn't call or write home, and I didn't visit. My father made no effort to contact me. Michael moved to Washington after his clerkship ended and we found an apartment near Dupont Circle with a small, fenced-in yard in which we read poetry to each other and selections from Proust and other great writers, whose books offered more emotional support than my family.

That year I didn't visit my parents for the holidays. I didn't care if Mother would be depressed. She'd been a coward, staying home while her husband waged war, trying to snuff out something I had longed for, a love that seemed so right I wanted it to last my whole life. Unlike my father, she would send a note now and then, but it would be mailed to my office, not to the apartment. I would freeze up at the sight of her handwriting, at once so familiar and so remote.

At one point I wrote my father a long letter saying I loved him, explaining that the current state of affairs caused me great pain, and pleading with him to apologize to Michael and try for real to get to know him. Mother told me that my father didn't even open the envelope. He just put it in a drawer, commenting to her that he thought my letter would upset him.

Eventually, the outcome my father sought came to pass. After nearly four years together, Michael and I went in separate directions, seeing each other only sporadically and dating other people. Our differences had become more problematic and less alluring, especially the continuing lack of acceptance by my family. Michael moved to Philadelphia to teach law, and I moved back to Manhattan. It was there that I started having strange symptoms, the blurring of my distance vision, the loss of my period, and then sudden, intense pain in the ovaries on my way to visit a friend out of town. The pain was so severe I called my gynecologist, who advised me to cancel my plans and return home by way of the route with the fewest potholes. I lay in bed over Columbus Day weekend until the doctor could see me. It was his brilliant medical work that led shortly to the diagnosis of a tumor in the pituitary, the so-called "master gland."

At first I thought the tumor was just a stroke of bad luck, and maybe that's all it was. But after the operation, when the surgeon told me the growth had likely been going on for over two years, I realized what that meant. It meant that while Michael and I lived together in Washington, in a loving relationship that my parents regarded as a cancer, Mother labeling it sinful because I was violating Catholic dogma that love-making was meant for procreation, a tumor had started growing in the part of my body that controlled reproduction, making it uncertain if I would ever be able to have a child. A religious person might have seen divine punishment; a secular mind could rue the cruel irony.

The tumor brought Michael and me back together, and we lasted as a couple for over a year and a half. He moved in with me, and we discussed trying to have a child, seriously, not on bar stools. It wasn't an easy time, me coping rather silently, sometimes poorly, with the endocrine changes and working too hard at my job. I wasn't at my best, but in the end, what Michael came back to was the difference in our heritage, which my father's nasty words at the restaurant had turned into a dark cloud that never really left Michael and me, though we had many good times together by averting our eyes and looking instead at the horizon—or each other.

"I can't see beyond the bris," Michael said in one of our last talks about the future. The cloud had grown too big for him to ignore, and soon thereafter I said it's best we part. How could you play roulette with a baby as the ball?

At the rented beach cottage, just a few weeks after Michael had moved out of my apartment, I would look back at our time together in Washington and the feeling I had then of being pulled apart by two strong opposing forces, romantic love and family love, and I would wonder about cause and effect. I would remember feeling that the divide between my parents and Michael was the first significant, ongoing problem I had encountered that couldn't be fixed through action or buried by denial, and I would wonder if the enormity and persistence of the resulting stress had affected me at a cellular level.

When parents don't make sense, a psychologist told me once, children go to great lengths to make it seem otherwise, often at great internal cost. As I was sitting at the picnic table, angry at the turns my life had taken, I couldn't help but wonder: Was the tumor my cost?

chapter thirteen

THAT OTHER HEMISPHERE

DAD ASKS ME again for the keys to his car, oblivious of his own state. There's been a blowout in that other hemisphere, the right one. He is paralyzed.

It's been seven years since the tumor came out of my head, five years since I found Judge Goddard's decision in the *Vestris* case. Michael is married to a Jewish woman whose father adores him and they are raising a child. I'm about a year into my new life as a writer, living in eastern Long Island a mile from the ocean in a small house I've bought not far from the cottage I had rented. I am still single.

Now Dad spends his days in a hospital bed in the same house where I once scrawled "Are you my father?" with a pen between my toes. His bed is situated in the ground-floor den where he used to watch golf, sip his martinis, finish *The New York Times* crossword puzzles, and answer my questions about Walter Lindberg. An aide sometimes sits in the white leather recliner in which Dad will never sit again.

THE END OF THE RAINY SEASON

I tell Dad once more that, sadly, he cannot drive a car. I explain again that his left side is paralyzed as a result of the stroke that made him fall onto the kitchen floor six months earlier.

"Nonsense," Dad says, "you just won't give me the keys and I don't know why."

"Okay," I say. "Why don't you get up then?"

He puts his weight on his right arm but cannot lift his large torso more than a few inches off the bed. He falls back, grimacing, out of breath.

"I can't do it," he says, like this is brand-new information.

"I know," I say. "I'm sorry this is how it is."

The left side of the body takes orders from the right side of the brain. Think of a marionette with crisscrossed strings. More than that, Dad's stroke occurred in the right pre-frontal cortex and parietal lobe, the area of the brain that receives sensory signals from within the whole body and relays them to the "thinking" left hemisphere. This is why Dad thinks he can still drive—if only I would give him the keys. His right brain isn't being honest with his left brain, updating the paradigm of Dad's self-image with the new information that he cannot move his left leg or left arm, sit up on his own, or stand.

"The doctors put something in my legs," Dad tells me on a good day. On a not-so-good day he asks for the phone so he can arrange a foursome. It is June, after all, a nice month for golf on Long Island.

Neurologists call Dad's condition "anosognosia," Greek for "disease of knowledge." Anosognosia is a difficult brain condition to treat, largely because of the challenge inherent in helping patients who cannot accept that they are impaired. For this reason, Dad has been fired from outpatient therapy.

One of the first evenings Dad is back in his house from the rehab center, I am standing in the den as darkness falls outside the sliding glass doors and he calls my name from the hospital bed.

"Get me my clothes," Dad requests with urgency. "Please, Marian, I can't be in the club in my pajamas."

I tell him he's not at his country club, he's at home.

"Look around," I say. "It's your furniture, the furniture in your house."

"No, they've redecorated. They have the same furniture we do."

Whoa, I think, we've got a real maverick of a brain here, pure left brain it seems, having an idea and warping reality to preserve the idea, rather than modifying the idea to correspond to reality. How much of this outsized left brain state has always been my father's way, and how much is the disease? Later, I will see a link between this "disease of knowledge" and the Walter story. Now, the story just sits inside me, like the second spinal column it's always been.

I'm able to spend days and nights at my parents' house because I no longer have a salaried job. There is irony in this state of affairs. Dad had a fit when I quit my law job with the media company in order to write. He asked to read a story I'd written and called it "rubbish." Now I have no interest in writing and couldn't concentrate if I did, but because I no longer have an office job, I have time to help Mother take care of Dad.

Gone is the anger toward Dad that I wore like an extra layer of skin for years after the attacks he directed at Michael. I've moved from fighting Dad's attempts at domination to turning him from side to side and taping up his diapers.

When I got the call from Mother and drove eighty-five miles to the hospital, Dad was lying in the intensive care unit and the first thing he asked with great labor and slurring was "How is Luna?"

That's when the anger left me, slipping off like snow from a warming roof. That this big, downed man could be so injured and yet inquire about my golden retriever took my breath away.

As a result of Dad's stroke, he changed, and so did I. He lost part of his brain and I found some new parts of mine. Any troubles I previously thought I had amounted to nothing, and nothing mattered except his recovery.

The door labeled "family" in me had been closed for a long time, going back to the harsh words to Michael. Dad's stroke swung the door wide open, but the landscape on the other side was upside down. Dad could no longer seek to control me, and at first I had absolutely no idea how to coexist with him in such a place, but I learned. I also saw his strength as he came off a respirator not once, but twice, something that fewer than 10 percent of patients are able to do, according to the doctor who saw it happen.

The same man who survived the influenza that killed half his family had done it again. I saw him in an entirely new light and realized that despite his childhood "Lucky" nickname—after Charles Lindbergh—Dad's seeming invulnerability had never been luck, not when he was a toddler, not when he led men in World War II, and not now when he was fighting for his life. He had grit and great strength, reflex, and instinct. All this I could see now, free of defiance and self-interest. What I saw most clearly was a brave soldier. Yes, he had used his strength inappropriately with Michael and me and it had been a terrible error with painful consequences, but that was over now. It wasn't like the negligence of the captain of the *Vestris*, or, for that matter, of its owner. No one had died.

Eventually Dad stopped asking for the keys, but what he never did was complain, at least not to Mother and me, the ones who gave him daily care. Sweetness came over him, and he was grateful for the smallest thing, like his scrambled eggs arriving with tarragon. What he wanted for breakfast became a regular topic of conversation between us. "Don't forget the ketchup," he would say almost every morning. Whereas before it annoyed me that Dad seemed to close himself off to emotional experiences that might upset him, sealing his world so that nothing could upset him became my daily mission.

Dad started showing whimsy. I asked him what he would do if he was on the moon and he said, "I'd throw rocks at the earth." One day he recited verse:

The Walrus and the Carpenter
Were walking close at hand;
They wept like anything, to see
Such quantities of sand:
"If this were only cleared away,"
They said, "it would be grand!"
"If seven maids with seven mops
Swept it for half a year,
Do you suppose," the Walrus said,
"That they could get it clear?"
"I doubt it," said the Carpenter,
And shed a bitter tear.

I'd never heard my father recite poetry in my life, but clearly the lines were in him. One hears of people who undergo personality changes after a stroke, but Dad's transformation seemed like something else, as though an outer layer had been removed, revealing a far more sensitive man inside.

This was shown in another way, in Dad's frequent requests that I order him the New York University course catalog. He wanted to take classes to get the college degree he'd never obtained. Why it had to be NYU I do not know, but I do know that Dad had never before expressed the desire or need to take a college class. To the contrary, he exalted the school of hard knocks and belittled Michael's academic achievements and choice of teaching law as a career. Now I had reason to wonder if Dad's criticism arose from insecurity about not having a college degree, as if he'd taken my choice of Michael as a stinging rejection.

Dad even started complimenting my writing when enough time passed and I managed to finish a story. He asked to see the story and I was reluctant, recalling his criticism, but I gave it to him anyway. He was sitting in his wheelchair in a white polo shirt, as white as my knuckles as I prepared myself for a repetition of the past.

"Marian, this is a real page-turner," he said to me. I fought back tears as I thanked him, because that's really all he was doing—turning the pages—unable to read full lines of print since his stroke. Still, he wanted to compliment me, and he did.

I hadn't met a man after Michael with whom I wanted to get serious, yet the reality of my father's neediness was so all-encompassing that I couldn't help but think about my future as a single, childless woman.

Dad only touched my big belly once.

"I'm pregnant, you know," I said.

"That has nothing to do with me," he replied. I laughed. From my standpoint it actually had a great deal to do with him. Because of the stroke, Dad became the father I remembered having as a girl, and that helped me see into myself. I could remember waiting inside the garage door for his car to pull in from the station, planting corn and beans with him near the old house in a patch we cleared together, playing Ping-Pong in the basement and laughing so hard at his jokes I could hardly swing the paddle. I could remember when being a child to my

Daddy seemed a joy, and I wanted to be on the parental end of that kind of joy.

Caring for Dad gave me the courage to get pregnant using anonymous donor sperm. If Dad could endure paralysis with such fortitude, I could surely raise a child by myself. This resolve was Dad's parting gift to me, as paradoxical as it was beautiful.

Two months after Dad died, I gave birth to an eight-pound boy. "See the woman without a pituitary in labor," said the doctor to the medical students who filed through the birthing room, but I didn't mind, I was so happy. The absence of a pituitary had necessitated many trips to a fertility clinic, but it hadn't made conception impossible.

I gave my son Dad's initials, JML, the M standing for Melville, Dad's original first name. I was now a single mother with an only boy—just like Grandma and Dad, before and after Walter Lindberg, the man whose story grabbed hold of me once again after I moved back to New York City and settled into parenthood well enough to start work on a new novel.

A novel takes its writer from friends, community, and entertainment—on top of the day-job hours if you need to get your income elsewhere, as I was now doing by practicing law part-time for a firm in midtown. You have to want to write what you're writing as much as you want to eat your favorite food, and this calculation must persist all the time. Because Walter Lindberg was that mental meal that could never sate me, I created a fictional world that allowed me to feast on the story day and night.

I wasn't ready to write about my father, his illness and death too raw, but I created a protagonist with a Scandinavian last name, Isabel Norgaard, to whom I gave a grandmother who had gone mad after her husband disappeared in the Amazon. The madness was, as far as I knew, not true to Grandma's experience.

I speculated about Walter, what he looked like, and what the lack of certainty about his demise did to the wife he left behind. I read about Amazonian tribes, gold, and explorers, and I wrote. Eventually a character based on Michael showed up on page one. Isabel and Simon argued, and she let him go off to Chiapas, Mexico, site of my last trip with Michael, while Isabel stayed at her job at the Metropolitan

Museum and worked on her photography, hoping she would never go mad like her grandmother, but then she got a pituitary tumor and went crazy after all. A lot was going on in the plot, too much. I was stitching together many tangents from my past, trying to make a coherent whole, but it wasn't quite right. During this time, a close friend died, and as executor of her estate I was drawn into intimate and stressful matters involving her affairs and her siblings. Sometimes I would wake after a vivid dream that featured Michael and wonder why was he still showing up in my brain—had he come to symbolize love, or was it more?—and finally I was pushed not to madness but to pick up the phone and find out where the *Vestris* docket was stored.

I wasn't Isabel Norgaard. I was a person named Lindberg with a son of the same name and too many questions still unanswered—not about the plot of my novel, not about the death of my friend, not about any of the hundreds of people whose stories I'd told as a reporter, but about me.

chapter fourteen

GROWING UP

BY THE TIME I found Otto Ulrich's testimony, when my son was six, I didn't actively wish that Michael and I had stayed together.

If we had, there wouldn't be the happy boy in my life who loved Legos, trucks, and pyramids, whom I walked to school every day and adored. There might have been another child, but that child was purely theoretical, whereas my child slept in the next room, held my hand, and engaged in very real acts such as sprinkling fern fronds on the head of his first piano teacher as the man squatted to pet our dog.

There were many beneficial aspects to raising a child on my own: uniformity in matters of discipline and schooling, no vacation scheduling problems, reduced interference with the attention I could offer, and a bond between parent and child that more than exceeded my hopes. Still, I was often alone among couples, and missed the steady companionship and love of an adult. I had been good in relationships. Michael had not been my only long-term boyfriend, though he had been the last. As my son grew, and the years without a partner entered double digits, I never stopped wondering why Dad hadn't been able to accept the man I'd chosen. Why had Dad preferred to shut out his only child rather than let Michael in?

I also wondered why Dad hadn't always been able to behave like the kind, whimsical person he became after his stroke. Clearly, those qualities were inside him, buried somewhere beside his religiosity. Why had it taken a brain injury to make him stop behaving like a bully?

In the weeks after finding the Ulrich transcript, I felt that my search for Walter Lindberg was, indeed, bringing me closer to answers. My instincts had been right: There was more to the Walter story than Dad ever let on. Maybe I was making too much out of a possible romantic liaison with Emmy Kern, and maybe I wasn't, but there was no denying peculiarity in Ulrich giving her an active role in the expedition, hardly mentioning Grandma, and not mentioning Dad at all. These matters were at odds with Dad's account, and for a time they made me angry with Walter. He wasn't the man he was supposed to be.

In addition to Mother, I talked about my extraordinary find with several friends, including one who worked as a law librarian. I brought him to a benefit dinner for my son's school and my friend sat next to me like a writer's patron saint listening as I rattled off details from the Ulrich testimony. My friend said he hadn't heard me so excited about something other than my son in a long time. He thought I would be good at researching the many clues embedded in the transcript. He said I should keep on going. That's what I did.

The truth was that I did not want to give up on Walter. That would have approached the emotional equivalent of self-amputation. He had been part of me almost my entire life, but for many years as a caricature, a little girl's idea of a hero. Only now was I starting to see a real man. Through Ulrich's testimony, Walter Lindberg had stepped outside the simple children's story told by my father and started to become completely human.

Yes, it hurt to think that Walter may have been cheating on Grandma— for unlike Mother, I never felt deceived by or about Grandma and only loved her—and I wondered what sort of subterfuge at home allowed Dad to form such an attachment to Walter.

Yes, the story of Walter Lindberg—something good and pure I had shared with my father, something about our family I had been proud of—now seemed less pure.

Yet, assuming my inferences were correct, Walter wasn't the first man to find himself torn between a wife and another woman, and there was childishness in my clinging to the original story when I'd told myself I wanted to know the truth. You can't begin a research assignment and then turn away when your findings don't affirm your initial hypothesis. That's like a scientist refusing to accept results of an experiment, like a man refusing to read a letter from his daughter expressing her love and begging him to accept the mate she's chosen.

I had to admit I had no idea what Grandma had been like to live with as a spouse. Perhaps the differences in Walter's and Grandma's ethnic and educational backgrounds became as much an abyss as the differences between Mother and Grandma, or maybe Grandma fell out of love with Walter first. There were many possibilities.

To get any accurate reading on the past, I would need to use the same attribute that made me a decent lawyer—the ability to see a situation from multiple points of view. For all I knew, when he went to Brazil, Walter might have been trying to get away from Emmy Kern and give himself a cooling-off period with the possibility open that he would return to Grandma and Dad.

An objective reading of Ulrich's transcript suggested some virtuous behavior by Walter. Dad had said Walter helped the families of his partners after the *Vestris* sank, and Ulrich confirmed this. Walter was waiting at the pier in New York when the rescue ship carrying Ulrich arrived, and Ulrich said Walter did not express anger about the equipment losses. Nor did Walter press Ulrich to pay back any of $1,600 in cash that was lost—not even by dipping into the $700 of Ulrich's money he claimed to have saved in his shirt.

By Ulrich's account, Walter did not dwell on the disaster, other than making lists of the lost equipment for the court case. Rather, he looked to the future and spoke with Ulrich about undertaking another expedition.

But Walter could not afford to replace the lost equipment, Ulrich testified. Dad had put it more strongly, that Walter was now indebted to the lenders from whom he had borrowed funds for the Goerz camera, box of tools, fifty grams of pyramidon, surgical instruments, surveying and riding equipment, and all the other articles in the "five large wooden trunks, one small wooden trunk, three large leather trunks, two small leather trunks, four leather brief cases and one large canvas sailor bag" that went down with the ship.

Nor did Walter succeed in enlisting partners for a new expedition, at least not partners willing to leave as soon as Walter wanted to travel. Ulrich said his wife's injuries required him to remain in New York, but he testified that he told Walter he would raise money, buy new equipment and scientific instruments, and join Walter in Brazil as soon as he could. He did none of those things.

"You mean you gave up Lindberg, is that it?" interjected the special master, obviously impatient with the witness.

"No," responded Ulrich calmly. "I remained here on account of the sickness of my wife."

Ulrich was not eager to be portrayed as a man who reneged on his promises, but the defense lawyers and special master kept coming back to Walter's situation in Brazil in 1929 waiting for Ulrich to join him. Early in his cross-examination, Ulrich was asked how soon he was supposed to meet Walter. "It was agreed that I should follow as soon as possible," he had said.

Yet later in the deposition, Ulrich indicated that in his own mind, the possibility of joining Walter was much more uncertain.

"Did you expect to go on the expedition?"

"I expected that I might follow."

"About how long afterward?"

"That depended entirely on the state of health of my wife and the fact if I could procure the money to follow at all."

The words "might follow" convey a very different state of mind than "it was agreed that I should follow." Clearly, Ulrich was adept at bending words to suit the question. However he characterized his intentions, it didn't appear that Ulrich tried very hard to raise the funds to buy the items on which Walter was counting.

"And where were you to get the money to finance [the equipment]?" a defense attorney asked him.

"Through an acquaintance," he said. "I was to buy the instruments, but I could not get the money together to buy them."

"Well, is Lindberg still waiting for you to come down with the instruments and the equipment?"

"Since I was unable to go down, Lindberg got tired and he started forth alone."

"Where were you going to meet Lindberg if you had been able to get a new expedition equipped?" the special master interrupted.

"He was going to write that to me; either at Sao Paulo or at Campo Grande."

"Did he write to you and say where you were to meet him?"

"No; he only wrote me one letter from the West Indies and that was the first and last letter, as far as I recollect."

"How did he know that you did not go down there?"

"We had arranged that I would write or telegraph to the American Consul General at Sao Paulo about my arrival, and when this would be."

"Did you write or telegraph to the Consul General when you found out that you could not go down?"

"As far as I remember, I have written a letter that my coming probably would not materialize."

"Did you write a letter to the Consul General that you would not come?"

"Not to the American Consul General but to Mr. Lindberg, care of the American Consul General."

Ulrich had received no reply.

That ended the special master's line of questions. He was as speechless as Walter must have been upon reading that letter. What was left to ask?

Remarkably, after writing Walter in 1929 that his "coming probably would not materialize," Ulrich successfully raised funds for an expedition to Brazil in the fall of 1931, claiming to have received transportation, personnel, and lodging courtesy of the Brazilian government.

He testified that he led the expedition and that it included a man whose name had already been mentioned, Carl Zimmerman. Ulrich identified Zimmerman as his "secretary" when questioned by his own lawyer, but under the pressure of the defense attorney's well-researched cross-examination, Ulrich admitted that Zimmerman was, like Ulrich, an orderly at St. Vincent's Hospital.

"Yes, sir. I worked during the day and he worked during the night," Ulrich conceded.

It had never occurred to me that Amazonian explorers would have jobs as hospital attendants. But I could try to accept the world's reality and marvel at its unglamorous gears. I was old enough now to understand that a person could work by day and dream by night, just as I was earning money as a lawyer during the day and writing after my son went to sleep.

What did Walter Lindberg do alone in Brazil? Did he follow Ulrich's 1926 route to the Rio Juruena in search of gold and amazonite?

Though Ulrich was adamant that the maps sank with the *Vestris*, he said the maps' absence would not have mattered had he made it down to Brazil to join Walter in 1929.

"We would have gone in the direction of the old territory," Ulrich said, "because the region is so great that exploration work can be done anywhere."

The special master asked what Walter could do alone in Brazil without any scientific instruments, records, or maps.

"Lindberg could do a lot," Ulrich declared. My back unhinged with pride.

"What?" asked the special master.

"Lindberg was one of the co-builders of the famous Madeira-Mamore Bahn, Amazonus," Ulrich told the master, referring to the Madeira-Mamore Railroad. According to Ulrich, Walter "was very well known in these regions, and therefore he was always in a position to carry on exploration of any description."

"Exploration of any description" seemed like a good way to put it, because Ulrich revealed that Walter had changed his mission and gone looking for a tree—the babassu palm.

Ulrich said this information came to him in 1930 in the form of a letter from Alfred Rackebrand, secretary at the Condor Air Line in Rio de Janeiro. Rackebrand wrote that Walter "had gone to the interior and that he was up to a big proposition that he was planning the exploration of the Babassu palm nut."

"Is that a river or a territory or a company or what?" asked one of the attorneys.

"That is a region in which a palm grows which is called 'Babassu' palm," Ulrich replied.

Ulrich said he received no further information about Walter, though in advance of the deposition, knowing that he would be asked about Walter, he inquired both at the Explorers Club and at the apartment on 86th Street where Walter had lived with Grandma and Dad.

He learned nothing at either place, saying curtly that "the wife moved out; she is not living there anymore."

Still, Ulrich asserted that Walter might still be alive: "Unless he is in New York, he can only be in Brazil."

My eyes read the sentence a second time, and then a third. The notion that Walter could still have been alive when Ulrich gave this part of his testimony in January 1933 defied what I'd heard from my father—that Walter died within a year after going to Brazil. It also conflicted with sworn testimony from someone I trusted even more than Dad—my grandmother.

An affidavit that she had signed, which I had not read in years, was stored in a drawer in my house in Long Island—with all the other court documents from when my parents tried to get rid of the Lindberg name once and for all.

chapter fifteen

THE GROOM'S CHANGE OF NAME

"JEANS AND DENIM of any color are not acceptable at any time."

So says a recent rule at the Bath and Tennis Club in the beach town of Spring Lake, New Jersey. In the 1940s, Jews fell into the same category as jeans and denim: barred and shunned, in practice if not in the written rules. The name Lindberg, misperceived by some in heavily Irish Spring Lake as a Jewish name, therefore had to go. It presented a problem for a young couple seeking acceptance. My father and mother were the victims of anti-Semitism.

There were at least two members of the Bath and Tennis Club who knew that the dark-haired, dark-eyed Patricia Ryan Lindberg was Christian, no matter what her new last name might suggest to others. They were Mother's brother John and my grandmother with the flapper dresses, Marion Kondolf Ryan, who had sold the family's Miami Beach house and bought a place in Spring Lake following her husband's death in 1939.

Mother and Dad were married in 1943, he 25 years old, she 22. The wedding's scale was small, befitting wartime, with a reception in the respectable St. Regis Roof. Thereafter, until Dad's deployment to Europe, the newlyweds lived in Camp Stewart in Georgia, quite a change for Mother. Dad used to joke that he taught Mother how to boil water. She certainly did a convincing imitation of a suburban housewife when I was a girl, but as I got older and learned more about her background—from my own investigation, and from fragments I managed to coax out of her—I understood the fall that her daily cooking, food-shopping, and cleaning represented, how much resignation was required for her to perform those tasks (though she rarely complained), and how completely her often absurd chores—ironing the dishtowels, for one—reflected an effort to re-create, on a modest budget, some of the attributes of the splendid environments in which she had grown up.

One day, sometime after Dad had died, Mother told me that two years into the marriage, she moved out. This story about the past didn't come in a cozy den while we were sitting down. Mother stood in the dining room and I stood a few feet away as she made an uncharacteristic disclosure, telling me in answer to one of my questions that she had tried to end her marriage to Dad due to the differences in their educational, economic, and cultural backgrounds. Apparently it hadn't been an easy adjustment for her, boiling water after so many years of other people doing it for her.

Mother said she turned to her mother for support, but none was given.

"She told me I'd made my bed and I had to lie in it." Ultimately, that's what Mother did. She returned to Dad and the marriage bed for fifty-one more years.

Mother did not put the two events together, but when I found the file I was looking for, I saw that the time of Mother's return coincided with Dad's hiring a lawyer and filing a petition requesting a change of name, which he did in 1946. I realized that he must have done so not only for the sake of acceptance by Irish beach lovers but also to placate Mother and forestall another fissure in the marriage. Dad couldn't change his poor background or his uneducated mother, but he could change his name. He had another at the ready, his real name.

Dad never talked to me about Mother leaving him, but he did show me the court papers, including the affidavits filed by him and Grandma and the judge's order declaring that Mother and Dad's marriage license was officially changed to read Mr. and Mrs. Melville Jean DePay.

I remember Dad calling me over as a teenager, at the bottom of the stairs in our old house, documents in hand, saying he wanted to show me something. He handed me the documents and asked me to give them back after I read them. It was the first time I completely understood that the man who disappeared in Brazil wasn't Dad's father.

After I read the documents, I asked Dad why he had gone to all that trouble to get his and Mother's names changed to DePay if we were still called Lindberg. He told me about the anti-Semitism he and Mother had encountered in Spring Lake but said it proved inconvenient to change his name at the bank, where he was already known as Lindberg. A child of two runaways who had lost two fathers by the age of eleven and had recently seen his new wife walk away, Dad may have felt that his career was the most reliable part of his life, the thing most worth honoring by holding on to the name by which he was known there. The bank rewarded Dad for his loyalty, promoting him to increasingly senior positions over a forty-year span despite his lack of a college degree.

Dad hadn't completely given in to anti-Semitism and dropped the Lindberg name, but he had tried, so when Dad claimed Michael's Judaism made him an unsuitable match, I thought back to the name change documents with disdain and even shame. Now the documents mattered to me for a different reason.

Walter figured in the court papers because Dad sought to establish that his "true and correct name" was and always had been Melville Jean DePay, as written on his birth certificate and church-issued proof of First Communion.

Dad explained in his affidavit that he had been known as Jean Melville Lindberg since age six because his mother and stepfather thought it would be "a matter of convenience" and in his "best interests," although he was "not formally adopted by his step-father, Walter Lindberg, nor was his name changed to 'Lindberg' by any legal proceedings."

He further asserted that "because of the confusion which has arisen in petitioner's affairs due to his use of the name of 'Lindberg' he is endeavoring at this time to correct any and all records which show his family name as 'Lindberg' instead of 'DePay.'"

"Confusion" in that context would appear to be a euphemism for prejudice.

Grandma also submitted an affidavit, dated October 24, 1946, stating that when her son started school at P.S. 6, she had registered him under the name of "Lindberg" and also reversed his first two names to "Jean Melville."

In the affidavit, Grandma swore that Walter Lindberg had died in August 1929.

She also stated that from the date of her marriage to Walter in 1923 until his death in 1929, they were both "at all times" residents of New York City. While down in Brazil, Walter was a resident of New York in legal terms only if he intended to return. That's what Grandma swore to, so presumably that's what she believed—and it could well have been true. If Walter sailed in March and died in August, he had only been away from New York for five months.

Putting the affidavit together with Ulrich's testimony, and the last news about Walter's whereabouts, my working hypothesis became that Walter had died in August 1929 while in the Brazilian interior searching for babassu palms.

The throttle in my brain was revving again. I was way past holding Emmy Kern against Walter. Thanks to Ulrich's testimony and Grandma's affidavit, I now had a whole new set of questions to investigate. I stopped revising the novel I was working on and embraced my new research.

Although Brazil had called to me since girlhood, I had done the opposite of Otto Ulrich. Whereas he boarded a ship to Brazil on one day's notice, I had only dreamed of going.

My first endocrinologist was cautious about my traveling. When Michael and I decided to see the ruins at Palenque in Mexico, the doctor insisted I bring my own canned food and wear a MedicAlert bracelet indicating which drugs I needed. She warned against dehydration from dysentery, or death if I was in an accident that left me unconscious and unable to tell medical personnel about the replacement hormones my body required. It wasn't as though I walked around with them in my pocket. One of the important ones, a liquid inhaled into the nostrils by means of a small plastic straw, required refrigeration.

Mexico went fine, but a few years later, traveling to Paris, I didn't bring canned sardines and I got sick, which led to dehydration, dizziness, and weakness. I knew I was in danger. The hotel summoned a lovely doctor, who spoke no English. Luckily, "hypopituitarisme" worked in French, and in a pretty satisfying display of two people trying to solve a problem quickly despite a language barrier, I got through it and resolved not to eat oysters away from home.

I had yet another scare while visiting a friend in Boston when my son was young. The whole house came down with a gastrointestinal flu, and I needed IV fluids at an emergency room.

Part of the magic of the pituitary is to help the body adjust to changes in the environment, so with a piece of fat instead of the gland, there was no denying that I occasionally suffered outsized reactions to things. I was okay with never running a marathon, and I learned the hard way that I couldn't take saunas anymore, but I was determined to live a full life.

As the years went by, I got much better at living without a pituitary. I gladly retired the nose straw when desmopressin acetate (synthetic vasopressin) became available in pill form, but I still needed to travel with a cold pack. Since 1997 I had been taking daily injections of growth hormone (approved by the FDA as medically necessary for hypopituitaristic adults), and the drug would lose its potency unless kept cool.

I reached a point where I would see my new, less cautious endocrinologist and she would say everything is fine, come back in a year. Sometimes a major trip required special planning, such as having liquid cortisone on hand, but mostly I traveled without giving much forethought to my condition. I took my son hiking and camping numerous times, not even thinking to look for the MedicAlert bracelet in my dresser drawer. So it really wasn't a fear of medical problems that had kept me from going to the Amazon. It was the fear of not finding what I wanted. I felt that changing thanks to Otto Ulrich. I felt Brazil getting closer.

chapter sixteen

WHAT'S WILD

BOTHERED BY FRIZZY hair or sagging skin? Try babassu palm oil.

That's what the Internet taught me about *Attalea speciosa*, the wonder tree that seemed to have lured Walter to his death. Virgin Airlines has even used babassu oil as jet fuel.

But what exactly did Walter have in mind with his "big proposition" in the Brazilian interior "planning the exploration of the Babassu palm nut," as the airline employee in Brazil had reported to Ulrich? Was Walter ahead of his time, sensing the palm's commercial possibilities back in 1929? Was he thinking of setting up a Lindberg line of skin creams or hair products? Or was he motivated by potential medicinal applications, perhaps dreaming of curing malaria with injections of babassu oil?

In the early part of the 20th century, it was mainly indigenous peoples and peasants who used the babassu for shelter (the fronds, woven into roofs, walls, and fences), sustenance (the oil-rich seeds and palm hearts, fed to humans and livestock), cooking fuel (the husks), emollients (the oil, made into soap and skin-care products), art (plaited baskets), and clothing items (buttons, from the fruit's inner layer). People have also made medicines, beverages, flour, and nutritional supplements from the palm's hard fruit—or "nut," as the man in Rio called it.

The babassu palm offered such versatility there was no telling what Walter had in mind, but one thing seemed clear: If Walter was last heard from looking for stands of palm trees, he wasn't hacking through the jungle in search of diamonds, gold, or amazonite on his last expedition. He may indeed have been killed by cannibals, or by native peoples who simply opposed his presence in their territory. The account of cannibalism that my father had reported to me could not, however, as he had believed, been a cover-up for betrayal. Who would kill over the location of an abundant plant?

I could see that Dad's account merged aspects of Walter's two trips, lifting the intended use of a treasure map from Walter's aborted 1928 expedition and ascribing the map as the reason for Walter's disappearance on the trip actually taken in 1929. Dad claimed Walter's "partners" had killed Walter to get the treasure map, but in 1929 it seemed pretty well-established that Ulrich was in New York with his wife, not in Brazil capable of stealing anything from Walter or killing him. Zimmerman, the other orderly and "partner," didn't go to Brazil until 1931. Besides, Ulrich had testified that all the maps sank with the *Vestris*.

Like some of the other details, the date Dad had given me for Walter's trip was wrong, too. In his last telling of the story, the one I wrote down on his seventy-first birthday, Dad said that Walter stayed in New York for two years after the *Vestris* sank and was reported dead about a year after that. My research showed that the actual times were much shorter: Walter stayed in New York for four months, and news of his death reached Grandma five months after that, according to the supporting papers in Dad's own name-change petition.

The conclusion was inescapable that Dad really had no direct knowledge of how Walter died. Dad was ten years old when Walter left; he turned eleven in August 1929, the month of Walter's death according to Grandma's affidavit. Whatever Dad did know had likely been conveyed to him by Grandma. Perhaps she wished to indulge her son's heroic notions of his stepfather. Or perhaps Dad knew about the map directly from Walter. Maybe he had visited Walter's office and seen it.

From another standpoint, though, the inaccuracies were minor quibbles. Walter Lindberg had gone into the jungle and never emerged. That much seemed confirmed—or was it? Grandma swore in her 1946 affidavit that Walter died in 1929, yet Ulrich testified in January 1933 that he thought Walter might be alive in Brazil. Someone besides Dad had his or her dates wrong, or else Ulrich hadn't heard, or wasn't convinced, of Walter's death.

I wondered what the relationship was like between Ulrich and Grandma, if they even knew each other, and why were they saying two different things about Walter's demise, both of them under oath. My two star witnesses were dead, so I couldn't assess their credibility based on body language and demeanor, like a judge presiding at a trial, and even though I had known Grandma, or thought I had, that was later in her life, and I was becoming open to the possibility that she had been a different person in the decades before I knew her.

I was left with different versions of Walter's exit from my family and the world, which only meant one thing. As my law-librarian friend had advised, I needed to keep on going.

I was propelled, in part, by a sort of competition with my departed father. I felt a satisfying sense of advantage at having learned more than he ever had about his stepfather. Like Walter before me, a sense of greed crept in. I wanted more, but it felt harmless, like boxing with a ghost. I was jab-jab-jabbing, not hurting anyone, and I rather liked the connection to the ghost. It was the way Dad and I had been as adults, often sparring. Why stop?

The Explorers Club did not always occupy one of Manhattan's best blocks in a lovely four-story house with leaded glass windows and interior walls of carved oak. The men who formed the club in 1905 met in rented rooms until 1912, when the club found space in a loft on Amsterdam Avenue on the West Side. The upscale brick and limestone house on East 70th Street wasn't purchased until 1965.

When I paid a visit to the current site, the ornate stairs to the library took me past a huge stuffed polar bear positioned in a standing pose on a landing. The bear was symbolic of the club's early fascination with cold places—Adolphus Greely, the club's first president, explored the Arctic, as did the three succeeding presidents. Of the thirteen men who comprise the club's "historical members," only Theodore Roosevelt had to bring along mosquito netting to where he was going—the warm middle of the earth. South America did not become an area of significant interest to club members until the 1920s, which only made Walter Lindberg seem like that much more of a pioneer.

But for the librarian and the aura of George Plimpton, the last person to have used the library according to the sign-in sheet, I had the place to myself. That suited me fine. I was in grave-digging mode, trying to learn from the dead about the dead. Silence was appropriate.

It was exciting to browse through books and papers associated with many of the world's greatest adventurers, and I wondered where in the club's records there might be buried a reference to Walter Lindberg. After a few minutes of self-service, I described my research to the librarian, who went into a back room to see what he could find. He emerged with nothing but an apology. Walter Lindberg, he informed me, was never a member of the club and there were no records about him. The same was true for Otto Ulrich and the other men in Ulrich's account.

There was finality to the librarian's information, which I didn't like. I felt my standing fall at once. I was no grandchild (or step-grandchild) of a recognized explorer. Nor would I ever be a writer of George Plimpton's stature. I was just another member of the public doing genealogical research. None of this disapprobation radiated from the librarian, who remained pleasant. It was my own psyche registering a radical decline in my importance.

My optimism about finding clues had fallen, but I wasn't ready to leave. I still harbored hope of stumbling upon a mention of Walter—or even Ulrich or Zimmerman—in the club's minutes or in the accounts of South American expeditions. After all, that had happened to me before, in the National Archives when I found Walter's name in the last file on the *Vestris* cart.

I sat down at a desk with files describing the missions of club members in the 1920s and early 1930s. My attention hugged the material like a long-lost friend. Walter was my reason for spending that week's writing day in the library of the Explorers Club, but he didn't have a lock on my brain. He couldn't prevent me from being captivated by the world of exploration even if it didn't concern him.

It was not long into reading members' reports from Walter's era—one about a 1925 trip down the Amazon, which had revealed the process of "reducing and curing human heads by the Jiveros of eastern Ecuador," another concerned with collecting specimens—that I realized the reason why Walter, Ulrich, and their treasure maps never would have belonged at the club: The club's mission was defined as scientific and anthropological exploration. Its members proclaimed their single-minded concern with the advancement of human knowledge and held themselves above prospecting for gems and any other goal of pecuniary enrichment.

Nothing about the club's self-image, then or now, jibed with Otto Ulrich. While he had testified about his interest in one of the native Brazilian dialects—Guarani—and claimed to have written a book entitled *In the Land of Monkeys and Parrots*, his primary passion seemed to be for wealth.

The Explorers Club rules state that its flag may be loaned (it is always loaned, never given) for an expedition or field research project the purpose of which "will benefit exploration and science." The flag will not be loaned if the expedition is primarily a competitive event, solely for commercial purposes, or one that "acquires artifacts intended for sale." Otto Ulrich's desire to acquire gold to sell for cash would have disqualified him, but what about Walter's cartography interests and his search for the babassu palm nut? Could Walter have had scientific goals in mind? I found no trace of him that day to suggest it, nor to suggest that any club member had ever gone searching for babassu palms. Ulrich had testified that the club had no information about Walter's whereabouts in 1932. That was still true.

Energized but also dejected by my hours in the club library, I walked out of the elegant headquarters into a spring evening in New York City, thinking that Walter must have been but a small player in the world of exploration that enthralled the Americas and Europe in the early 1900s. I was only sixteen blocks south of where Walter, Grandma, and Dad had lived in what was then a German epicenter, but other than perhaps the

German Louis Schellbach, the club secretary whom Ulrich said he had consulted, it was more likely that members of the Explorers Club had traveled in the same social circles as John and Marion Ryan than those of Walter Lindberg.

That wasn't true in the world of commerce, however.

A record in the Explorers Club files mentioned Major Anthony Fiala, of Fiala Outfits, on Warren Street in New York, explaining that "Major Fiala has been the outfitter for some of the most famous expeditions that have ever left the American continent, including Roosevelt's famous exploratory trip into the then unknown regions of the River of Doubt. Major Fiala was one of the official leaders of this expedition."

Fiala Outfits was almost certainly the store that Walter and Ulrich hurriedly visited the day before the *Vestris* sailed, after Ulrich received the letter from Alexander Alexandrovitch saying to come to Brazil immediately. Unlike at the Explorers Club, one didn't have to have a high purpose or social connections to shop at Fiala Outfits. One only needed cash or credit.

After my visit to the Explorers Club, I bought an old Fiala catalog online for $25, a plain business-like document compared to today's glossy catalogs, consisting of black-and-white photos and small type. It offered boundless possibilities, from "soft fluffy camp blankets" ($6.75 each) to the "pocket snakebite outfit" (fifty cents), and "freight canoes for exploration" ("prices furnished on application"). There were cameras and lenses like the ones Walter bought and put aboard the *Vestris*, and surveying equipment of the sort Ulrich had packed in trunks, a sextant for measuring degrees of latitude, and numerous types of altimeters and compasses.

Fiala offered services beyond equipment: "If you are contemplating hunting or hiking in a place that is not well known or correctly mapped—and there are many such places—write or visit us for instruction in sketch mapping if you are not familiar with the subject. We can help you so that your exploration may be placed on record and your trip be made worth while."

On the back cover, the Fiala Outfits logo showed a polar bear standing on top of a globe of the earth, the same animal that greets visitors at the Explorers Club, only the Fiala bear is twice the size of the continent of North America. Its mouth is open and its teeth are bared.

In 1927, when the catalog was published, the polar bear must have symbolized absolute wildness, triumphant nature which humans could only hope to reach and explore with gear of the sort offered in Fiala's "Adventure Shop":

Here in the "Spot of Romance," surrounded by the roar of the world's greatest town, are piled queer scientific instruments for desert wanderers. There are great parkas, to ward off Arctic cold, and khaki tents, waterproofed to withstand torrential tropic rains, sleeping bags for cold wilderness nights, mosquito bars for jungle insects, dog sledges, camp stoves, Bowie knives, barometers and swimming suits. Lined along the wall are guns of every description—elephant rifles, pistols, target guns.

It couldn't have been imagined when those words were laid in type in 1927 under the photograph of a polar bear guarding its ice haven that in the not-too-distant future, through actions of the same species that might wish to buy Anthony Fiala's queer scientific instruments and mosquito bars, the polar bear would face extinction, its habitat of northern sea ice melting into the Arctic.

It couldn't have been anticipated that in less than a century after the brochure was printed, no part of the earth would remain untouched by human activity, by emissions of carbon dioxide and methane warming the world and beginning to disrupt the very triggers that make it rain in the rainforests.

The catalog boasted that the shop "dispatched and outfitted Capt. Dyot to Brazil, and explorers to every part of the globe. From here trains of adventure lead to the known and unknown."

In my lifetime, however, the unknown itself had ceased to exist. Sons of explorers had become purveyors of eco-tourism trips safe enough for children and retirees. At the Explorers Club, I had read of the specimen collector George Cherrie, who experienced a gun accident in Ecuador in 1921. He marched five days with a huge wound on his arm. This is not what is asked of people who travel to the Amazon today. We have gained access, but lost much of the mystery, at what cost to our individual and collective ability to feel wonder?

The Fiala catalog sang to me of that mystery, even though I knew that much had changed in the Amazon since Fiala's day, with highways, cattle ranches, and vast soybean farms where trees and vines once stood. Much had changed even since the 1960s, when it was still possible for a girl in a suburb in the developed world to believe that wild places would stay wild just for the sanctity of what her father told her they sheltered, a special man's remains.

The Amazon had first come to me in story form, and as a parent I saw how the books we read our young are filled with colorful plants and animals, but I didn't want nature to be just a story we tell our children.

I took my son to the Galapagos Islands, where Charles Darwin collected his famous finches. I enrolled in conservation biology classes and began volunteering in the mammalogy department at the American Museum of Natural History, where I relabeled bat carcasses, read Latin American explorers' journals, and studied giant maps of Bolivia and Brazil while scientists conversed in the halls about evolution. And then, two years after finding out that the story of Walter dying in the jungle appeared to be true, I left the law to join an organization that regards the earth as its client.

chapter seventeen

THE FOREST FOR THE TREES

"SAVING THE PLANET" may be a tongue-in-cheek phrase, but The Nature Conservancy takes its work very seriously. With over 3,500 employees in thirty-three countries, the organization seeks to operate at such a large scale that making a difference at the planetary level is an avowed goal, whether the step is purchasing 175,000 acres in the Adirondacks to protect the land from development, or buying huge ranches in Australia and returning the land to aboriginals, whose traditional practice is to use controlled burns to reduce the risk of wild fires.

The Conservancy had an office three miles from my house on Long Island, where I became a member of the land protection and coastal teams, while my son, Justin, started fourth grade in a new school. Mother's health was declining, another reason to leave Manhattan, as she had moved into my house a couple of years after Dad's death while Justin and I remained in New York City, seeing her on weekends and during the summer.

My work as an "enviro," as the local politicians called us, began at a small scale, negotiating deals to protect nine acres here, seventy-eight acres there, mainly in the maritime moorlands of Montauk and around Accabonac Harbor, where the open views of the tidal marsh and blue water inspired Jackson Pollock, Lee Krasner, Willem de Kooning, and many other artists who moved to the area beginning in the 1940s.

Accabonac Harbor is not the Pantanal or an Amazonian tributary. Babassu palms do not grow there, but spartina grasses, bayberry, and marsh elder do. And when the young osprey cry from one-hundred-pound nests on the tops of wooden platforms, and the steamy air rises from the tall grass, when white-tailed deer trot in the distance, and one spots animal bones in the grass, eastern Long Island can seem wild enough.

Scientists like to say that tidal marshes are as biologically productive as rainforests; you just can't see the activity. It's only a matter of morphology, not intrinsic worth, that ribbed mussels will never be snakes, and saltmarsh sparrows and willets will never be toucans and macaws. In my first year and a half working for the Conservancy, I repeated this comparison to donors, interns, and town board members and tried to sound convincing. I told them how salt marshes filtered water, sequestered carbon dioxide, and helped protect communities from flooding and storm surges. I wanted people to care as much for the marshes of Long Island as for the forests of Brazil.

But did *I*?

If Walter Lindberg had met his end clamming near a Long Island salt marsh, would the story have had the same resonance all my life? No, Brazil made the story what it was, and that very point was expressed by a former classmate, an artist, after I had a couple of glasses of wine at my high school reunion and trotted out the story of Walter Lindberg.

"What does Brazil mean for so many people?" my former classmate asked. "What does it connote throughout the world, and what has it connoted?"

Those were great questions, presaging the protests that would erupt in 2013 and continue through the 2014 World Cup in which millions of Brazilians demanded a greater role in determining what Brazil should mean—good health care and schools, for many of the protestors, not just a place vying for international status by hosting major sporting events.

The Brazil of the story I had for so long told about Walter meant something else altogether: dangerous places teeming with natural riches and home to native peoples.

So it was that shortly after my high school reunion, when an internationally recognized conservationist and photographer, Cristina Mittermeier, spoke to our staff about her work in Brazil with the Kayapo people, I couldn't resist bringing out the Walter Lindberg tray of hors d'oeuvres and offering her a bite. She had just told us how the Kayapo tribal lands and way of life were threatened by the construction of dams over the Xingu River, the main purpose of which would be to provide electricity to a Chinese mining company. She had recently founded an organization devoted to advancing environmental protection through photography.

Cristina listened politely and encouraged me to go to Brazil. "There are areas open to tourists now," was how she put it, and I bridled at the phrasing.

Two of my colleagues were standing next to me, and after Cristina moved on to speak with someone else, they each took an appetizer off the Walter tray. They told me I should go to Brazil and bring along an interpreter, someone who knew the ins and outs of the country's government.

I wanted to follow this advice, but I still didn't know what I would do in Brazil—or even what I was looking for. Then, a few weeks later, a senior leader from the The Nature Conservancy spoke to us about his recent assignment in Chile and how well it had gone even though he didn't speak Spanish. That got me thinking that maybe I could work for the Conservancy in Brazil even though I didn't know Portuguese. To discuss this possibility, I coordinated a meeting with a leader of my organization's Amazon program, an Irish expat named Ian Thompson, who had originally gone to Brazil with the British government to do development work, married a Brazilian, and now lived in Belem.

Ian was visiting New York to meet prospective donors and I felt fortunate to be given some of his time. He thought I could help by editing a conservation plan for the Amazon program, and we had a wide-ranging conversation about goals and objectives, and how the Conservancy could help bolster native people's inherent interest in protecting the rainforest as well as work with farmers, ranchers, and big agricultural companies to enforce Brazil's laws limiting the amount of rainforest that could be cleared.

Ian was pragmatic. Roads were going to be built through the rainforest. The question was where. The road down from Acre didn't need to go up to Peru into a pristine area. Success meant getting a shorter road, not no road at all.

I didn't take much of Ian's time talking about Walter Lindberg, but when I told him the route that Ulrich had described, leading to the area between the rivers Juruena and Ji-Paraná, Ian volunteered that it was a place where diamonds could be found. I asked him about the babassu palm and he was dismissive of the tree. "It survives fire," he said. "It's found in the eastern part of the Amazon. Women make soap out of it." He couldn't imagine why a man would have gone to his death looking for babassu palms.

I edited the business plan Ian forwarded to me, started to take lessons in Portuguese, and entertained the idea of an assignment in Brazil. My son was in sixth grade now, an increasingly serious musician, not all that interested in change or world travel, but I hoped that I might be able to find a good international school for him in Brazil.

Then Mother fell in the kitchen again and I began to see what I was doing. I was creating a fantasy, an escape from the day-to-day pain of watching her slow crawl toward death. Given her condition, there was no way I could leave home for more than a week, much less a year, with or without my son. Each morning I would wait to hear if her bedroom door opened and her walker tapped the floor, affirming that she hadn't died during the night. She never wanted to talk about her health or see a doctor or say hello when I walked in the door from work and she was listening to a vile talk radio host spew vitriol at full volume as she made her dinner, after which she would wash the dishes by hand. The entire process took about three hours, during which period she would peer at me like I was a tornado speeding in her direction, seconds from jolting her off her feet, if I so much as entered the kitchen for a glass of water, much less started cooking a meal for my son and me. Who wouldn't rather be in the Amazon, shielded under a thick canopy from a tropical downpour?

The Walter Lindberg story was like a beach read I never had to put down, a book whose cover I would never have to shut, a magical world I sometimes wished I could somehow swap with my own.

I saw this in myself, and yet felt powerless to change it. Walter Lindberg didn't need me, but I seemed to need him. Perhaps I always had.

Seven months after my meeting with the head of the Amazon program, the eastern division of the Conservancy was summoned to Norfolk, Virginia. Scores of employees assembled to learn from each other and hear more about the organization's global priorities. Me, I would sneak out of one of the afternoon sessions to go to the public library.

Norfolk is an important city in the conservation world, low-lying and increasingly flooded due to sea level rise caused mostly by warming temperatures, but that afternoon, Norfolk mattered to me for a different reason. Norfolk had played a prominent role in the Walter story, though not the one Dad said. Dad told me Walter was supposed to board the *Vestris* in Norfolk on its way south, but that was wrong. Norfolk was a place to which survivors were brought after the *Vestris* sank.

In the dim light of the microfiche machine, headlines blared from *The Virginian-Pilot* dated Tuesday, November 13, 1928: "NO TRACE OF BOATS FROM LINER VESTRIS" and "ROUGH SEAS AROUSE FEARS THAT ALL ON BOARD ARE LOST."

Soon I found myself staring at the face of Marie Ulrich. There she was on the front page of the next day's newspaper under a three-decker headline: "BATTLESHIP WYOMING ARRIVES WITH SURVIVORS FROM VESTRIS: OFFICIAL INVESTIGATION BEGINS."

As *The Virginian-Pilot* put it:

Three women widowed by the sea, three Negroes mute from the horror they had seen and lived through and two more women too shocked to talk, with two American seamen of the battleship Wyoming crippled in the rescue, came to the Norfolk Naval Hospital last night, living evidence of the tragedy that accompanied the sinking of the Lamport & Holt passenger steamer *Vestris*.

Mrs. Ulrich was shown in the photograph standing with three other women, two of whom lost their husbands, unlike Marie Ulrich, whose husband was taken to New York and met by Walter at the pier.

The fifth woman rescued by the *Wyoming*, Mrs. Teruko Inouye, "was too ill to pose for the photograph," according to the caption. She was "a tiny Japanese [who] came borne upon a stretcher, so much had she suffered from exposure and the shock of having her husband die in her arms."

The four women in the photograph did not look particularly well themselves, or pleased to have been asked by a photographer to pose for public viewing after all they had endured.

Marie Ulrich stands on the far left, mouth closed, looking down and to the left, not at the camera. Her short, dark hair is matted, and she wears a baggy, long coat presumably given to her on the rescue ship. She looks like she is about to fall forward into a long, deep sleep. I understood why. Her testimony came back to me, how she spent an afternoon and night in rough seas holding onto a capsized lifeboat until the number of people still alive from the port lifeboat with the poorly patched hole dwindled from sixty-eight to four, how she had swam the next morning for hours after the seas yanked the boat from her weakened grip. She was one of the lucky passengers who had been given a life preserver and hadn't lost consciousness. She was also, obviously, a person of unusual strength.

Next to her stands Marian Calvin Batten, now the widow of the famous racecar driver from Dayton, Ohio. All she said to *The Virginian-Pilot* reporter was that "if it hadn't been for Gerald, we wouldn't be here." Gerald Burton, first-class fireman, was one of the three "Negroes" rescued by the *Wyoming*. According to the paper, he had "cheered the women for new courage when they became despondent and ready to die after more than twenty hours in the water," their lifeboat having capsized and splintered into pieces.

At least Mrs. Batten fared better than Ann DeVore, the widow of the other racecar driver, Earl DeVore. Mrs. DeVore and the couple's dog survived, but Earl did not, prompting hate mail to Mrs. DeVore as "the woman who saved her dog and abandoned her husband."

Mrs. DeVore tried to explain: "What was I supposed to have done, hold [the dog's] head under water until she drowned?"

Disasters are made-to-order media stories, and this was as true in 1912 and 1928 as it was in January 2012, when the *Costa Concordia* changed its course, hit a rocky reef, and capsized off the coast of Tuscany, costing thirty-two people their lives.

Captain Carey may have contributed to the sinking of the *Vestris*, just as the captain of the *Costa Concordia* may have been negligent taking the ship into shallow water, but Captain Carey paid the ultimate price, going down with his ship. The captain of the *Costa Concordia* was alleged to have left his ship before all the passengers and crew disembarked, and that is what people spoke about in judgmental tones in locker rooms, coffee shops, and on their commutes to work. The captain's behavior was an outrage, an extreme moral lapse, for we humans expect captains of sea vessels to be heroic. The captain would be charged with multiple counts of manslaughter and causing a maritime disaster.

In 1928 Virginia, heroism was apparently not expected of African-Americans at sea, so Burton's life-saving actions were newsworthy, as was the total lack of heroism of many white crew members.

"CREW of Vestris took best boats, says WITNESS—Sobs as He Relates Story of Horror," cried the headline of *The Baltimore News* on November 15, 1928.

The star witness in question, testifying a week after the sinking, was Fred Puppe, the man on his way to a new job in Buenos Aires whose wife and seven-month-old child perished. Puppe testified "in a broken voice" that members of the crew took the best lifeboats for themselves "wink[ing] at their friends to join them." Crew members grabbed the working flares, "fixing a few [lifeboats] with proper equipment, planning to ride in them themselves."

Puppe also corroborated Ulrich's testimony that the baggage was mishandled. Ulrich had complained that he could not insure the expedition baggage; Puppe said his family's luggage had not been delivered to their cabin, but was instead dumped in the hold. He spoke to other passengers who had reported similar experiences. "The handling of the baggage was absolutely careless," he was quoted as saying.

Yet other efforts I made to corroborate Ulrich's testimony failed.

Ulrich had testified that Walter worked on the Mamore-Madeira Railroad, one of the most deadly railroad projects during the rubber boom, but the head of the Mamore-Madeira Railroad Society told me via the Internet that there was no record of any employee by the name of Walter Lindberg.

I tried to find a newspaper column by a writer for the Hearst syndicate based on Ulrich's book about his 1926 expedition, mentioning him and Alexandrovitch by name. I knew the column wasn't a fabrication because one of the lawyers introduced it into evidence at the deposition, only the article wasn't attached to the transcript copy in the National Archives. It used to be said that today's newspaper is tomorrow's bird cage liner, and that seemed to be true for all copies of the Hearst article just as it was true for the Damon Runyon piece about John William Ryan. I couldn't find it anywhere.

Nor could I locate a copy of the book itself.

When all was said and done, the only well-documented aspect of the Walter Lindberg story seemed to concern where Walter hadn't been. He hadn't been on the *Vestris* when it sank, attracting much publicity. As a result, I had a photo of Marie Ulrich, but not of Walter.

I also had a letter from New York City stating that a marriage license between Elsa Roth DePay and Walter Lindberg matching the date in Grandma's affidavit could not be found.

With so many dead ends, I had every reason to give up on Walter Lindberg and Brazil and concern myself fully with the future of Long Island's tidal marshes, my mother, myself, and my son.

For a time, that's what I tried. I put all of my information about Walter Lindberg into a box and stuck the box in a closet—but not for long. The past wasn't done with me, nor I with it.

chapter eighteen

DOCUMENTS FOR CHRISTMAS — HOLY S---!

I HAD KNOWN for many years that Walter Lindberg wasn't the only missing person in our family. There was also Mother's youngest brother, Cornelius, whose absence my Aunt Connie used to bring up on Christmas after a scotch or two.

Aunt Connie was as talkative and warm as Mother was reserved. Aunt Connie always gave me love, and sometimes she gave me tantalizing information, for even though her husband, my mother's other brother, didn't talk about the past any more than Mother did, Aunt Connie had been married to John for many years before I came along and had her own recollections. However, Aunt Connie tended to repeat herself at our holiday gatherings. Year after year, we would hear the same information about Cornelius, known as Neil—an account of Aunt Connie's last phone conversation with him.

"I suppose every family has its black sheep," Mother would respond with aristocratic detachment and Tolstoyan sweep, as though she had done an exhaustive study of families the whole world over. Then Mother would reach for a cracker and ask someone else a question. That would put a lid on any discussion of Neil until the next Christmas.

A new generation joined our holiday observances, Aunt Connie switched from scotch to white wine, and the content of that last talk with Neil eventually turned a decade old.

That's when I hired a detective. I'd left journalism for law by then, and I knew some professional investigators. By then I also knew that we didn't have a black sheep in the family. We had a lost sheep. A black sheep would have been a gambler, a drunkard, or a felon. We had absolutely no idea who—or where—Neil was.

It wasn't that I wanted to find Neil out of affection. I didn't know him at all. He was a hole in my life, his absence depriving me of a significant percentage of my close blood kin. I had only met him once, on my way home from college via New York's Penn Station. After her mother's death, Mother had sold her interest in the family stores to Uncle John—a wise decision on her part, because unlike the poshness of the stores' first address, the original Pennsylvania Station, men's clothing stores in the new, mostly subterranean Penn Station were sad affairs.

By the time I was a teenager, in the 1970s, not too many people were shopping for suits and overcoats while rushing for commuter trains to New Jersey or Long Island, but whenever I traveled by train from Poughkeepsie to Long Island, I would stop in one of the remaining two Penn Station stores to say hello to Uncle John. One time Neil was behind the counter in the lower level store. We were such strangers that Uncle John had to introduce us. That's why I never could bring myself to call him Uncle Neil.

Later, I was told that Neil stole from the cash register, and Uncle John fired him. Eventually, Uncle John closed both stores and began a career in academia, which suited him much better. Neil and the stores became ancient history, but it seemed wrong to me that neither Mother nor Uncle John knew where Neil was. I'd come across an old album that included pictures of Neil with my mother and father, and Mother seemed to prize the Atmos clock that Neil had given Dad and her as a wedding present. The very fact that she told me its provenance was a testament to its meaning, which could also be inferred from the prominent place she gave it in the living room, and her regular dusting of its glass case. I concluded that Mother still had feelings for Neil, even if she didn't want to say much about him.

All she ever told me was that Neil was spoiled and overly dependent on their mother, so that when she died and Neil had to live on his own, he couldn't handle it. In other words, Neil hadn't managed to adjust to the real world, as Mother believed she had done, however painful it may have been pretending to almost everyone that she hadn't grown up in a family so well off that chauffeured limousines escorted them to country clubs during the Great Depression.

I thought there might be more to Neil's story than I was being told, but the detective I hired said he couldn't find an address or place of employment without Neil's Social Security number, and neither Mother nor Uncle John had it. There was talk by Aunt Connie of a locked trunk somewhere in Westchester County that might contain a document bearing the number, but neither the trunk nor the document ever materialized.

After that, I made a few phone calls and wrote letters, without success. According to Aunt Connie, in her famous last conversation with Neil, he said he was working in the mail room at either Pratt or Pace. She couldn't remember which college it was, so I wrote both. Either way, a clerk's job was a huge fall from Neil's upbringing, far more of a plunge than Mother's.

"What happened to the money?" was a question posed to me by Uncle John's Princeton roommate, Taylor Bigbie, when I met him for lunch during a trip to London in the 1990s.

"Time," was the best answer I could muster, to which Taylor shook his head and said, "They just lived so well."

"Isn't that your answer?" observed his intelligent wife.

Uncle John always expressed the hope that I would find his brother, just as he hoped that I would find the Damon Runyon column, but as hard as I tried I wasn't able to accomplish either goal, not before Uncle John's death in 2001, nor before Aunt Connie's in 2006.

In 2009, too late to set the record straight with my aunt and uncle, I discovered through a website that Neil had predeceased them both, having died in the 1980s. Neil died alone in an apartment in Brooklyn. According to the funeral home, a few days elapsed before anyone found his body. He was buried by the government at Calverton Military Cemetery on Long Island because of his World War II service. No friends or family attended.

At least Mother was still alive, residing with my son and me, and I told her the sad news about her long-lost brother, which didn't entirely surprise her. I said I wanted to take her to the cemetery where Neil was buried. Mother agreed, as long as we could stop for a nice lunch on the way. I said fine, but I had an unusual amount of weekend work that fall, and the first open Saturday was several weeks away. When the day arrived, something else happened. Mother died.

She had fallen in the bathroom and injured herself internally, in ways that went undetected for nearly a week, despite her being in the hospital. The end was so in keeping with everything about her—a final secret, borne with the utmost dignity, which was what I tried to leave her with, deciding not to authorize a very risky operation after a CAT scan showed how bad things were.

The November night Mother slumbered into death, my cousin Dwight and I clinging to her hands, I returned home from the hospital in the middle of a nor'easter. I could hear the surf pounding from the back patio, which only happens when the ocean is particularly rough. Somehow, the sound of the waves taking my beach away wasn't nearly as loud as the echo of Mother's last breath, which seemed to come from a deep, dark corner of her being, with a foul, dank smell, perhaps the place where she'd stored all those feelings she cared not to express, or could not, except in rare moments, in the way she would sometimes say "Good night, dear," when she played the piano and I was young and sat upstairs in my room listening to her heart speak through the notes of Chopin and Debussy. At the end, it was as though Mother was finally exhaling the first breath she had ever taken, a breath she'd held, tightly and with exceptional self-discipline, for eighty-eight years.

Having my mother die on the day I was to bring her to her brother's grave dampened my interest in researching the dead—for a while. I grieved. I busied myself in the details of her estate. Then, as the forsythia flowered and my mourning began to subside, I took the box of records about Walter Lindberg out of the closet. As had happened during every major transition in my life, Dad's story about who we were took hold of me again, and now, with my caregiving duties ended, I actually had more time to devote to the search for Walter. I planned to review the documents thoroughly while my son was away at summer camp and see what leads were left to pursue.

Somewhere in the Catskills, on Route 17, after I'd said good-bye to Justin for two weeks, the idea of records at the State Department came into my mind like a friend from the past unexpectedly knocking on the door.

For decades I had known about the Freedom of Information Act (FOIA), the law that compels the United States government to make official records available upon request unless the documents are classified or otherwise exempt from disclosure. As a reporter, I used the law to obtain records, and as a lawyer I reviewed FOIA court opinions and often advised reporters on how they could use the law. What had stayed out of consciousness all those years was the idea that the statute could help me find Walter Lindberg.

That seemed obvious once I thought of it. If the spouse of an American citizen disappeared in a foreign country, it would be natural for the Department of State to get involved. Why hadn't I recognized that earlier, even before I waded through the *Vestris* docket?

It didn't occur to me to contact the State Department about the dead until I had a respite from feeling responsible for the living, and that was enough to alter my course.

Within hours of pulling into the my driveway, I was seated at a computer sending e-mails to the United States consulate in São Paulo and completing an online FOIA request with the National Archives, keeper of old State Department records.

With both of my parents dead, there was no excuse to avoid the truth any longer.

Half a year later, my son and I had a white Christmas, not having to do with snow. A large white envelope arrived at the post office and buried the holiday in an avalanche of surprises.

My son was seated in his favorite spot on a stool in the kitchen in front of his laptop when I walked in from the garage and announced, "They're here."

"What?" he asked, looking up.

"The documents from the State Department. The ones about Walter Lindberg."

"Oh, wow," he said, really looking at me now. "That's weird, on Christmas Eve."

Justin had grown up listening to the story of Walter Lindberg just like I had, only I was the one telling the story, not Dad—and there was another difference: I told Justin many stories, not just one. Having wished my parents had spoken more about the past, if anything, I went to the other extreme, offering a steady stream of anecdotes, photo albums, and visits to friends and far-flung cousins, a couple of whom I didn't find until my forties.

I'd told Justin about my interest in Walter, about the research I was doing, and the request to the State Department, so Justin knew right away that the large envelope I waved at him was important to me. I walked over to the kitchen table, which Mother had brought with her when she moved into my house. It was the same white table on which I'd written "Are you my father?" with a pen between my toes. Opening the envelope, I had no idea how pertinent a question that would prove to be twenty-three years later.

chapter nineteen

FRAUD IN TRÊS LAGOAS

THE ENVELOPE FROM the State Department contained thirty-six pages. First was a letter dated November 30, 1929, from a man whose title was special agent in charge. He worked for the US Department of State in its New York City office. His name was Burr.

Burr's letter absolutely confirmed that 1929 was when Grandma received word that Walter had died in Brazil. In fact, the letter informing her of Walter's death had reached her on her birthday, August 28, which happened to be the day after my father's birthday. One didn't need to be an astrologist to wonder about the timing.

Grandma sought help from the New York City Police Department, which called in the State Department.

I always wondered how Grandma heard about Walter's death, and Burr's letter provided the answer.

Elsie Lindberg residing at 1275 Lexington Ave., this city, has a report that her husband, Walter Lindberg, who has lived in this country 15 years but [is] still a citizen of Denmark, was killed in Brazil near a place called Treslagoas, where he has been for several months. This information came to her August 28th in a letter from Hans Joachims of the above place.

It appears that she has communicated with the Brazilian Consul here and paid for a cable to the Chief of Police of the above named place for confirmation of the story of her husband's death, but has received no reply. . . .

Burr referred the matter to the US consul in São Paulo, C.R. Cameron, who sent letters to the mayor of Três Lagoas and chief of police of Mato Grosso, the state in which Três Lagoas was located, requesting information about both Walter and the man who had signed the letter to Grandma, Hans Joachims.

Cameron cautioned his colleagues in the United States that "communication with Matto Grosso is very slow, letters addressed to that section being frequently ignored."

A reply came in January 1930 from the mayor of Três Lagoas, reporting that Walter's name did not appear in the "register of deaths of persons buried during the past year in the Municipal Cemetery of this City." As the consul noted in his report, "this is very limited information and would not necessarily settle the question as to whether Walter Lindberg did or did not meet his death within the Municipality of Tres Lagoas."

A few months later, in June 1930, new information came to Cameron's attention in the form of a letter from the delegate of police of Três Lagoas, Antonio Alves de Siqueira. The delegate scoffed at the assertion that Walter had been "assassinated in this Municipality on the 28th day of August of last year":

From the information obtained from trustworthy sources, I can assure your excellency that such assertion was absolutely inexact. . . . [I]t appears that such news was spread by the citizen Walter Lindberg, known here by another name, and who has in New York a wife called Elsie Lindberg, in whose favor he took out a large life insurance with a

North American company, and spread in person the news of the supposed assassination, so as to share later in the product of his chicanery and fraud.

Reading these words I made gasping noises and involuntarily released a profanity. Justin looked over from across the kitchen and asked what was wrong. How could I tell him that Walter Lindberg might have faked his death to scam an insurance company?

I was familiar with insurance scams. Shortly after I returned to New York from Washington, after the first break-up with Michael, I'd been a member of a team that successfully litigated a civil racketeering case against a ring of insurance salesmen, adjusters, auto body shop owners in Brooklyn and Queens, and even bankers who were making money off phony accidents involving cars insured under fake policies. Later, at the media company, I had permitted a television reporter to go on air with a story of alleged insurance fraud that probably cost a man the mayoral election in a major city. I was relying on the protections for journalists secured by the very professor whose class Michael and I had taken. A lawsuit followed. I was questioned under oath in a deposition about my discussions with the reporter. Aside from winding up in a mental ward or having a client executed, one of the last things a lawyer wants is to be questioned under oath about conversations with a client. Eventually, on appeal, the suit was dismissed and the TV station prevailed.

I thought that was it for insurance fraud and me. I was an environmentalist now, dealing with the sediments of estuaries, not the grit of crimes. I was relieved to read that Grandma wasn't having any of the delegate's "chicanery and fraud" pinned on her.

She confirmed the existence of insurance policies, but that was all, according to a memo sent back to São Paulo by the special agent:

Five or six years ago he [Walter] did take out three insurance policies with the Prudential Insurance Co., for $5,000 each, on which she has been regularly paying a $79 premium every three months, but this she is unable to keep up much longer. She reported her husband's alleged death to the Prudential Insurance Co., and was informed that the company would take no action towards payment of the policy until proof of her husband's death had been submitted.

No body, no money. Who could blame Prudential for that decision?

It did not sound like Grandma participated in any deception, but while that shock was quelled, there remained a few more. First, there was the distinct possibility that Walter hadn't died in 1929. Second, Grandma told the special agent that Walter worked as "an automobile mechanic and had several jobs" in New York City, and "then she paid his transportation down to Brazil."

An automobile mechanic? That didn't jibe with Dad's story or Ulrich's testimony, but Grandma certainly confirmed that Walter had no money back when he sailed for Brazil. In fact, she was the one who had paid for his passage on the *Van Dyke*.

During my last stay with Grandma in her Ft. Lauderdale trailer, she told me how, in her early years in New York, the male supervisors at the factory where she sat in front of a sewing machine all day used to walk by and pull on her long auburn braid as though it were a rope not attached to a human being. I had assumed that at home, with her new husband, Grandma had a respite from that sort of demeaning treatment. Emmy Kern provided the first hint that my picture was wrong, and now the words in the State Department's documents put the picture through a shredder. As Special Agent Burr reported of Grandma:

> She has a boy 12 years old by her former marriage, but she has supported herself and boy ever since her marriage with Mr. Lindberg, who has never contributed one cent toward that end.

It seemed that my hunch based on Ulrich's testimony had been correct. Dad's early home had been far from happy and loving. Grandma sounded bitter indeed.

Grandma told the special agent that Walter sent her "one or two letters" from Brazil, one with a photograph of himself and two friends. I longed to know what Walter looked like, and the special agent wrote that he was attaching a copy of the photo to his memo, but when I turned the page, the photo wasn't there.

Instead, there was a verbal portrait of a very different life in Brazil than the one I had imagined for Walter. In February 1931, this was what the United States learned, courtesy of Brazilian authorities:

This Delegacia de Policia having received your letter of January 31 of the current year relative to the citizen Walter Lindberg, I have to advise you that the citizen referred to worked for some time in this city in the office of the Light and Power, afterward taking passage for the State of São Paulo with destination to Port No. 15 on a steamer of the Navigation Company with head offices in São Paulo.

The consul explained in his cover note to Washington that Port No. 15 "is the port on the Paraná River on the west bank opposite Porto Tibirica." He went on to say he had inquired about Walter's employment with the Três Lagoas Light and Power Company and received the following reply concerning Citizen Walter Lindberg:

[W]e have to communicate to you that this gentleman was not really employed in this plant but he performed the construction of a fence on the property of the Cia. Feira de Gado, of which we are the representatives, and later on undertook still another service, the construction of a corral, the latter belonging to this firm.

In July of the past year he left this city for an unknown destination but later on we heard that he had gone toward the upper Sorocabana, but we do not know to what city of that district.

So much for the great explorer. According to the documents, Walter had spent his time in Brazil building a fence and corral. Did his engineering experience qualify him to provide those services, or was it his work as a mechanic? Perhaps it was his familiarity with design as a result of inventing the mobile home?

I didn't know what to believe.

Agent Burr shared the 1931 correspondence from Brazil with Grandma, as he had done with all the documents, which confirmed that my seemingly simple-minded and sweet grandmother had indeed lied in the affidavit she signed in 1946. She knew Walter had not died in 1929. She knew that in July 1930, almost a full year after his reported death, Walter had traveled on a steamer down the Paraná River, and that as of February 1931 he was living in Brazil, perhaps in a place called the upper Sorocabana, perhaps somewhere else.

It didn't really matter.

What mattered was that in my digging for the truth about Walter Lindberg, I had discovered something that opened up a crater in my gut. I had discovered that Walter abandoned Grandma and Dad—and that my grandmother knew it and never told Dad. This was a far greater deviation from the original story than Emmy Kern had led me to consider. Dad hadn't just created greatness out of a man who may have cheated on Grandma. Dad had created greatness out of a man who had used Grandma's earnings to get to Brazil, then faked his death, changed his name, and started a new life. Grandma knew this, and withheld it from Dad. Not only that, she had lied about it in a sworn affidavit in 1946, averring that Walter had died in 1929 at a time when he—and she—considered New York to be his place of residence. What my father had relayed as a story of heroism was a story of his own abandonment. He was right that there was betrayal in the story. It just didn't arise from any theft of treasure maps.

To say the truth hurt is literally true. My typically strong stomach spasmed with pity for my father, idolizing a man who deserted him. Walter hadn't let the *Vestris* sail without him to spend more time with Dad and Grandma, and he hadn't been prevented from returning to them by a tragic, untimely death.

With this new information, my father became a child in my estimation, not a fool, not a simpleton, just a naif. It was an entirely different way of assessing and understanding a person I'd known for over forty years. I looked right through the towering man and saw a wronged little boy, deserted by the only father he ever knew and lied to by his mother.

I didn't know yet how I felt about Grandma. Mostly, I was amazed she had gone to her grave never divulging the secret to Dad or me, her only blood relatives in the United States.

As a result of the stroke she suffered, Grandma was unable to talk for the nine months before her death. Dad and I would visit her in the nursing home when I was home from college, and she would groan miserably when we walked into her room. Perhaps she was trying to speak the truth then. Dad and I would turn on the television in her room and try to find a Mets game because she and her third husband, the barber, had been Mets fans. That's what we'd talk about to my grandmother, speechless with a huge secret inside: baseball.

chapter twenty

TWO CHAPS IN HATS

THE NEXT DOCUMENT from the State Department regarding "Alleged death of Walter Lindberg" bore a date of 1934. Three years had passed since the last correspondence. My father was now a public high school student in New York called "Lucky" by his classmates.

The memorandum came from C.R. Cameron, still the consul general in São Paulo. Another familiar name jumped out from the second paragraph, none other than Otto Ulrich.

As Cameron explained, Ulrich had tracked down Walter in Brazil, and then gone to the American consulate to tell them all about it:

On January 16, 1934, this Consulate General was visited by Dr. Otto Willi Ulrich who gave his address as Caixa Postal 1339, São Paulo, and stated that Mr. Lindberg is alive and residing in Nova Danzig, State of Paraná, Brazil. Dr. Ulrich further said that Mr. Lindberg now goes by the name of Dr. Waldomiro Lindberg, and that he is working as an agent for the Northern Paraná Land Company (Companhia de Terras Norte do Paraná).

I sat back and exhaled, not like Mother's last breath, but my lungs did a powerful job. They released a lot of time, all the years I'd believed so many things that were not true. As a conservationist dedicated to rainforest protection, I did not have a good feeling about the Northern Paraná Land Company and Walter's association with it. I did not think their mission was to preserve land in its natural state. And why was Otto Ulrich, whose last words in the deposition expressed ignorance of Walter's whereabouts, showing up again in the narrative?

I learned by reading further in the document that Ulrich had gone all the way to Brazil to find Walter, now Waldomiro, because of the *Vestris* court case. Ulrich wanted Walter to give testimony in support of his claim. Walter was perfectly willing to do that, but told Ulrich "that he would never go to New York."

In connection with his claim against the above steamship company, Dr. Ulrich informed that a Mr. Knauth of the law firm Smith, Demming & Griffith, 27, William Street, New York City, is his lawyer and that Mr. Knauth is informed regarding Mr. Lindberg and his connection with the claim case of Dr. Ulrich.

Knauth was the lawyer who represented Ulrich in his testimony before the special master, so my search had come full circle, back to my first big find on Varick Street, the Ulrich transcript. Had the lawyer counseled Ulrich to find Walter? That was a logical conclusion to draw. The last transcript of Otto Ulrich in the *Vestris* file was dated January 8, 1933. The volume ended with a note that the questioning of Mr. Ulrich would resume the next morning, but the file cart contained no transcript from January 9 or any later day. I had asked the archivists about the possible whereabouts of other transcripts, to no avail. Now I wondered if Ulrich ever showed up for the session on January 9, 1933, or if he and his lawyer realized it wouldn't have been worth their time without producing testimony by Walter.

If the latter, it took Ulrich a full year to find Walter—and there wasn't any evidence in the *Vestris* file that Ulrich's trip to Brazil led to testimony by "Waldomiro" Lindberg. Had Ulrich wasted his time and precious money? Dad said that none of the *Vestris* claimants recovered anything, because of the shipping company's bankruptcy or inadequate insurance. That was fairly close to the truth. The disaster and court case forced Lamport & Holt into reorganization and disgrace. Nearly all of the company's assets were sold to pay legal bills. I read of a small out-of-court settlement negotiated by a British accountant, but there was no way of knowing whether any of those English pounds made their way into Ulrich's bank account, or into his trousers or shirt pockets. It seemed quite likely that Ulrich had gone all the way to Brazil to find Walter Lindberg for nothing.

In his 1934 memo, after explaining Ulrich's reason for locating Walter, Cameron referred to a photograph "furnished by Dr. Ulrich of Messrs. Lindberg and Ulrich taken about a week ago according to Dr. Ulrich. The man in the picture wearing glasses and a cap is said to be Mr. Lindberg while Dr. Ulrich is the other."

I quickly looked at the next document, hoping it would be a copy of the photograph. It was not, so I returned to Cameron's memo and continued to read:

> There is enclosed also a form used to grant free railroad passage to persons wishing to visit the land of the above-mentioned company [on] which form it is seen that Mr. Lindberg now calls himself Dr. Waldomiro Lindberg.

The form was attached to the next document. Typeset in Portuguese, the form stated that "Snr. Dr. Waldomiro Lindberg" was an "agente" of A' Companhia de Terras Norte do Paraná. The form included a line where an address of the bearer was supposed to be inserted. The line was blank, as was the signature line and date, other than the year, 1933.

Cameron filled in a different blank, though. He ended his memo with the suggestion that Walter wasn't a Dane.

Dr. Ulrich further informed that Mr. Lindberg, although he is German, possesses a Danish passport obtained from the Danish Consulate in New York City.

There were so many times I'd said Lindberg was a Danish name because that's what Dad told me. Dad said Walter had been educated in Denmark and Germany, but came from a Danish family—though Swedish friends of ours insisted Lindberg was a Swedish name. Now Ulrich was saying Walter was German, but traveled as a Dane. Was anything certain about the man?

I looked up and told my son what I had just learned from the contents of the white envelope, as best I could. The intricacies were complicated for a boy who had only turned fourteen a week earlier, with references back to the *Vestris* sinking and the lawsuit, the reappearance of Otto Ulrich. So much of the impact was in my head, on a mental trail I'd been blazing since childhood evenings with my father. The trail had become hopelessly forked and unmarked, leading me to a cliff from which I was now falling, watching the rose-colored apples and pears on the kitchen wallpaper go by as I plummeted.

Justin listened well. He closed his laptop. I had tried to raise my child to be connected to me, and having him with me that day as truth turned to falsehood and honor to amorality made all the difference in the world. I was fortunate that he was home from boarding school on winter break when the documents arrived from the State Department. Justin wasn't the one who had sat in the National Archives seven and a half years earlier discovering Ulrich's testimony with joy, thinking then that it was the beginning of proof of Dad's story, but he was the one person who could throw me a rope as I fell from that high point. Like me, my son had grown up with the story. Like me, he bore the last name of the story's protagonist. But unlike me, Justin hadn't invested his emotions in the story's being true.

"So your step-grandfather wasn't eaten by cannibals," Justin said, matter-of-factly.

"No," I replied. "He wasn't."

The whole affair could have ended there, but it didn't.

There were still a few pages left to read. The open question, for me, was the reaction from Grandma once presented with the information in Cameron's 1934 letter.

The documents ended where they began, with a letter from Special Agent in Charge Burr to his boss. Burr wrote on March 29, 1934, that he had "located, although with some delay, Mrs. Elsie Lindberg," and showed her the photo "of two men, one of whom is said to represent Dr. Waldomiro Lindberg and the other Dr. Otto Willi Ulrich."

Grandma did know Otto Ulrich, after all. As Burr wrote:

> Mrs. Lindberg promptly identified the one wearing cap and glasses as that of her long missing spouse and the other as a Mr. Ulrich, whom she knows but detests for some reason she did not see fit to divulge.

I knew the reason why Grandma detested Otto Ulrich, the man who had cajoled Walter Lindberg into traveling to Brazil with his treasure maps and talk of getting rich. I was a mother to a boy sitting across the room, and I could well imagine his pain if back when he was just shy of eleven, a man he loved had taken a steamship to Brazil, never to return.

I realized, too, how embarrassing it must have been for Grandma to have the faithlessness of her husband revealed by an agent of the government of her adopted country, a man who for nearly five years had been an ally in her search for the truth about Walter's supposed death. There was little more to be said at that point, as Burr made clear with an economy of words in his final paragraph: "I may say that the Police Authorities of this city are no longer interested in the case."

Burr added that he was returning the photo and railroad pass. I turned the page. Finally, after so many years, I was staring at the face of Walter Lindberg.

Tan and slender, Walter stands to the right of his former partner. He is a good-looking man. That much of Dad's story was true. He wears jodhpurs and polished leather riding boots up to his knees. He is standing in front of a wood porch with a slatted railing. His left foot rests on the soil, his right foot positioned on the bottom of the three steps leading up to the porch. The raised leg and bent knee give him a casual, if affected, appearance, a posed nonchalance. A button-down shirt is tucked into belted pants, sleeves rolled up above the elbows. He is looking to his left, not at the camera, holding something in his right hand while his left hand rests in his pocket. He has an engaged look on his face, not smiling but not frowning either, as though he is pondering something deep. The bright sun illuminates the right side of his face under a white cap with a visor.

He looks like a man who cares about his appearance, possibly even vain. He looks like a man pretty sure of himself, possibly even smug. He looks like a man who could tell a good story, possibly even lie. Still, he looks like a man who could brighten your day and make you laugh if he felt like it, a man you might want to know, especially if you were a boy wondering if you'd ever grow up to be big and charismatic like him.

Next to him stands Otto Ulrich, obese, wearing jodhpurs twice the size of Walter's pants, more cistern than trouser. His boots are short and covered in mud, not tall and polished like Walter's. His shirt is stretched flat against his enormous stomach. He holds a cane in his right hand and wears a dark felt hat creased in the wrong place as though someone has sat on it. He looks rumpled. He has two chins, a small mouth and small nose, bland cheeks. He is looking at the camera, but the brim of his hat casts a dark shadow above his nose. It looks as though he is wearing a black mask over his eyes, like a bandit.

I stood up from the kitchen table and walked over to Justin. I hugged him, tears in my eyes, feeling a sense of resolution, as though a tonic chord had finally been played after so many years of fourths and fifths.

What an extraordinary week it had been. There was a great deal of new information to process, not only the discoveries about Walter, Grandma, and my sadly deluded father.

There had been a discovery of a wholly different sort made a week earlier. Thanks to an online donor sibling registry, I discovered that my son has a half-brother, a child of the same man, a boy born one month after Justin.

At roughly the same age my father was abandoned, my son had gained a half-brother. It had taken me decades to find out the former, but only minutes to discover the latter. The information made a very good birthday present, one my son will never forget.

chapter twenty-one

THE MISSING FATHER, ONE WAY

AND ANOTHER

A GOOGLE SEARCH for "Waldomiro Lindberg" produced only one hit, a document in Portuguese containing names and monetary amounts that appeared in the *Diário Oficial do Estado de São Paulo*, the official journal of the state of São Paulo, on June 17, 1939.

I couldn't tell whether the matters listed were court actions, license applications, or something else, but it seemed clear that as of 1939 Walter was still living in Brazil, in a place called Paraná, a full ten years after word of his supposed death reached Grandma in New York.

In 1939, Dad turned twenty-one, surely old enough to travel to Brazil if he had wanted to, if he knew what he would be looking for, the actual man whose surname he bore, alive with a real address in Paraná, a state in central Brazil south and west of the state of São Paulo.

If Grandma had told Dad the truth about Walter's still being alive, Dad would most likely have been surprised, angry, and hurt to find out that he and his mother had been deserted. Most likely, Grandma believed she was protecting her son from feeling the sting of rejection by the man he considered his father, but by withholding the truth she also prevented her son from learning how to experience and process real feelings, vital anger, hate, regret. Instead, she left him with an incomplete story: Walter's sudden disappearance, at foul hands in one way or another, to which the natural reaction by a boy of eleven would be despair over loss and endless concern that Walter had experienced a painful demise.

If I sat in the bathtub as a girl imagining Walter being boiled alive, never having met the man, what horrible notions went through Dad's mind as a child, hearing that the father figure he had lived with for half of his young life was the victim of tribal headhunters?

How did that make Dad feel about the general safety of the world— and of himself and his loved ones? Had I found the explanation for Dad's need to dominate, for his tremendous trust in himself in a time of crisis? Had I found the reason why Dad's first instinct during my psychosis was to keep me at home, under his control, when I needed medical intervention?

If it did nothing else, finding out that Walter was alive would have ended the worries in Dad's mind about Walter's death. Had the truth been divulged, perhaps Dad would have traveled to Brazil to confront Walter. If Otto Ulrich could find Walter in Nova Dantzig,* Dad could have found Walter, too. I had no idea how Ulrich had managed to trace Walter, but someone in his circle in New York or Brazil must have known Walter's whereabouts. Dad could have tapped into that knowledge.

Or maybe Dad would have written a letter. Venting his hurt feelings might have done him good. Perhaps Walter would have replied, offering an explanation, an apology, and a good story or two. Wouldn't that have contributed to Dad's healthy development?

Instead, Dad's emotions never grew up. They were blocked by a wall that I could imagine his mind building higher each day to seal off the all-consuming nothingness, not even a body or a funeral. Some say the Amazon was formed when an inland sea became blocked and

---

* The Brazilians spelled the city "Nova Dantzig," whereas the Germans called it "Neu Danzig." Occasionally, as in the State Department documents, the two versions were combined to result in "Nova Danzig."

the build-up of water caused a breach of the land blockade, the giant river and its many tributaries spilling forth because the water had no place else to go. So it seemed with Dad's emotions. His anger sometimes roared like river water defying any and every impediment.

From time to time I felt the torrent of his outbursts, and I'd seen how Dad otherwise avoided emotion or discounted it, as he had discounted the importance of my feelings for Michael. I couldn't help but reassess Dad's hostility to Michael based on the new information in the State Department documents. It seemed quite possible that an irrational but deep-seated fear of abandonment lay within Dad all of his life, causing him to see Michael as an enemy, justifying, even requiring, Dad's solitary journey into New York the night of our infamous dinner. I could see now that Dad was probably afraid I wouldn't go on loving him if I loved Michael, and Dad's reaction was to try to hold onto me more tightly, not understanding that love wasn't like the military commands he excelled at giving in his army days. You couldn't order people to stick around in your personal life.

I felt sad and stunned in the days following my review of the State Department documents, sad for Dad, and sad for me, sad for us both that he hadn't learned he could trust someone who loved him as much as I did to treat him fairly.

In the years after Dad's death, as I conducted my research, I had wondered whether the Walter story enthralled me because it made me feel close to Dad, even via competition. Now the story was having the opposite effect: It was putting a huge distance between us. I knew intimate, harsh truths that Dad never knew, and those truths made me feel sorry for him. The information and the pity gave me a certain power over my father that felt unasked for and peculiar, shearing the height off his frame, obscuring our years together, and leaving me staring at a traumatized boy whom it seemed I had never really known.

Grandma wasn't looking so good now, either. Sharing the truth might have fostered closeness between Dad and his mother, so I wondered about the converse: What impact did Grandma's withholding of the truth have on her relationship with Dad?

Though I understood her desire not to cause her child pain, I had to wonder about the choices she had made.

To be sure, child-rearing practices were different in the 1930s. Parents were less likely to confide in their children than they are now on a range of issues, but child therapists say children are brilliant at sensing when they are not being told the truth, and that probably wasn't much different in the 1930s. Rather, the old expectation of being seen but not heard gave a child a lot of quiet time to ponder what he or she wasn't being told, and to learn to pretend that it didn't matter.

It may well have been from his mother that Dad learned the lesson that serious personal matters, emotional matters, were not to be openly discussed and addressed with the aid and counsel of others. They were to be buried. The letter from your daughter stating her feelings belonged in a drawer, not in your hands being read, not in your brain mulling it over and wondering if you erred and how to make things right. A doctor shouldn't be consulted about your wife's depression because her mood might improve when your daughter comes home for Christmas vacation.

I wondered whether Grandma had found it hard to keep her secret from Dad. I would have found it unbearable, which is why I said no to a friend who offered his sperm on a confidential basis when I was seeking to get pregnant. I didn't want any secrets between my child and me, and I strove to be open about why there was no dad in our house.

The way I first explained it to Justin was that I had borrowed the part of a man that helps make a baby. When Justin was in kindergarten I tried a new formulation: "We don't have a daddy. I know that sometimes you wish we had one. Sometimes I wish we had one, too. But we do have a dog, and we are so lucky to have her!"

Positive reinforcement for that strategy came one day when my son was crossing West End Avenue after school with his friend Ethan Chen and I was walking behind them. Ethan said to Justin, "Tell me again why you don't have a dad," and Justin replied, "I don't know, Ethan, but how come you don't have a dog?"

When I posted our information on the donor sibling registry, I never expected to find a sibling or Justin's biological father. I simply thought the website would be a good vehicle for talking about the absent father during Justin's teenage years. Of course, the Internet didn't exist in the 1930s. Grandma couldn't find a new family member for her son by typing on a keyboard.

Mother was the other person who required reassessment after I read the State Department documents. I realized with a bolt of clarity and remorse why she had stood up to leave the room during my father's recitations of the Walter story. It wasn't because a chore needed attention. It wasn't even because she lacked interest in an exciting story—or in me, as I had sometimes thought. Somehow Mother knew or strongly suspected that the story was a lie. She'd already seen Dad's propensity to exaggerate when it came to Grandma. She wouldn't be complicit in lying to her child, but she wouldn't cast aspersions on the story either. She let me have that shimmering connection with my father for as long as it would last.

Her forbearance had been an act of quiet love, the hardest kind.

chapter twenty-two

BASKET CASE

ONE REMAINING QUESTION was how much longer the phantom of my search survived after 1939. The Internet would not surrender a death certificate, not for Walter or Waldomiro.

Several public record websites advised consulting a Brazilian lawyer, advice I found galling. In the United States, almost anyone could request an official record. Besides, I had a law degree. Why did I need to know Brazilian law to get my hands on a routine piece of paper?

Wary of hiring a lawyer from so far away, concerned about the cost and the possibility of being bilked, I felt I had no choice but to go to Brazil myself, a plan I announced to my son one afternoon toward the end of his winter break.

"Why?" Justin asked right away. "Why do you need to go to Brazil?"

I had to admit that I didn't have a logically compelling answer. I wanted to go to Brazil. I felt I needed to go in some deeply essential way to finish what I had started, but what was I actually going to do there? Travel from clerk's office to clerk's office when I didn't even speak

Portuguese? Sure, Brazil seemed like the next rational step, but to depart at once would be like rushing out of the city room to cover a fire without knowing the address of the burning building. If I had unlimited time, I could go to Brazil, hire a translator, and see where leads took me, but I couldn't get away for more than a few weeks. I had a job and a child.

I put off doing anything about Walter Lindberg's death certificate. There was the matter of the new family member, one who was alive. Over Presidents' Day weekend in February, Justin came home from school and his newly discovered half-brother, Corby Rider, visited us from Pennsylvania with his mother, Betty. It was one of those mid-winter weekends when the chill of the air and low angle of the sun, not to mention the absence of people, make the blueness of the sky over the beach more stark and vivid than in summer. We showed off our life, the crashing waves, the golden water dog, the bluffs and hoodoos of Montauk, the World War II bunkers covered in graffiti, the shorebirds, the history of a place where art and nature have fused for 150 years, the lighthouse preserved from the era of George Washington.

Betty and I marveled at the boys' similarities and their differences. Their bodies were duplicates, tall and thin, similar to what we had been told about their biological father. Their tastes were akin—strong aversions to insects and condiments—but their faces linked them unmistakably to their mothers. Corby with his fair freckles and straight, sandy hair—like his mother—looked nothing like Justin, whose dark, wavy hair resembled mine, and whose deeply set, large eyes appeared to have come straight from his great-grandmother Marion.

At the end of the weekend, after Corby and Betty left, I drove Justin back to school in Massachusetts and said in the car what a satisfying and peaceful feeling it was to know there were new people in the world who would always love him.

"And you, too," he said sweetly.

I imploded the next week.

My neighbors' two dogs were staying with me. Early Sunday morning, I was standing in the kitchen when I heard the crunching of dry straw in the living room. I walked in to find the younger lab chomping on the Indonesian basket my father had bought me at the 1964 World's Fair. The lid lay on the floor, surrounded by sequins. The tattered bottom sat nestled between Miele's large front paws. What short-lived fun her nails and teeth had known.

It was an old, dry, and dusty thing, not worthy of despair, and yet sounds poured out of me the likes of which I had never heard. Was I so unstable as to be undone by the destruction of a basket? Wails turned to whimpers and I could not stop. Miele sat and looked up at me with confused eyes. This wasn't the usual reaction she got when playing with a toy.

I walked back into the kitchen and started to write, standing up at the counter. I didn't know what else to do. I'd always told my son not to invest physical things with meaning. That's what Nana did, I'd say, and here I'd done the same. My dog started to whimper in response to my moans, and that upset me all the more. What kind of owner was I, upsetting a dog over a shredded basket? And yet my chest tightened, and my cries continued. I knew the basket was a thing, but what a thing it was to me. I'd chosen it to house my fondest memories of my father and put it on a shelf, and I liked it very much that way. I liked those feelings tucked away in a container with a lid.

Now the lid was off.

I texted a friend, an artist who gets up early, and told her I was having a meltdown. Monica Banks called right away. She passed no judgment about the fact that I was crying over a gnawed basket. Monica's stunning copper wire sculptures sometimes include pieces of fingernails and dead flies, and she is married to a poet whose book called *Failure* won the Pulitzer Prize. There were no off-limit places in her world, which is probably why I turned to her at such a vulnerable time.

"When things like that happen to us," she told me, "we just use it in our work."

In the days that followed, I reconsidered my objection to hiring a Brazilian lawyer. At that time in my life, the investigation into Walter

Lindberg was my work, as much as, if not more so than, my paying job. My strong reaction over losing the basket had shown how deeply the contents of the State Department documents had penetrated—to my core. I didn't know what to believe about the past. In the case of Walter and Grandma, I was the descendent of dissemblers. In that of my father, I was the offspring repository of the delusions of a reject.

Even the basket, that hallmark of Dad's goodness, had been tainted, now symbolizing the almost pathetic actions of a man using his daughter's affection for all the wrong reasons, doing anything to get and keep my love, from taking me to a World's Fair six times to pushing away the man who might otherwise have been my husband. The Walter Lindberg story wasn't just a lie. It was a cover-up for an emotional maiming that had begun in my father's youth and lasted his whole life.

Given the strength of my emotions, I no longer thought I could go it alone. I felt beaten down and uncertain. If there was anything I'd come to rely on about myself, as a parent, head of household, and career woman, it was a hearty appetite for problem-solving, aided by an ability to lay out logical next steps, but I couldn't see where my feet, or mind, or organizational skills could lead me now with respect to Walter, nor did I have a desire to continue on my own. I needed help, the help of an expert, a person who spoke Portuguese and knew some inside tricks, namely how to request a death certificate and other relevant documents. Having a lawyer on site would allow me to travel to Brazil in an efficient way, visiting places mentioned in the documents, talking to key people identified and contacted in advance. I thought a lawyer in São Paulo would be best as that was the location of the US consulate which investigated Walter's disappearance. But how could I find a lawyer in another hemisphere who would do a reliable job without costing a fortune?

Spring came and I found myself thinking for no particular reason about someone I'd known in high school and once visited in New York but had not seen or heard about in many years. I contacted him through Facebook and asked where he was living now. São Paulo was the remarkable answer. Soon his friend John McNaughton, an American expat practicing law in São Paulo, received my wired retainer. I could have bought more than a few new baskets with the money, but considering how much the search meant to me, the lawyer's fee seemed quite reasonable.

While my new lawyer in São Paulo worked the Brazil front, I climbed upstairs to the attic. I sensed that I still had some digging to do at home before I could give a good answer to Justin's question and say why I needed to go to Brazil.

I found a cardboard box of Grandma's belongings that my father had packed long ago. In it were early photos of Dad and Mother standing with Grandma and Joe Hess, probably one of those times when Mother was thinking to herself how Dad had deceived her about Grandma's background. Mother looked so pretty and elegant, in a tailored dark suit with a white ruffled blouse and high heels. Grandma wore a loose floral shift.

I knew now that Dad wasn't the biggest liar in those photographs. However he may have stretched the truth about his social status, it paled compared to the secret Grandma was keeping, that her husband lived on. Grandma's marriage to Joe Hess probably wasn't even lawful so long as she was still married to Walter Lindberg. Had Joe known this, he could have saved himself the trouble of a divorce, for which he filed in his seventies, and sought an annulment instead. Perhaps her desire to marry again was one of the reasons why Grandma never told anyone that her second husband hadn't really died in August 1929.

It wasn't pleasant entertaining the idea that Grandma may have kept Walter's non-death a secret mainly so she could marry again. Since reading the State Department documents, I had finally obtained a copy of the New York City marriage license application between Walter and Grandma by using the year 1924 rather than 1923. The application listed Grandma's name as Elsie Roth, her maiden name, and next to the box that said "Single, Widowed or Divorced" was the word "Single." So much for Dad's father, Melville DePay. Was this, too, the practice of the day or advice Grandma received, to keep things simple, to avoid the need to produce proof of one's former husband's death? Or was Grandma just naturally inclined to keep secrets, especially when they pertained to the existence of prior husbands?

Something else had struck me about the marriage application. Walter's occupation was listed as "mechanical engineer" and I wondered if that had something to do with the State Department's reference to

Walter as an automobile mechanic. Did Grandma not understand the difference between a mechanical engineer and a car mechanic, or had she tried to say "mechanical engineer" but her English was so poor she was misinterpreted? Even my faith in documents seemed misplaced, so easily do we humans make mistakes that can be carried forward through repetition, until no one is around to make a correction.

There were some very old photos in the box of Grandma's things with Hungarian type on the reverse, either taken before Grandma left home or sent by her sisters. There was a small, heavy box of five-by-seven glass negatives, one of which had been printed and showed a gathering of fifteen people of all ages standing on rocks in front of a waterfall, the girls and women in long cotton dresses or white blouses and dark skirts, the boys and men wearing jackets, neck scarves, and hats. Maybe if I went to her hometown of Kikinda, now part of Serbia, and handed out copies of the photo, the way TV detectives do when they're searching for missing persons, local residents could direct me to the waterfall and perhaps provide names for some of the faces. I doubted I would ever do that. I never felt the same curiosity about the life Grandma left behind when she fled Kikinda for Trieste, and sailed across the Atlantic at the age of eighteen, as I did about Walter Lindberg.

Grandma must have spoken to me about her relatives, about the people who gathered in front of a waterfall for a family portrait, but nothing lingered. No stories gave those relatives life in my imagination, only the story of Grandma leaving them in search of love and independence. I was told she had run away to avoid an arranged marriage. She went to a lot of trouble to gain the right to choose a mate. She exercised that right three times, losing one husband to death, one to desertion, and one to divorce. She had Dad, and she had me, and I wondered, looking through her things, whether she thought we were enough, enough to justify all she'd been through and all she'd left behind.

In Florida, visiting Grandma once with Dad, I asked her why she never went back to see her family. She planned to go, she answered, but "the ship sank."

I had always thought it odd the power with which ship sinkings had forged our family history.

Having re-read my journal entry summarizing Dad's recounting of the Walter story on his seventy-first birthday, I now understood that Grandma wasn't referencing a second ship sinking. Until then, I had forgotten that Dad said he and Grandma were intending to sail to Europe to see Grandma's family when Walter went to Brazil. Once the *Vestris* sank, Walter couldn't meet Ulrich in Brazil, and Grandma and Dad did not sail for Europe.

It turned out that I *had* discussed the *Vestris* with Grandma, not even knowing it at the time. There was so much I might have asked after she told me "the ship sank." It was an opening to ask her all about Walter Lindberg. I squandered that opportunity out of ignorance and youth, never dreaming that later on I would spend years trying to get at the same information in other ways.

Most likely, Grandma would not have told me the whole truth. Besides, by the time we were sitting in her trailer with her third husband gone, she was beginning to suffer from dementia, so who knows how much she had forgotten. There's no way of knowing what she might have told me had I used my cross-examination skills better with her than I did.

Of all the things I found in Grandma's box, three black-and-white photographs stood out.

One photo shows a man elegantly dressed in a dark suit standing in front of a ship railing. He's wearing a white straw hat. His face is tilted toward the left but his pupils stare at the camera from the corners of his eyes, giving him a shifty look. This man is Walter Lindberg. It's the same man who appears in the photo with Otto Ulrich, and he's looking off to the left in a similar way as in the photo that came from the National Archives. In the ship photo, he appears younger and trimmer than in the 1934 photo with Otto Ulrich, not surprising as the photo of him on the ship must have been taken in New York Harbor either in November 1928, when he boarded the *Vestris* to see off Otto Ulrich, or in March 1929, when Walter boarded the *Van Dyke* to sail away himself.

In my judgment, it's the latter. This conclusion is suggested by the second important photo, which shows three people standing in front of the same ship railing. One is a fairly young woman, wearing a dark coat, looking to the left. Next to her is a more buxom woman, crouching slightly and staring at the camera. In front of both women is a boy with sandy hair. He is wearing knee socks below a dark double-breasted sailor's coat, and on his head is a sailor's cap. His right shin rests against the left leg of the tall woman. He is my father, his face uncharacteristically emotional, as though the camera had turned quivering lips into still ones solely through shutter speed and artifice.

The tall woman is my grandmother, quite slender and pretty, not stocky with drooping skin like when I knew her. I wonder whether the other woman is Emmy Kern. Is it possible that both Grandma and Emmy Kern went to the pier to say good-bye to Walter when he sailed away forever? Did Ulrich just forget to mention Grandma, or did he know that she detested him?

Both photos were torn out of an album. Blotches of black paper are stuck to the back corners. Had the album been Grandma's? If so, why did she save these two photos and throw away the rest? Or did Dad do that?

The third photo is completely different, brown in its tints. The contrast has faded significantly over the years, but there is no mistaking the man sitting on the white horse holding the reins in his left hand. He is Walter Lindberg, and he looks imposing and grand sitting in the saddle. On the back there is handwriting: "Tres Lagôas. July 1929."

Walter must have sent this photo from Brazil. Just one month before he faked his death, Walter was thinking about his family back in New York. The photo was likely his means of saying good-bye before having word of his death sent up to New York. The pose was certainly not accidental, but the extent to which it was staged to conform to his stepson's notions of him as a hero I couldn't say. There are trees in the background, and a fence, perhaps even the fence Walter built for the power and light company. Maybe he just borrowed one of the company's horses, mounted it and asked someone to take a picture for the folks back home. Who would know? Certainly Walter never could have guessed that the daughter of his stepson would be nosing into his affairs over eighty years later.

There were days after the State Department documents arrived when I felt completely duped by Walter Lindberg, times when he seemed like no more than a delusion I'd shared with my father. Here he was, pictured in the flesh, a man on a white horse in Brazil, astraddle of story and myth.

If he was only a delusion, why did I feel so much anger toward him?

In the fall, after I'd spent many a summer evening dancing with our dog while my son played "The Girl from Ipanema," new information started to arrive from Brazil.

First there was the excited report by my lawyer that he had been introduced to a woman in Cambé, where Ulrich reported finding Waldomiro Lindberg in 1934 when Cambé was called Nova Dantzig. The woman, Isabel dos Santos, was a retired school teacher who was said to be fascinated with my project, having already visited cemeteries looking for Waldomiro's name. My lawyer had sent her the State Department documents, and I wrote a letter of thanks to Dona Isabel, marveling that years after I had created an alter ego named Isabel in my novel, a real Isabel was searching in my stead for evidence of Walter Lindberg in Brazil.

As I waited for more information, my attitude toward the story began to shift. I began to recognize my own centrality in the myth of Walter's death: When I was a teenager telling what I thought was the true story of Walter Lindberg, I was incorrect in believing that people were responding enthusiastically because of Walter's heroic adventures. In fact, they were responding to me, the storyteller. I was the one offering the entertainment, the escape, not Walter. He was most certainly dead by then. "How can we tell the dancer from the dance," Yeats wrote in "Among School Children," a question I strove now to understand in a new way.

I realized, too, that even though the Walter story had turned to myth in my hands, that didn't mean I had to change. True or not, the story had influenced me. If a false jungle story had driven me to care about conservation and rainforest protection, so be it. Many a paleontologist started out as a child obsessed with dinosaurs, and dinosaurs haven't existed for sixty-five million years.

❧

When all the oak leaves on my property had fallen, a few days after Thanksgiving, when my son was back at school and I was alone again in the house, I opened the world atlas early one morning. As coffee brewed, I studied South America's largest country, tracing Otto Ulrich's route through Mato Grosso—the one he and Walter would have taken if the *Vestris* had not sunk all those Novembers ago—and the route that Walter actually took: Rio de Janeiro to São Paulo to Três Lagoas, down the Paraná River, then east, ending up in Nova Dantzig, now called Cambé.

That very day an envelope with six bright stamps was waiting for me at the post office, an envelope from Cambé.

"My name is Helio Rebello, Mrs. Isabel dos Santos' son in law," began the letter inside. "She asked me to summarize and report to you her efforts in order to find out evidences of the supposed life of Mr. Walter/ Waldomiro LINDBERG in the State of Paraná (PR), Brazil. As I have been aware of all the documents you have sent to her and as I have been watching Mrs. Isabel's moves through Mr. Lindberg's clues, I feel free to sometimes show my mind on the subject."

Isabel's son-in-law went on to explain that he was enclosing a photocopy of a page from what he described as a "North of Paraná pioneers book." He said I would find WALDOMIRO LINDBERG listed on the page "among other German names that came to the region in the early 30's. It is Mrs. Isabel's best finding so far. In fact, this evidence verifies that both the railroad pass and Mr. Ulrich witness are to be trusted."

I turned to the attachment. On the first page was a reproduction of a painting showing three men standing next to saddled horses on a patch of cleared land surrounded by trees.

Underneath the painting was a caption in Portuguese, and above the painting were two paragraphs and a heading in capital letters: "ALEMÃES VIERAM COM SONHO DE CULTIVAR A PRÓPRIA TERRA." In handwriting, Mrs. Isabel's relative provided an English translation: "GERMAN PEOPLE CAME WITH THE DREAM OF CULTIVATING THEIR OWN LAND."

The next page contained a long list of names arranged alphabetically by last name. The page began with "JUCHEN, Fritz" and ended with "PLAPPER, Aron." In the middle of the page, underlined in pen by Helio, was "LINDBERG, Waldomiro."

Right next to that was "LINDBERG, Frieda."

I was back on the case, with questions that could only be answered in Brazil.

I made plans to go to Brazil at the end of the rainy season, not the beginning, like Walter and Ulrich. I would make two pilgrimages, one to Paraná, where I now knew Walter had lived, and one to Mato Grosso, the part of the Amazon where I'd always thought he had died.

I had honored my son's request not to rush off to Brazil, but now it was time. People were waiting there for me, and I could articulate questions that begged for answers, such as why Walter's name appeared in a book about northern Paraná pioneers, and whether Frieda Lindberg was a woman he purported to marry in Brazil, while his American wife lived on in New York, also pretending she didn't already have a spouse.

Justin still did not want me to go, but he would be at school during my trip, with more "house parents" in his dorm than he had at home. I had attended the same school and trusted the smart and caring adults there. I knew he would be fine.

If Justin had asked why it mattered to our lives whether my father's stepfather had a secret wife in Brazil, I would have told my son that he didn't understand.

It was I who didn't understand, but I didn't know that yet. I could rationalize all I wanted to about the need for factual accuracy and completeness, but there was something deeper drawing me to Brazil. I hadn't realized what.

PART TWO

Chapter twenty-three

BOA TARDE, BRAZIL

SLEEK OFFICE TOWERS. Glass-fronted clinics where skin wrinkles are made to disappear. This is São Paulo?

I want to see the São Paulo that Walter Lindberg saw, not this modern city built by Brazil's prosperous financial sectors. I want to see old, but on my first walk through São Paulo, only the huge banyan trees with their elephant-skin limbs and ancient, sprawling roots seem capable of transporting me to 1929.

Some of the trees have been collared by cement or asphalt, no soil visible around their trunks. That they continue to live seems a miracle. Their roots must go deep, to another place entirely, a place of nourishment that sustains them in this vast metropolis with twenty million residents, the largest city in South America.

The tree near the entrance to Ibirapuera Park is as wide as a truck. I imagine Walter Lindberg passing it on his way from the United States Consulate, having picked up Otto Ulrich's message that his "coming probably would not materialize." Was Walter furious to find himself on his own, or matter-of-fact, mulling over his options?

I'm not on my own on this cloudy, cool Saturday. Roberta Steele is with me. An old friend, she's flown from San Francisco to join me on this journey. She and I have taken many a hiking trip together, but never one searching for a dead man.

Walking to keep from sleeping after spending hours in planes, we stop for refreshments in the park. A woman cores a fresh coconut and pours its contents into a plastic bottle. Now that's more like it, something I can't buy in Central Park, certainly not for two reals, or about $1.

May is autumn in the Southern Hemisphere and many Brazilians are wearing coats and boots, though to us the temperature feels comfortable, perfect for walking.

The swans here are reversed, just like the seasons, from a north-of-the-equator point of view. The birds glide across the lake, black-feathered, their beaks bright red. Perhaps Roberta and I look exotic in our new context because as we sip our coconut water, two men half our age stop to talk. We met them earlier outside the park at the large stone Monument to the Bandeiras, the bands of seventeenth- and eighteenth-century mineral and slave hunters who pushed westward from coastal Brazil, making Portugal rich, wreaking havoc on indigenous tribes, and creating many of Brazil's early white settlements in places such as Mato Grosso and Minas Gerais.

The two men know less English than we know Portuguese. One asks "where from?"

"*Eu Nova York*," I say. "*Ela California.*"

"Cal-ee-for-nya?" the bearded one repeats with awe. He looks at Roberta and the age difference vanishes. Everyone likes a good-looking woman from California, especially a blonde. So far, we have not seen many fair-haired women walking around São Paulo. In the few hours since our arrival, Roberta has received many glances. Me, I like to think I can pass for a *brasileira* with my dark hair and hazel eyes.

We do not linger with the real *brasileiros* who want to practice their English. I have an agenda of old places to see in Centro, the original downtown, including the 1911 belle-époque theater modeled after the Paris Opera. I also want to see Theodore Roosevelt plaza, because *Through the Brazilian Wilderness* is part of the canon of old Brazil.

The theater, ecru and brown, glows with golden light from chandeliers visible through the large arched windows of the second floor. People have congregated on the steps.

We follow the sounds of an electric guitar into a McDonald's in the lobby of a 1920s art-deco office building across from the theater. Fast food is what has become of this elegant structure from Walter Lindberg's day, but the McDonald's is also a music club. People are dancing the bossa nova and samba in a big open space surrounded by tables. The guitarist sits in the center on a platform. We join the spectators, not the dancers. Roberta buys an ice-cream cone, and I take photos for my son, a fan of McDonald's in any setting.

Being from Nova York, I should be the street-smart one, but at dusk it is Roberta who sees the danger first, whispering "that boy has a knife" as we walk across Se Plaza, toward old St. Peter's Church, the shops closed and gated, the sky darkening. We don't seem to be the boy's targets but that could change fast; we are obviously foreigners, walking a few feet away from him with cash-flush pocketbooks. Nearby, a woman has just pushed her male companion into the street screaming "*voce, voce*"—you, you. A man on a motorized scooter zooms past us followed by several barking dogs, and I notice more people standing next to sleeping bags than not. I realize I'm so intent on reclaiming the past that I may get us hurt.

"Let's turn around," I whisper. There is one car parked on the street at the end of the plaza, a taxi as luck would have it. We get into the car and I say in bad Portuguese, "We're happy you are here." The driver gives us a thumbs-up.

"So, what do you hope to find out?" Roberta asks over dinner at Figueira, named for the enormous fig tree in the outdoor seating area.

The wine glass can't get to my lips fast enough. I'm not sure I can articulate to a professional litigator a clear purpose for why I dragged her to Brazil, as though we are a couple of prosecutors investigating a crime. I am tempted to point to the tree and ask isn't it enough to want to be in a place where a fig tree's branches can grow into a canopy covering forty tables?

Roberta is waiting for an answer. Do I respond as a reporter working on a story, an environmentalist wanting to see more of a country with major significance for the planet's future, the step-granddaughter of a man who fled New York for this place, the accomplice after the fact to a woman who kept a secret from her own son, the daughter of a man who was hurt, or the daughter hurt by him?

"I know this is really unlikely," I begin, not wanting to sound like a dreamer, "but the jackpot would be to find out why he did it, why Walter abandoned Dad and Grandma. Why he didn't care enough about them to stick around or come back."

Roberta doesn't say a word. She just looks at me. She is used to asking questions in depositions and hearing all kinds of answers. It's part of her job not to respond with what she is really thinking. I am traveling with a woman who practices cross-examination for a living, but for now she doesn't question my answer.

"The other thing," I add, "is why Brazil? Why did he wind up here?"

Roberta nods at this. She wanted to visit Brazil wholly apart from Walter Lindberg, despite her two sisters' concern about the Amazon portion of our itinerary. They asked me to take good care of Roberta, and I promised to, but the truth is she usually manages just fine on her own. When I first met her, clerking for Judge Harold Greene in Washington, she worked as the judge's secretary and was in the midst of a divorce. I was one of the people who encouraged her to go to law school, but first she needed to finish college. She did that, excelled in law school, and then became a partner in a civil rights firm, specializing in employment discrimination cases. She is a frequent speaker at bar association events throughout the country.

I didn't see the need to remind Roberta's younger sisters that I am the one with the chronic health condition. I have a note from my doctor explaining why I travel with hypodermic needles, and I am wearing the MedicAlert bracelet that I usually leave in a drawer, but that's the extent of my accommodation. It's been years since I had a travel problem.

Roberta and I have one thing in common: We are both grieving recent deaths. Roberta's mother died a few months ago, and she is grappling with being the oldest person alive in her immediate family. I am hoping this trip will help her heal.

Michael died of cancer six weeks before my departure. I attended the memorial service, marveling at the poise of his daughter, a college freshman, and his adopted son, a few years older. I hugged Michael's wife, and then happened to use the restroom before the service at the same time as his daughter. I had not seen her since she was a girl. Within minutes we were crying. "I promised myself I wasn't going to do this," she said. I want to think that this helped her, coaxing the tears out in private before six speakers eulogized her father's brilliance and compassion and shook their heads over how much he had suffered, the cancer raiding his jaw, making it hard for him to talk, impossible to swallow. For months near the end, this man who always chose the restaurants and cared about ordering well, this man with whom I had traveled through France, drinking wine and eating cochon, was receiving his calories through a feeding tube.

In 1928, after Colonel Fawcett disappeared with his son and a friend, the British Royal Geographic Society hired a leader for the search party and sought an assistant through an ad in English newspapers. According to author David Grann, writing in *The Lost City of Z*, some twenty thousand people responded—twenty thousand men from over a dozen countries, but not Brazil. The Brazilians knew better. If a young military man from coastal Brazil, "civilized" Brazil, received a posting to the interior, his family mourned his death in advance. In the 1910s, if one was assigned to work with Colonel Candido Mariano da Silva Rondon building the telegraph line through western Mato Grosso, all that seemed in doubt was how one might die—of parasites or poisoned arrows. Though the jungle conjured up romance in the minds of those from afar, to civilized Brazilians, it was a horrid place.

Things haven't changed all that much, a Brazilian employee of The Nature Conservancy tells Roberta and me over dinner during our second night in São Paulo. Brazilians from the coastal cities, she explains, don't vacation in the Amazon or the Pantanal seeking out wildlife. Those with money to travel prefer the United States or Europe. Tatiana, a lawyer turned fundraiser, says it is especially hard to raise money in Brazil to train indigenous peoples to protect their native lands. Our organization's training center in Manaus, a joint project with the association of indigenous peoples, has temporarily closed for lack of funding.

Not everyone in São Paulo feels antipathy toward the Amazon region, I discover the next morning. The receptionist at the Melia Jardim Europa is wearing a pin that reads WWF—World Wildlife Fund—the organization selected to receive a portion of the hotel's revenue this month as part of an ongoing campaign. When he learns that I work for The Nature Conservancy, he asks for my card. He will propose to his boss that the Conservancy be a future recipient.

WWF and The Nature Conservancy work together in some countries, independently in others. It's a big world with no shortage of environmental challenges, plenty to be divvied up—though all of the major "enviros" work in Brazil, along with numerous smaller groups, on account of the country's phenomenal biodiversity. Nearly one-fourth of all plant species on earth are found in Brazil—an estimated sixteen thousand different tree species alone—not to mention all the animals and insects, many of which remain unstudied and even unnamed.

The hotel receptionist is navigating streets with his finger on a city map. He calls over a concierge. I have an appointment in less than an hour with the lawyer John McNaughton, whose office is supposed to be within walking distance, but still the receptionist checks Google Maps and prints a page as the concierge points at my polka dot, travel-size umbrella and shakes his head. He hustles across the lobby and returns with a large black umbrella, suitable for a golf foursome. It's the end of the rainy season on the calendar, but outside it's pouring. If I am going to insist on walking instead of sitting in a taxi in Monday morning traffic, the hotel staff is going to make sure I am well-equipped.

"*Obrigada,*" I say and the concierge instantly replies, "*Da nada.*" It's nothing. A Brazilian would never think of withholding those two words after someone says "thank you." I've only been in Brazil a few days but already I understand that for Brazilians, "*da nada*" is a reply almost as reflexive as breathing.

It is crowded as I walk along Boulevard Brigadeiro Faria Lima. I seem to be the only person wearing sandals, but that's okay because the sandals have platform bottoms, which elevate my bare feet above the splattering mud more common than pavement along this stretch of new offices, banks, and parking garages.

I am not dressed in a manner befitting a client about to meet her attorney. The decision to travel with only a carry-on bag meant the sacrifice of business attire. I am wearing white capri-length pants.

At least I have one accessory like everyone else's—a large, black umbrella. In return for the kindness of the concierge, I am operating the umbrella carefully, tilting it often, attempting to avoid all the other black umbrellas and the bodies of those carrying them.

At the correct building on Faria Lima, I climb the steps to the reception desk, announce my *encontra* with John McNaughton, and take the elevator to the third floor. Fast Portuguese comes from inside the door marked 301. At precisely 10 am, I knock. A man dressed appropriately for an autumn business meeting opens the door. Tall and lean, with neatly combed longish hair, he wears a button-down shirt, gray cardigan sweater-vest, and dark jacket. His face puts me at ease immediately. His eyes sparkle and he smiles, reaching his hands forward to greet me and take my wet umbrella before it drips all over his office.

"Marian, welcome," he says, offering a kiss on the cheek and a hug. He introduces me to Valdir Macenco, his accountant, who has broad shoulders and apples for cheeks.

Valdir has already helped me. I am not sure why, only that he chose to do so. My mother found it difficult to accept help from people. If someone did something nice for her she would promptly go out and buy a gift in order to reciprocate. I do have a small gift for Valdir, a Nature Conservancy baseball hat, but I did not feel it was required. Preparing for this expedition into Walter Lindberg's life when he was supposed to be dead, I have learned to accept the help of total strangers with a simple but genuine *obrigada*.

Valdir shakes my hand and bows his head as I express my gratitude for all he has done, putting me in touch with his aunt, Isabel dos Santos, and her son-in-law, Helio, with whom I have since had several communications.

John motions for Valdir and me to take seats across from him at his desk. John taps a stack of documents and says, "Waldomiro Lindberg. There ought to be a movie about his life."

I sit back, pleased with my choice of attorney.

chapter twenty-four

A CHANGE IN THE CURRENT

"I'M LOOKING AT this as a Brazilian," John begins, and that's how he thinks of himself, notwithstanding his American roots.

John moves the pile of documents to the center of the desk. He starts with Walter's arrival, saying he tried to obtain passenger lists from the ship that brought Walter to Rio in March 1929. He flips through a binder with notes and documents neatly organized inside plastic page protectors. It's obvious he's put in a lot of time.

John believes the passenger lists no longer exist, but he hands me printed material about the ship. That's how I learn that the ship's name was *Vandyck*, not "*Van Dyke*" as the court reporter typed it in the Ulrich transcript.

Like the *Vestris*, the *Vandyck* was owned by Lamport & Holt, which inaugurated its Liverpool, Brazil & River Plate Steam Navigation Company in 1865 to provide service to the east coast of South America. (The third ship in the fleet, the *Vauban*, took Percy Fawcett to Rio for his final expedition in 1925.)

It turns out that Walter sailed on one of the *Vandyck*'s last voyages to South America, John tells me. After the *Vestris* disaster and all the legal claims, the Lamport & Holt shipping enterprise collapsed, the New York–South America service was discontinued, and in 1930 the *Vandyck* was rerouted to Southampton, England. She became an English military ship and in June 1940, off the coast of Norway, she was bombed by German aircraft and caught fire. Most of the crew escaped ashore, where they became prisoners of war, and the ship sank the next day.

I tell John I'm not disappointed about the absence of passenger lists from the *Vandyck*. They would not have added anything significant. There is no doubt that Walter arrived in Brazil in 1929. Thanks to Ulrich and the State Department, I already know that after arriving in Rio, Walter first headed southwest to São Paulo, at the time a small coastal town, where he received Ulrich's letter. From there Walter went to Três Lagoas—Three Lagoons—which meant heading west through lands marked "unexplored" and "inhabited by wild Indians" on the era's maps.

Today, Três Lagoas is accessible from São Paulo by means of a highway passing through Bauru and Araçatuba, but Walter likely made his way by rail. It was the Noroeste do Brasil Railroad that caused elimination of the "wild Indians" and began to change the geography of western São Paulo state from "unexplored" to "explored" in the early twentieth century. During that time, workers intent on extending the railroad westward from Bauru to the Paraná River, joined by settlers and land developers, waged war on the Coroada and Kaingang tribes. The whites won. Between 1910 and 1934, the population of the area increased 350 percent.

At the westernmost point of São Paulo state, Walter would have crossed the Paraná River to get to Três Lagoas. The word "paraná" is a shortened version of the Tupí phrase for "as big as the sea," and the Paraná is the second-longest river in South America after the Amazon.

John has several points to make about the delegate of police of Mato Grosso, the man who reported that Walter's supposed assassination was "false information" because Walter was still living, only under the name of Waldomiro. First, John says, I need to understand that the *delegado* wasn't a career police officer. The *delegado* would have been a law school graduate, someone who chose being top dog in a frontier town over practicing law, someone who liked to throw his weight around. He would have been one of the most educated people in town.

The *delegado* offered fraud as the reason for Walter's staged death, writing to the US consulate in 1930 that Walter "has in New York a wife called Elsie Lindberg, in whose favor he took out a large life insurance with a North American company, and spread in person the news of the supposed assassination, so as to share later in the product of his chicanery and fraud."

John sees it differently.

"My reading of the death claim is that it wasn't a fraud," John says. "It was intended as a means to support his wife. Waldomiro may have decided to stay in Brazil, but he wanted her to recover some money. I see it as a humanitarian gesture. He probably thought no one would know the difference. It was very . . . *Brazilian*."

This idea is so completely fresh that all I can say is "Really?" It has never occurred to me that Walter faked his death out of concern for the family he left behind.

I am certain that Grandma wasn't a co-conspirator, as the *delegado* alleged. If, as she told the State Department, she was paying $79 a quarter in premiums—not a small amount at the time—why shouldn't she have reported the death to Prudential and sought to recover? And if she was in on a scheme, why did she keep coming back for meetings with the State Department even after Prudential refused to pay?

The surprising thing, John says, and I agree, is that a Brazilian authority knew about the insurance policies and the name of Walter's wife. That information could only have come from Walter, which means he told someone in Brazil about the policies, perhaps even boasting about how he had made sure his wife and stepson in New York would be provided for. If Walter went on living and working in Três Lagoas for eleven months after his alleged death, as indicated in the State Department documents, he obviously wasn't too concerned with what people thought in Brazil. The audience for his "death" was in New York. Probably Walter had no idea Grandma would question the report the way she did. Likely he also had little knowledge of how insurance companies processed claims, and that without a body or any proof of death, a payment was unlikely.

Grandma told the State Department that Walter "never contributed one cent" toward supporting her and Dad, but now my representative in São Paulo was suggesting that perhaps Walter had tried.

Sitting in John McNaughton's office, the idea that Walter may have been attempting to help Grandma and Dad alters something in my brain. I put down my pen and notebook and stare at John, then at Valdir, who smiles back at me. It's as though the current has suddenly changed, and the river steamer that is my anger at Walter sputters and starts to slow. With this change in direction comes a different way of looking at the timing of the staged death. I tell John and Valdir my new supposition, that in his mind, Walter may have been sending Dad and Grandma a present, the best and last one, and that's why he chose their birthdays for its delivery. Until now I have been thinking the timing showed heartlessness and hostility. Recast through John's interpretation, the timing may have reflected a final act of duty, if not affection.

This is so aberrant it would never have occurred to me on my own. I haven't even finished talking to my expat lawyer, but already it's as plain as the Paraná River is long that looking at things like a Brazilian may adjust my course.

chapter twenty-five

THE TOP OF THE HEAP

JOHN ISN'T MAKING money as he sits behind his desk analyzing the case of Walter Lindberg. He hasn't charged me anything beyond the initial retainer, and clearly he has done a great deal of work. When John tells me a little about himself, I begin to understand.

According to John, he was a twenty-four-year-old sculptor living in New York City when a friend invited him to the Soviet Union to interview circus clowns for a book. John had been jilted by his girlfriend and seized the opportunity to do something new, but the two men never reached their destination. Their car crashed in East Germany, injuring the friend, but John, sitting in the passenger seat with a bag of laundry in his lap, was saved by the dirty clothes. He took a long detour to Italy, where he knew someone, and there he met and married a Brazilian woman. She brought him to her home city, where he taught English, learned Portuguese, and eventually went to law school. São Paulo has been his home ever since.

The turns in John's life—leaving New York for Russia, winding up in Italy because of a transportation accident, meeting a woman and moving to Brazil—are not dissimilar to the turns in Walter's life, and I reflect on how lucky I am to have found a lawyer with a bit of Walter in him, a smart man working on the Walter case out of interest rather than business.

John explains that back in the early 1930s, northern Paraná was "really the frontier, very much like the Wild West, a place for a certain kind of person who was asking, 'Where can I make a fortune?' There were the stories of Theodore Roosevelt shooting game in the Brazilian interior, and those went around the world. The earth was rich in Paraná for farming. The soil was very good for coffee. There weren't that many other places where you could come to get rich at that time. This coincided with a series of migratory movements toward that area."

I'd read in the Museu Paulista the day before that after slavery was abolished in 1888, the elite's desire for more whites and coffee plantation owners' need for workers coalesced in an advertising campaign directed at Europeans, offering to pay for their cross-Atlantic travel. The largest number of coffee hands came from Italy, but many came from Spain, Portugal, Germany, and Eastern Europe. Some stayed in São Paulo; others went elsewhere, such as Paraná.

John says that many worked off their debts and were thrifty. "When the 1929 crash came," he says, "they were able to buy land and marry the daughters of their former patrons."

Japanese immigrants also came, beginning in 1908, bringing with them the practice of cultivating vegetables. Indeed, São Paulo today has the second largest population of Japanese outside of Japan. Many live in a neighborhood called Liberdade—"freedom" in Portuguese— where lanterns hang over the sidewalks and sushi restaurants sit four to a block.

John says that Germans drawn to the promise of Brazil included political refugees and "the adventure type," which makes me think of Otto Ulrich's compatriots, Alexander Alexandrovitch and Otto Herbinger, who left Germany for Brazil in the 1920s and invited Ulrich to join them on their 1926 expedition. Ulrich described Herbinger as a chief forester in Germany, work that would have prepared him well for the jungle. In contrast, John points out, the political refugees often lacked practical skills. Some were highly educated, such as lawyers and judges. Germans were fleeing tensions of several kinds, not just the Nazi build-up. Ulrich, for example, testified that he originally left the German city of Graudens "because I was expelled by the Poles and they took everything away from me."

Nearly four hundred surnames, including Lindberg, appear on the page Helio sent from the "North of Paraná pioneers' book" about the early German community, people who came to the area with a "dream of cultivating their own land."

No one can say what dream took Walter to Três Lagoas, but what he wound up doing there at first, according to the State Department documents, was manual labor, not the usual stuff of dreams. Then he took a steamer heading south on the Paraná River, disembarking at Porto XV, about 160 kilometers away, still in the state of Mato Grosso.

Perhaps that was when Walter's dream shifted to "exploration of the Babassu palm nut" as described by Alfred Rackebrand, the American expat in Rio who worked for Condor Air. Being associated with an airline at the start of air travel in Brazil would have put Rackebrand in touch with many people from different locations, and thus he could well have learned about Walter's plans either from Walter or someone else.

Today, an eight-ounce jar of "pure babassu oil" sells on Amazon.com for $35.99. The hair and skin care company Aveda supports a community of babassu "nut-breakers" in northeastern Brazil to obtain palm oil for its products. Other proponents of the plant claim that pelletized babassu palms could make a viable coal substitute for power companies.

Walter may have been ahead of his time with his ideas, but he didn't die looking for babassu palms, nor did the trees make him rich. Instead, he wound up in Paraná, a place where trees were being felled for the fertile soil on which they stood, not sought for their nuts.

The State Department documents said Walter headed toward the "upper Sorocabana," a railroad district in the western part of São Paulo state, defined by the expansion of the lower Sorocabana railroad west from Botucatu to the Paraná River. Like the seventh zone to its north, this eighth zone was settled by whites who fought and ousted the native population.

Construction of the upper Sorocabana railroad made the region a "moving frontier" in the 1910s and 1920s, according to the author and professor John Woodward.* In 1924, the goal of expanding the railroad westward all the way to the Paraná River was reached, with a station opening in Presidente Epitacio, across the river from Porto XV. Walter must have realized that if he grew tired of looking for babassu palms, all he had to do was cross the river and he could board the upper Sorocabana railroad.

If Walter did work in the Brazilian rail industry before coming to New York, perhaps he relied on his old knowledge of railroads when he traveled across Brazil after arriving in Rio. Maybe he encountered people he'd known from his pre–New York days, and maybe they were the ones who helped fill his mind with new dreams as he congratulated himself on the fine life that he assumed his wife and stepson were living in New York on the insurance payoff.

I never could find proof that Walter had worked on the Mamore-Madeira Railway, as Ulrich stated, and the timing doesn't match up, but Percival Farquhar, the same controversial North American capitalist who invested heavily in construction of the Mamore-Madeira Railway, also managed the Sorocabana for a time, perhaps leading to confusion in Ulrich's mind.

The fortunes of the Sorocabana were much improved when it stopped carrying cotton and started carrying coffee from the new farms of northern Paraná via the lower Sorocabana line, one of whose passengers into Paraná must have been the man now calling himself Waldomiro.

In northern Paraná, Waldomiro encountered Brits who were creating a "little London" one scorched acre at a time. They were in the process of removing three million acres of forest to expose the *terra vermelha*— rich, red soil full of iron. First, the large and plentiful trees were cut for timber, often by hand. Then the brush was burned, leaving the soil ready for planting.

There in Londrina, headquarters of the land company's operations, the man I grew up believing to be a great explorer of the Amazon took a

---

* Woodward, James. *A Place in Politics: São Paulo, Brazil, from Seigneurial Republicanism to Regionalist Revolt*. Durham, North Carolina: Duke University Press, 2009.

job offering for sale parts of a different forest, the Atlantic Forest. Such was the true "chicanery and fraud" in my mind—the hero of my father's story revealed as part of a deforestation effort on a scale so grand, and with adverse ecological and social consequences so profound, that many organizations, including my own, have undertaken a massive restoration project—over twelve million new trees planted to restore the Atlantic Forest since 2008 toward a goal of one billion.

Today, the trip by car from Três Lagoas to Londrina takes two hours. In the early 1930s, it apparently took Walter two years. His arrival date in Londrina—1932—is no secret. It's inscribed on a city monument, which I knew before sitting down with John and Valdir thanks to Helio and his mother-in-law, Isabel. A few months after Helio first contacted me, he e-mailed a photograph of Isabel pointing to a name and date on a plaque: "Waldemiro Lindberg 1932."

I show Valdir the photo of his aunt pointing to the plaque. He is not surprised to hear of her efforts on my behalf.

"She likes to help people," he says simply.

John unveils a book of photographs depicting Londrina's colonization.

He opens to a black-and-white photograph of a large arch carved out of wood and painted white, with "WELCOME" across the top in old English letters, and above that the royal crest bounded by British and Brazilian flags. The sign had been made in preparation for a visit by the Prince of Wales, an investor in the British company that was clearing the forest.

In the photograph, the *arco de boas vidas*—arch of good lives, as the caption puts it—sits atop a mound, reached by twenty white steps, the ornateness of the design completely incongruous with the setting: barren earth, a simple, one-story wood building behind the arch, and the perimeter of the forest in the background.

The *arco* was an arch of triumph, triumph over the forest and all that went with it—the animals, the heat, the insects, the diseases, the natives—and when Waldomiro arrived, he became a card-carrying member of the enterprise.

The Atlantic Forest once stretched from northeast Brazil into Argentina, an area twice the size of Texas. As its name suggests, the Atlantic Forest was near the coast, which made its land accessible for building settlements and farming. Moreover, unlike the Amazon, where the soils can be poor for agriculture, the soils of the Atlantic Forest offered great promise for crops.

The consequent investment opportunity was realized in the mid-1920s by a Scottish man named Simon Fraser, also known as Lord Lovat, the leader of a British land development syndicate.

John tells me another Scottish man with the last name of Thomas handled the negotiations. When Thomas was through, the Northern Paraná Land Company owned 13,600 square kilometers, more than three million acres. Most of the land was sold to the company by the Brazilian government, which happened to owe a great deal of money to English banks arising out of World War I debts. To have those debts extinguished, and to gain additional investment capital, the government was willing to sell to a foreign company 7 percent of the state of Paraná, mostly *floresta virgem*.

Following the 1929 stock market crash, the development model embraced by the company involved the sale of small plots to many people, rather than big plots to a few. That's why agents such as Walter were needed to sell land.

"Snr. Dr. Waldomiro Lindberg" is how the name was laid in type on the small Northern Paraná Land Company document sent by the State Department. The US Foreign Service officer referred to the item as a "railroad pass," but John says the document was something more. It was a form that Waldomiro, as a *companhia* agent, would have handed to a potential buyer to confirm an offer of land. John surmises that Waldomiro had a book of forms, allowing him to tear off a page as needed.

With Ulrich, Walter had planned to travel to Brazil to get rich off of the land; had he, as Waldomiro, finally realized that dream not by removing its gold from riverbeds, but by removing its trees? According to John, Waldomiro would have been paid commissions on tracts he sold, which "would have been sizable amounts. Even if he only sold two, that was a lot of money."

John speculates that Waldomiro might even have owned land himself. Perhaps he employed a family to farm for him, as many of the small landowners did.

One thing John is sure of is that Waldomiro had status, as indicated by the *companhia* use of the word "Dr." in the agent book, which connoted a university education of some sort.

"It means he was respected, a distinguished person."

Along with such status went certain obligations, John continues. Such a person was expected to be a community leader and "to resolve problems for poor people."

"Waldomiro was at the top of the heap," John says, "and Brazil was a paradise."

John shows me more photos. Here are the hacked trunks of trees and gnarled vines awaiting "civilizing fire" to take the land from forest to naked soil; here are five men trying to free an overloaded truck from its trap of mud, the men dressed alike, in linen jackets and fedoras. A woman in a skirt carrying a baby looks on. They are her family's belongings in the truck, on their way to a new home, but the same red dirt that bestowed economic opportunity became "a slurry of red mud" during the rainy season, according to the text.

The soil gave the immigrants of northern Paraná both promise and hardship. It also gave them a name. They were called "red feet," though some of the red feet lived better than others.

Here are a white man and woman waving at the camera as they swim in the Rio Cambé, a waterfall behind them. Here are families of darker-skinned workers with dirty faces and ragged clothes standing in front of shacks, and on another page are three well-coifed women dressed in tailored, dark suits, each seated in a chair, each with a man in a khaki suit standing next to her. These three couples, photographed in Nova Dantzig, were members of the German community.

As John puts it, "The English had tea and the Germans had string quartets."

There's one photo in particular that he wants to show me, a photo of nine people standing on the veranda of a one-story wooden building. John points at the latticework of the railing around the porch, noting how similar it looks to the railing on the house in the photo of Walter and Ulrich, with a Japanese style to the open squares.

The building in the book was the region's first hospital, built in 1933, one of the earliest buildings constructed of *peroba rosa*, pink mahogany.

The hospital is larger than the structure in the Ulrich photo. They are not the same building, but they are definitely products of the same time, perhaps even the same hands.

John turns a few more pages, to a photo of a man sitting on a mule. The caption gives the man's name as Jose Licia. John picks up the page from the pioneer book that Helio sent and shows me the name LICIA, Jose, on the same page as LINDBERG, Waldomiro.

John is nothing if not thorough.

According to the text, Licia came from Austria and lived in Londrina until the age of one hundred. If Waldomiro had stuck around Londrina or Nova Dantzig anywhere near that long, there might be a street named after him, John says. So far Isabel and Helio haven't told me about any Lindberg Street, though I'll soon be able to see for myself. Londrina is our next stop.

John apologizes that he has to return the photo book to the British library, but he has made copies of each photo and hands them to me.

The next item we discuss is the 1939 "protest" from São Paulo state that pops up online. John says it was a step short of a lawsuit in which a person claiming a debt made a formal request for payment. Waldomiro is listed as the buyer but John has not been able to determine if he was the person filing the protest or being protested against. John notes that Waldomiro's address in the document wasn't Londrina or Nova Danzig. It was Rolândia, a town further west.

John also hasn't obtained a death certificate. I'm a little disappointed to hear this, remembering that my interest in a death certificate was the reason for hiring a lawyer in Brazil, but that seems like a long time ago. Obtaining proof of death is hard, John says, without knowing the state in which Waldomiro died. If he stayed in Brazil during World War II, Waldomiro may have been fingerprinted, and those records might be available. We'll see. John asks me to let him know what I find on the rest of my trip. Maybe there will be more leads to investigate.

I ask John what I owe him.

"You don't owe me anything," he answers right away. I invite him to lunch, but he has another appointment. He recommends that Valdir and I get some food at the mall up the street.

As we prepare to leave, Valdir shows me a photograph of his wife and daughter. I take out a photograph of my son. John shows me photos of his children, including a beautiful daughter and her polo-playing husband. I also show John and Valdir a photograph of my father with Arnold Palmer and they linger over this image of the famous golfer, who was under contract to play an annual round with the executives at Chase Manhattan Bank. I like the picture because my father looks happy.

John's Mandarin instructor arrives and Valdir and I head to the door, John handing Valdir an umbrella as a last thought.

Outside, Valdir puts on the baseball cap and thanks me for the gift. He laughs, telling me he intended to bring a hat when he left his house, but he forgot it, and now he has one. When we walk into the mall, Valdir takes my umbrella and inserts it into a contraption that sheathes it in a narrow plastic bag so that it won't drip through the modern shops and food concessions.

Valdir lets me buy him lunch but puts little on his plate. We talk about our children, agreeing in many ways about how we are raising them.

We part in the rain on the sidewalk. Valdir has taken the day off from work to be with me. He'll return John's umbrella, then drive home. At this point we're actually not sure which umbrella is John's and which one belongs to the concierge. They both look alike.

I make my way to the hotel in the rain, past the banyan trees in their cement collars. Walking gives my brain time to adjust. I need to find my way across eighty years.

Roberta is drying her hair when I enter our room. While I was meeting with John and Valdir, she used the hotel gym. She turns off the dryer and asks me how it went.

"Really great," I answer, and my voice sounds practically manic.

Roberta asks if the attorney found a death certificate and I say no. She asks if he confirmed that Frieda was Walter's new wife. I say no.

"What then?" she asks.

"He gave me some fascinating history, and a lot of photographs."

"Of Walter?"

"I don't know. They're copies. It's hard to tell."

She is silent.

"It wasn't really facts that he gave me," I say, groping to establish a basis for my high spirits. "It was more the context. He had a fresh way of looking at things, like a whole new take on why Walter faked his death."

"Oh," she says. "I'm glad you were happy with it."

We each finish packing. Downstairs, we order wine while waiting for our taxi to the airport. We are alone, sitting in the courtyard, under an awning that protects us from the rain.

Roberta tells me she spent some time writing in her journal, but she still has a lot to add. She is writing chronologically. She's covered our visit to the park and what we saw in the museums. She's up to Tatiana and Brazilian pizza.

I don't want to say anything critical about something as personal as a journal, but it strikes me that Roberta has been writing only about facts. I wonder how she really feels, and how she is going to heal from her mother's death through a mere recitation of her days' activities.

"Just the facts, ma'am" is an old journalistic expression: Don't tell us what you thought or how it made you feel, just tell us what you saw.

Sitting in humid São Paulo after my *encontra* with an American who thinks like a Brazilian, I feel myself wriggling inside my reporter's skin. I don't know about Roberta, but I feel a lot smarter than I did when the day began, and it's not because of any new facts that John gave me. John may be a lawyer, but he drew on a whole lot more than legal training in our discussion.

For all the facts that I've gathered about Walter, it seems I'm only just beginning to get to know Waldomiro. He's escaped from my father's story into a life of his own. I'm eager to follow his trail of red feet, not sure where it will lead.

chapter twenty-six

ALTERNATIVE REALITY

DOWNTOWN LONDRINA IS deserted when we arrive at night, riding in the car of a driver sent by a woman I have never met, who expressed concern for our safety if we hailed a cab at the airport.

Luciana Walther is a local mother of three whose cousin is the sister-in-law of a friend of mine in Connecticut. This is a not a close connection, but since my introduction by e-mail to Luciana, she has been answering my communications faster than my blood relatives. She made our hotel reservations, offered advice about airlines, and provided the cellphone of her aunt in São Paulo in case we ran into trouble there.

Luciana is part of a wholly unexpected alliance of helpers that grew over the months before my trip, both in the United States and Brazil, assembled through friends and co-workers. It turns out that a great many people know or are related to Brazilians, and a great many Brazilians are kind and generous with their time.

Kindness has its limits, though. The lone person sitting in the small restaurant at the Bourbon Hotel declines to turn off the TV, so Roberta and I leave the hotel to find dinner elsewhere. We wind up down the block in a no-frills place where the fish comes with capers, the manioc is fried, and Brazilian Portuguese is the only language choice.

Thanks to a CD crash course in Brazilian Portuguese, I can speak with some confidence about engineers' meetings, managers' speeches, and multinational corporations' problems, but asking if the fish is fresh is beyond my ability. The course was geared to business travelers.

Fortunately, my language skills are not a problem tonight. The fish and manioc taste great and the *cerveja* is cold.

After dinner, we walk through a plaza ringed with closed stores and banks, so quiet we hear our footsteps on the cobblestones. The only other person is a man pushing a grocery cart full of empty cans. Around a curve we find a *farmácia* turning off its lights. Across the street is another plaza, empty except for a few teenage boys around a bench. I understand why Luciana sent a driver. It is eerily quiet for a big city, as though its residents are in hiding.

The next morning Londrina is alive with people and cars. I've got my running shoes on, and I'm headed downhill, following the street map for the Monumento ao Viajante. City workers in orange uniforms are receiving their instructions for the day in a small park across from the modern Catedral Metropolitana. Down the hill, banks and clothing stores give way to open-air bars. People are sitting outside in plastic chairs drinking coffee. I pass a pet shop, cages of birds stacked on the sidewalk.

I come to a major intersection with cars backed up bumper-to-bumper in every direction. Across four lanes of traffic, down an incline, sits a giant round spaceship of a building. It is the Terminal Rodoviario de Londrina—a bus station—designed by Oscar Niemeyer, Brazil's signature architect.

The traffic light lets me cross, and when I walk down the steps toward the station I see way off to the right a metallic monument rising high in the midst of a large lawn encircled by more highways. There are no traffic lights, no pedestrian walkways, no visible means of passage to the lawn. I can tell very quickly that this isn't the Pioneer's Monument where Waldomiro Lindberg's name is inscribed. From afar, the monument's shiny surface doesn't show any bronze plaques bearing names and dates as in the photograph Helio sent me. The monument isn't bronze at all; it is silver.

I make my way back up the hill, telling myself that the exercise was worth the early rising, even if I have made a mistake.

2

Bruno Sanches finds us in the hotel's breakfast room in time for coffee. His assignment for the day is to drive, translate, and help us avoid errors like the one I just made.

Bruno is young and lithe, with a graduate-student stubble. He and Roberta find something to laugh about right away, and I feel glad she is with me, my cover for not being crazy on this search for a man whose DNA I don't even share.

But Bruno doesn't think I'm crazy. He is writing a master's thesis about the people whose names appear on Londrina's street signs.

Introducing Bruno to me by e-mail was Helio's last act before leaving with his wife and son for France, where he teaches philosophy every year for a few months. I'm disappointed I won't meet Helio. "Now I can really say that I could leave Brazil at ease," Helio wrote a few days before he departed. "I would like to tell you that I finally found someone to guide you around over here."

We are in excellent hands with Bruno. Lindberg Street or not, Bruno has already done research, and he's got news.

"Waldomiro had a store," Bruno tells us.

"A store?" I repeat, practically spilling my coffee. "What did it sell?"

Clearly, I can still get excited about facts.

"All sorts of machines, agricultural equipment, and other things. There's an advertisement in an old magazine."

Bruno proceeds to tell us that the store was located in Rolândia, the same town mentioned by John McNaughton, two towns to the west of Londrina, past Nova Dantzig/Cambé.

"There's no street address, just a post office box," Bruno says. "I looked at the other ads and that's the way they all were. They sent around a postal address. People would write and say 'I want a machine.'"

Waldomiro as mail-order pioneer is completely new information—
another new dream?—but it jibes with what John said the day before,
that Waldomiro was involved in commerce by the time of the 1939 legal
protest.

I ask Bruno where he found the magazine.

"At the Historical Museum. We can go there this morning."

I am eager to see the advertisement, but first I want to finish the
botched attempt to see the Pioneer's Monument. I show Bruno the
place on the map where I walked and he shakes his head. That was the
Travelers' Monument, sensibly located near the bus terminal. What I
want is the Pioneer's Memorial, which is a short walk from the hotel in
a different direction.

Bruno leads us there. Like many Brazilians, he walks with elegance,
his posture erect, his pace moderate and uniform. He walks like a fashion
model on a runway, and next to him, I feel elegant, too.

We come first to a series of rectangular cement kiosks, each one about
seven feet tall. Bruno calls them totems. The totems are laid out diag-
onally from one another on a narrow brick plaza along a city street.
One walks from totem to totem as one might walk from tree to tree
in a woodland. Bruno says that a small park used to be situated here.
How fitting that more trees should have been cleared to commemorate
northern Paraná's original tree-clearers.

A brass plaque is affixed to each totem's four sides. The first totem
gives the official name, Memorial do Pioneiro, and the date of comple-
tion: 2006. Perhaps the memorial's relative newness explains its absence
from the city map, or perhaps the memorial is not considered of interest
to most visitors. It is an unusual memorial, to be sure, offering an apology
for the actions of the very people whom it honors.

The apology is a short one, a tribute on the first totem to the indigenous peoples whose relationship with the forest was severed when the
white settlers arrived.

The native peoples of northern Paraná, originally part of the Gê
group, were familiar with intrusions. The forest gave them cover into the
1900s, but "most of them . . . had been rounded up by the Brazilian government and, about 1914, established in several reserves," according to
the renowned anthropologist Claude Levi-Strauss. The reserves proved

a failure, Levi-Strauss wrote. Most of the native peoples abandoned the government houses and returned to a nomadic existence in the forest.

Some historians contend that the Northern Paraná Land Company hired squads to kill and disperse the native peoples. Others say that the government did the company's dirty work for it. Either way, the pioneers' memorial certainly attests to the pivotal role played by the company in the area's transformation. As stated in another plaque entitled *Os Desbravadores*—"the trailblazers" or "pathfinders," translated as follows:

Even before 1929, when the first caravan of the Northern Paraná Land Company arrived, some brave men ventured into the great forest that dominated the red earth. They were trailblazers of the future Londrina. To them [go] our respect and admiration.

As Bruno puts it, this text commemorates the "unknown pioneer." The "known" pioneers are synonymous with the Northern Paraná Land Company because the names laid in type on the remaining totems came from the company's property records.

There are 2,500 names on the totems, 2,500 people whom the memorial lauds in poetic language that Bruno translates for us:

They came from various parts of Brazil and the world. They were men, women and children. They crossed the forest and rivers. They braved the mud, dust, diseases, isolation, difficulties. They all came in the name of the dream. And the dream was to build a city for all and happiness for everyone. With the memorial to the pioneer, Londrina pays tribute to the characters in the colonization of the red earth between 1918 and 1939. Here are their names and surnames, so different from each other as the ethnic composition of our people.

The plaque ends with an expression of hope, "That the citizens of the future can read in each of those names . . . the translation of the eternal human strength."

Near the end of the walkway, the sun is shining bright on the "W" plaque, making the raised letters look white. In the right column are five Waldemars, one Waldeonor, two Waldirs, four Waldomiros, and one

Waldemiro Lindberg—spelled here with an "e." Across from his name is the year "1932."

"Eternal human strength" is what I'm supposed to perceive gazing at these names, but what I actually experience is more out-of-body. It is so very strange to see this proof of an alternative reality, a tribute to Walter/Waldomiro/Waldemiro Lindberg surviving "diseases, isolation, difficulties" to build in the red earth a "city for all and happiness for everyone" in the same year that my father was starting out at DeWitt Clinton High School in the Bronx, believing his stepfather to have met a tragic death. At DeWitt Clinton, students would begin calling my father "Lucky," after the aviator Charles Lindbergh, underscoring the one connection to Walter that Dad still had—a shared last name.

The story of Walter the explorer had him dying a lonely death in the jungle, possibly at the hands of native inhabitants, but the mistruth underlying that fable is cast in concrete and bronze all around me. On this plaque in front of my eyes, Walter is officially the holder of a new dream. He is a pioneer, even a local hero, as part of a collection of foreigners who cast out the native peoples and turned the forest into fields and towns. The true Walter is free from dishonor here in little London, home of the colonist.

I'm not so traumatized that I can't pull out my camera. I take a photo of Bruno and Roberta pointing to the name. Then Roberta takes one of me. I'm in the same pose as Isabel in the photo that Helio sent me.

When I first saw the photo of Isabel pointing to my step-grandfather's name, I could hardly believe it. There was the euphoria of discovery.

Now, I am not sure how I feel about Walter. Does he deserve any of the admiration my father and I gave him all those years?

How will I decide?

chapter twenty-seven

GREEN GOLD

THEY ARE EXPECTING me in the former train station, now the Londrina Historical Museum. The high gabled roof calls to mind a Black Forest chalet—and why shouldn't that be so, given the many Germans who came to northern Paraná in search of their dreams?

The three employees who greet us are fine examples of Londrina's ethnic diversity: Barbara Daher Belinati, the press officer, is of Lebanese descent and is married to an Italian; Rosangela Ricieri Haddad, a librarian, is Italian with an Arab husband; and Ruth Hiromi Shigaki Ueda, the other *bibliotecária*, is Japanese, married to a Japanese man.

Working together in a large, wood-paneled room on the second floor, the women have, over the past few months, experienced a surge of interest in the pioneer Waldomiro Lindberg. Bruno is the most recent person to have stopped by with an inquiry on my behalf. Before Bruno there was Isabel dos Santos, then Luciana Walther, and the librarians received a call from Klaus Nixdorf, a leading man in the city with whom I've corresponded, asking them to give me help.

So here I am, the instigator, and the mood is guardedly warm as Bruno facilitates introductions. School children are touring the downstairs exhibits about early settlers and coffee production, and the cheerful sounds of young voices waft up the stairs.

"She would like to see the magazine ad," Bruno says to Rosangela in Portuguese. Rosangela walks behind her desk and hands the old magazine to Bruno. I catch a date of 1938 on the cover. Bruno flips to the correct page and lays the magazine open on a table. Waldomiro's ad occupies half the page.

The name of Walter's store wasn't just "Casa Marumby," it was "Wal-domiro Lindberg's Casa Marumby." I ask Bruno what "Marumby" means and he confesses utter ignorance.

Was I looking at Walter Lindberg's Rosebud?

What a broad and unrelated mixture of items the advertisement showed Walter selling: "machines and belongings for the industries of sawmill, brickyard, bakery, blacksmith and mills, for the manufacture of lard and cassava flour," plus "articles for photography," "equipment for haberdashery," Underwood typewriters, stationery, "printed matter in general," and the final clause in large type at the bottom, "Representatives of machinery for farming—domestic and foreign."

I remark to Roberta that it's as though Walter was trying to compensate for all the equipment he lost when the *Vestris* sank. He couldn't retrieve those items from the ocean floor, but he could find replacements, sell them, and use the profit to buy more.

Rosangela and Bruno converse in Portuguese, and Rosangela takes a seat at a computer terminal. Soon I learn what she is looking at: the original records of land sales by the Northern Paraná Land Company, the primary source of the names listed in the Pioneer's Memorial. There are many pages, handwritten ledger sheets, which have been scanned into the computer.

I already know, thanks to Isabel and Helio, that the original Northern Paraná Land Company records are stored at a farm in Jussara, a town to the northwest, and that access to those records is restricted, controlled by a man who is descended from one of the company's founders. It's all rather mysterious. Rosangela confirms this, saying the museum had a hard time obtaining the records. I infer that influential people intervened, possibly in connection with erecting the Pioneer's Memorial. Had I come to Paraná before the memorial was completed, I may not have had access to the records, and then I would have missed the morning's second big discovery.

Rosangela motions for me to sit down so I can review a page on which "Waldomiro Lindberg" is written four lines from the bottom, below "Koisima Yonosuke" and above "Joao Torresan," all in the same attractive and legible script.

It's just as John McNaughton said it might be: Waldomiro bought land in his own name. He bought it on June 25, 1932, so that must be the source of the year next to Waldomiro's name on the Pioneers' Memorial. The record lists his nationality as Danish—he identified himself as such, as my father said, in spite of Ulrich's testimony that Walter was German.

Waldomiro is the only Dane of the twenty-nine purchasers on the page, the others who bought land in June 1932 being from Japan (12), Brazil (4), Portugal (3), Italy (3), Germany (2), Australia (1), Poland (1), Russia (1), and Spain (1). There are no people from the United States, but Waldomiro had lived in the United States for fifteen years and still reported himself as "*dinam.*" Possibly other purchasers had passed through the United States, or perhaps the British company limited its advertising to countries that hadn't rebelled against King George III.

Bruno looks at me and says "maybe you own this land now."

"That couldn't be true," I answer, "he's not a blood relative," but no one seems to think that matters. I am the next of kin, someone says. It's true that I bear Waldomiro's surname, and I've brought with me proof of his marriage to my grandmother. Am I going to use those documents to claim a piece of property in Londrina?

Goose bumps prick my skin. I ask where this property is that I might own. Bruno says he will need to consult the early maps he has at his home.

The price of the land is listed as 8,000,000. The monetary unit back then was the milreis, and each milreis was written with three zeros, so 8,000,000 probably meant 8,000 milreis. Bruno doesn't know how much money that would be in today's terms, but Waldomiro only had to pay 10 percent as a down payment, which was true of all the purchasers listed on the page. The plot was large, twenty *alqueires*, a Brazilian way of measuring land by its productivity. The value of an *alqueire* varied by region, but a quick, conservative computation puts the plot of land Bruno says I might own at 120 acres or more.

It's not clear what I should do with this new information, but I request a copy of the record and Rosangela obliges. I am recalling my pilgrimage to Miami Beach to see the house where Mother spent her winters in the 1920s and 1930s, the ludicrously named De Ryan Villa, only to find that the entire block of Meridian Avenue had become a department store. I am wondering what the land Waldomiro bought in 1932 looks like now.

Waldomiro's job was to sell land as an agent, but the librarians explain that records showing which agents facilitated the sales are not available. Rosangela believes they were destroyed, so I'll never know how many acres of the Atlantic Forest Waldomiro helped sell to people who had left their homes for new lives as red feet, how much money Waldomiro made in commissions, or how many times he handed out an offer from his booklet of pre-printed forms.

Responding to my question about Frieda Lindberg, Rosangela and Ruth bring files to the central table and start to leaf through them as Barbara looks up from her chair and asks why. Why have I come to northern Paraná to search for my step-grandfather?

I say, with Bruno's help, that Waldomiro's departure had a big impact on my father, and I want to understand more about it. I tell her the story of how Walter came to Brazil on his own, changed his name to Waldomiro, and wound up in Paraná.

Then Barbara looks at me and says *"Ele veio aqui para o ouro verde."*

I look at Bruno, who translates.

"He came here for green gold. *Ouro verde.* That's what they called coffee in Brazil."

"Yes," I say to Barbara. She is absolutely right. Walter followed the gold and didn't seem to care what color it was. He just knew it wasn't in New York.

"Now I understand," Barbara says, and I feel like I've passed some sort of test.

Ruth and Rosangela say there are no records for anyone named Frieda Lindberg. They have a file for Frieda Fleuringer, whose name we saw at the memorial, but she had a husband and his name wasn't Lindberg. The source of Frieda Lindberg on the page Helio sent remains a mystery. I show the page to the librarians and they recognize it; it is from a book by Klaus Nixdorf, whom I will be meeting the next day. I should ask him where he obtained the information, the librarians suggest.

It occurs to me to ask about the book of photographs, *Londrina Documenta*, that John McNaughton found in the British library.

Rosangela pulls out a copy from behind her desk. It turns out the Historical Museum co-published the book in 2010, and Ruth and Rosangela worked on it. The book is a compendium of photographs in the museum's collection by one of the earliest employees of the land company, George Craig Smith, who came to Brazil from London in 1925 and who, in 1929, brought the first group of settlers to Patrimônio Três Bocas (Homestead of Three Mouths), later to be called Londrina. There is a second volume of *Londrina Documenta*, published by the museum in 2011. This volume contains photographs by José Juliani, a photographer employed by the land company from 1933 to 1943.

I buy both books. Rosangela hands me a third book as a gift, about the museum's collection. I accept it gladly, knowing that three books are going to strain the capacity of my luggage, but I'm willing to leave behind some things to make room for this treasure—not gold ore or green gold, but pictures showing the real life Waldomiro lived in Brazil long after my father presumed him to be dead.

chapter twenty-eight

RINGING IN THE OLD

LONDRINA CELEBRATES ITS past in the old train station, but to see an actual dwelling from the past we have to leave the city. In the 1950s, Londrina began to replace its one-story, timber buildings from the 1930s and 1940s with taller, box-like structures of steel and cement. So, as Helio advised in an e-mail, if I want to "walk inside a house most like that one in Mr. Lindberg's photo," Bruno will have to drive us to the Casa do Pioneiro on the campus of the State University of Londrina.

In this way, Londrina differs significantly from New York or Chicago, Rome or Mexico City, New Delhi or Moscow, cities where vestiges of the past coexist with the modern. This is somewhat strange given that Londrina is a far newer city. To retain representative structures of Londrina's different periods would not have meant repointing centuries-old stone facades.

There are people alive who remember the place when it was all forest with a few small clearings such as the Homestead of Three Mouths (referring to rivers, not people or animals). In the 1930s, when builders in New York and Chicago were erecting fine stone apartment houses and art deco skyscrapers, settlers in northern Paraná were building one-story structures of wooden boards. As coffee money poured in and the economy grew, progress meant replacing the old buildings. The train station, opened in 1950, is one of the oldest buildings still standing in the city. Even the main cathedral has been rebuilt two or three times.

It is understandable that as the city grew, the original structures ceased to serve the population's needs. It's not as though New York City held on to its farms when the increasing number of people warranted apartment buildings, or didn't raze architectural masterpieces, such as the original Pennsylvania Station. Yet the near total obliteration of Londrina's past calls for some other explanations. Perhaps because colonization took place so recently, there was a certain taking for granted of older structures. People could remember the old buildings in their own minds. What need was there to keep them? The old structures had not become iconic yet, as the works of past generations who could only be imagined, not recalled.

Fortunately, a few buildings, such as the Casa do Pioneiro, were saved.

Bruno knows the way to the university. It's where he is studying for his master's degree. He also seems to know that the local custom is to interpret the word *pare* on red signs as a suggestion rather than a command. The way he zips onto the highway, barely looking out the window or slowing down, makes me grateful for Luciana's advice not to rent a car.

We find the Pioneer's House behind newer, block-styled buildings on the large campus. The house is a strong and handsome structure, its vertical wood planks thick and straight, its curved clay tiles placed evenly atop a thick wooden roof. If the materials and workmanship of this building were typical, it doesn't appear that lack of durability presented an excuse for wrecking so many of the original houses.

The house sits on wide pillars about three feet above the red dirt, and its veranda is edged by the same type of Japanese-inspired railing as the house in the Lindberg/Ulrich photo and the hospital in the photo John McNaughton showed me. After viewing the black-and-white photographs, it's a surprise to see that the house is painted bright orange-red with green shutters and accent walls. A motorcycle is parked outside.

Inside, people are holding a meeting. The building is not merely an historic attraction, but also a conference center for the university, so we do not linger. We cross the sidewalk to a wooden church, a replica of Londrina's first Catholic church with a high gabled roof and a trinity of windows above and to the sides of the wide door.

The original church was inaugurated on August 19, 1934, and Walter was likely present for the festivities, one of scores of people in front of the church in the photo of the inauguration in the *Londrina Documenta* book—men in hats and white or dark suits, women in dresses, children in shorts.

Bruno explains that the original bell was preserved. The bell is not housed in a belfry atop the church, but suspended in a simple wood frame, where it hangs about fifteen feet off the ground, daring one to pull on its rope.

I hand my camera to Roberta and walk over to the scaffolding and as soon as I hear the first clear ring of the clapper I realize I am hearing the same sound that Walter heard, calling people to worship, marking the hours.

I pull the rope eleven times, once for each year of my father's age when Walter staged his death, became Waldomiro, and started his new life in Brazil.

The bell has a loud ring. I wish the dead could hear it. What I'm thinking is that I wish my father could know I've traveled so far to ring this bell for him. Walter ran from Dad and changed his name, Londrina razed its past, and Dad reinvented himself as a golfing banker with no heritage, but the clanging of the bell cuts through all that flight. Each ring delivers my message across time: I've found you, Walter Lindberg. I know what you did.

It will take me a little more time to realize that the bell also tolls for someone else.

For now, when the bell stops clanging, I feel at peace. It's time for lunch, so we rejoin the twenty-first century at a mall restaurant. There are rules to follow: a scale next to the buffet, like at the restaurant where

I ate with Valdir. An attendant provides a piece of paper attesting to the weight of the food on my plate.

Over lunch, we talk about our morning, Bruno's research, and the way the menu sets forth the ingredients of each Brazilian beer along with calories and alcoholic quantity. When the waiter comes to settle our bill, I notice that Roberta does not have a piece of paper like mine. She didn't know about the scale, and her plate is empty now. She smiles sheepishly to the waiter while Bruno explains her infraction of the rules. I am preparing for the waiter to charge Roberta for the heaviest possible plate of food, like the penalty parking garages inflict back home if you lose your ticket: They don't charge you for an hour. They charge you for a day.

It's different in Brazil. The waiter laughs and says, "It's okay. You eat for free."

chapter twenty-nine

GOOD DEEDS IN NOVA DANTZIG

WE HAVE BEEN getting a lot for free in Londrina—help from Bruno and the librarians, a free lunch, and now even the parking lot seems generous.

As we exit the mall, I ask Bruno about the signs for the parking spaces closest to the doors and he explains that these spaces are reserved for the elderly. In Londrina, and maybe elsewhere in Brazil, you don't have to be handicapped to qualify for good parking. It is enough simply to have survived for a long time. This benevolent policy puts me in a good frame of mind for meeting altruistic Isabel.

It is a short drive to Cambé, the next town west of Londrina along a grid initially determined by the railroad tracks some eighty years ago as the line was extended west. Towns were set up along the rail line like marks on a ruler.

The mark that was Nova Dantzig, now Cambé, grew more slowly than Londrina. Today the population of Cambé is approximately 93,000, one-fifth the size of Londrina.

Cambé is a center for coffee processing, and we get a strong whiff of coffee through the open car windows as we exit the highway. Approaching the center of town, we pass one-story buildings and open lots serving functions such as animal feed storage or vehicle repair. The past has not been obliterated here.

The original Free City of Danzig was a semi-autonomous city-state between Poland and Germany established by the Treaty of Versailles and disbanded in 1939, a brief nineteen years after its creation. It included the Baltic Sea city of Danzig, now Gdansk, and some 315 villages and hamlets. Though affiliated with Poland, its population was mostly German, and the Nazi Party grew in power there in the late 1920s.

In the early 1930s, ten families from Danzig came to northern Paraná via the Northern Paraná Land Company. The company named the colony Nova Dantzig, or Neu Danzig in German, expecting many more people from Danzig to follow. In addition to Nazi persecution, there were economic reasons to leave Danzig, as was true of many places in Europe still trying to recover from World War I.

As a result of World War II, the German origins of the name eventually proved unacceptable to Brazilian officials, and the original Patrimônio Nova Dantzig evolved into the municipal district of Cambé, the same name as the river that flowed through the area. The indigenous peoples had named the river, linking the Tupí words for "tree" and "good hunting," giving the choice of Cambé for the town's new name a certain irony. The original namers, not to mention the trees and good hunting, were mostly gone.

When I meet Isabel, I want to be enough—enough to justify her adoption of my cause and her hours of effort searching for clues about Waldomiro. I've been a steady donor to charities abroad, but I am not poor, sick, or subject to persecution. Why do I deserve the help of a stranger from another country? In a place that distributes good parking places to all senior citizens, this is perhaps less of a mystery than in other places. One way I have tried to answer the question is to universalize my search for Waldomiro. So, on the card I plan to give Isabel, I have written, "We are all children of wanderers, searching for a meaningful past and future."

Still, I feel the same insecurity about my appearance that I did on the way to John McNaughton's office. In the morning, I wrapped my wet hair in a bun to avoid humidity-frizz, and I'm concerned that I look like a retired ballerina from the neck up and a tourist with sensible shoes from the neck down.

2

Isabel stands up from a metal folding chair as soon as we enter the director's office in the Museu Historico Cambé. She and I smile and embrace. We have the same color hair, only hers is short and wavy. She is wearing blue jeans and a purple shirt, the color of advent. She says words in Portuguese I do not understand. I introduce Roberta and Bruno, which I can manage.

Cesar Cortez, the museum director, smiles from under his bushy gray mustache. He is talking on the phone, standing behind a desk. Isabel explains that Cesar has been calling elderly residents who might remember Waldomiro. He is speaking with one now. His animated voice and long strings of words offer promise, but I've already learned that Brazilians are marathoners when it comes to talking. Conversations which in English would be long over, such as how to get from here to there, keep on going in Brazil. Bruno swears there is research showing that at the end of the day, the average Brazilian will have spoken three times as many words as the average American.

I take this opportunity to present Isabel with the small gifts I have brought. Bruno translates the card and she smiles. Now Isabel gives me a box, which contains two needlepoint towels, one that says "*Lembranca de Cambé*" in red and one that reads "*Lembranca de Londrina*" in lavender. Satin ribbon runs through eyelet binding above and below the lettering. I know I will never use these towels. As the words state, the towels are for remembrance.

Isabel also gives me a bookmark with a picture of a waterfall on the bottom, and words Bruno translates for me: "Life is beautiful when shared. May the Lord protect and bless your life, your home and your work."

I am not surprised to learn that Isabel is religious. When her nephew told me "she likes to help people," this was likely what he meant, that her charitable impulses are deeply ingrained and bound up with her faith.

On the back she has written the following, originally in Portuguese:

Dear Marian,

In this tireless search for your grandfather, I could tell that you are a friend, sensitive and courageous. I have not made a great discovery, but I can say that I found a friend. Always continue to be happy alongside your son.

Hugs from me,
Isabel

Cesar ends his call and comes around the desk to join us, full of positive, let's-get-it-done energy. He wears jeans and a white short-sleeved shirt, loose and comfortable over his barrel chest. With his mustache, expressive eyes, and stocky frame, he looks vaguely Russian.

The person on the phone didn't remember Waldomiro, but Cesar already made a big discovery before we arrived.

He explains to Bruno, and Bruno translates:

"The Germans formed an association to build a school in 1935. Waldomiro's name is on the list of members."

Cesar picks up a piece of paper and hands it to me.

All of the names are written in the same script, starting with "1. Erich Anger." In the middle of the second column is "46. Waldomiro Lindberg."

Entitled *Mitgluderliste*, this master list of people who helped build the first school in the German community is dated *24 Februar 1935*, a little over a year after Otto Ulrich reported finding Waldomiro in Nova Dantzig.

Cesar motions for me to step over to a computer. He points to a tall man in a dark fedora in the middle of a solemn-looking group of men and women in a black-and-white photo. Behind them are piles of felled trees, with the edge of the still-standing forest in the background.

Cesar is sure the tall man is Waldomiro Lindberg. He has made the identification based on the photo with Otto Ulrich, which Isabel provided.

I look closely. The cheeks are in shadow under the hat, but the nose, mouth, and chin are illuminated by the sun and they are the same features of the man in the photo sent by the State Department. As in that photo, the man Cesar has identified is standing with his left arm bent at the elbow, his clothing neat. He is wearing glasses and not looking at the camera. His gaze is fixed to his right, like in the photo of him sitting on the horse from Três Lagoas. The position of his face doesn't look accidental, not like he just happened to move his head as the shutter was pressed. Rather, he was staring off slightly at an angle, as was conventional for powerful men in photographed portraits.

But this is not a portrait. Twenty-seven adults—the other school association members who attended—crowd the frame. No one smiles. This was a serious occasion, the groundbreaking of the school. The eight women have on dresses and nice shoes. The nineteen men are wearing jackets or button-down shirts and ties. There is one small girl in a dress.

The hacked trees, gnarled branches, and huge stumps make an odd setting for the men and women in their finery. Waldomiro looks particularly elegant, in a slightly rumpled light linen jacket over a white shirt. He's the tallest and best-proportioned man in the group, taking over the woodpile just like Dad said he took over a room.

Cesar explains that he has a reason aside from the obvious physical resemblance for being quite sure the man in the light-colored jacket is Waldomiro. Cesar knows the names of all the other men in the photo, and they match the names on the association list. He'd always wondered about the identity of the man in the center.

Cesar is not as sure about the women. He knows the identities of a few of them, but not all. He points to a young woman, second from the right, last name Mueller, and tells me she died only two weeks ago. No one else pictured in the photograph is alive. I express regret that I missed her, but he says her memory was not very good toward the end.

Cesar says he is surprised he hasn't been able to learn more about Waldomiro.

"If you sell land, people should know you, but no one knew him," he says.

Part of the problem is that most of the people old enough to remember the mid-1930s have weak memories, especially for a man from so long ago who didn't stick around. If Waldomiro had remained in northern Paraná, Cesar says, people would know it. Cesar would know it. Every other man in the photo did stay in the area, though Cesar still wonders about one or two of the women. He points. Could this one have been Waldomiro's wife? She is standing to the left of Waldomiro. Like him, she is wearing a dark, brimmed hat. I explain about Frieda Lindberg's name appearing in the page Isabel found, and Cesar picks up the list of association members, combing it carefully as I look over his shoulder, but no one named Frieda is listed.

We leave the museum in Cesar's car. The director is taking the afternoon off. We are a sleuthing party of five, two English speakers, two Portuguese speakers, and one person who speaks both. This is when I find out that Cesar once worked as a journalist in Newark, New Jersey. He went to the United States to recover from a motorcycle accident and wound up working for a Brazilian newspaper, getting by with little English. What he learned, he's mostly forgotten. He's still a reporter, though; I can tell. He's chasing a story, and I'm right there with him. His enthusiasm reignites the fact-gatherer in me. I'm not so sure about Roberta. She's been quiet since we met up with Cesar and Isabel.

As we head away from the business area and through a residential section, Cesar slows down and points to a building on the right. It's the site where the German school once stood. The forest in the background of the photo is now gone, and the new building isn't made of wood. New structures lie on both sides of it, with driveways, fences, and gates.

Cesar stops the car. He remembers when there was nothing but forest around the school, he says. He attended the school when he was young. The wooden school built in 1935 lasted forty years—surviving World War II, when the Brazilian government confiscated property in the area owned by Germans. Two years after Cesar left the school, it was torn down.

My Portuguese rises to the occasion and I say to Cesar, "My grandfather helped build your school."

He laughs and says that's right. He adds that it's too bad the original structure is gone.

We continue driving and slow down near a cemetery, one of the places Isabel visited looking for Waldomiro's name on a headstone.

After a few miles, Cesar stops the car next to a wooded area on the edge of town, a park with trails. Close to the entrance stands a lovely one-story wooden house, symmetric and alpine in design except for the clay roof tiles. The house, dating to the 1930s, was moved to this spot to be preserved. Cesar explains that the entire house was built from the wood of one tree. In the *Londrina Documenta* book, there are photos of severed trees as wide as a person is tall, so I believe him.

As we walk toward the house we hear feline cries. There's a box of very young kittens on the veranda. Cesar and the park superintendent speak for a long time about the kittens, and as we tour the surprisingly large rooms inside the house, some of the windows still hung with lace curtains, I know that Roberta is thinking about the kittens. She has a cat back home. Walter is long dead and so are the prior owners of this house, but the kittens are very much alive. We all feel better when Cesar tells us that an employee of the museum has agreed to take the kittens home and try to feed them with a dropper.

The forest around the house is dense but it's new growth, Cesar explains. The timber used to build the first houses of Nova Dantzig came from this part of the forest, so the trees and vines we are looking at grew back in the last eighty years. In the absence of this information, we probably would not have known the difference.

Cesar tells us that a section of original Atlantic Forest, the *mata virgem*, still exists, but it's a forty-minute walk on a somewhat difficult trail. I would like to see it, but Cesar has other ideas. We compromise on a short walk through the new growth, moist, green, and shady enough to give us a welcome break from the heat.

Cesar points out the shallow roots of a palm tree that's been upended in a storm. We hear a stream running alongside the trail, about fifteen feet away. Isabel says the stream used to be much wider. I find myself wondering about the cause of the reduced flow. Perhaps there is less precipitation due to climate change or reduced tree cover. As Cambé's population has grown, larger quantities of water taken from the stream's source may also be a factor. What one knows for certain is that reduced stream flow is usually a symptom of change caused by humans, a phenomenon that is happening to freshwater sources throughout the world.

In the new growth forest of Cambé, I keep my thoughts to myself about the wide stream that has been reduced to a rivulet. I'm not walking with ecologists or climate scientists. I'm with people who are helping me out of generosity and kindness, people who are proud of where they live. I'm in a place where the man who abandoned my father is a pioneer who helped build a school.

chapter thirty

ONCE UPON A JUNGLE

THE AFTERNOON SUN burns our faces as Roberta, Bruno, and I pull tangerines from a nearby tree. The juice quenches our thirst and we spit seeds onto the red soil of Eduard Schulz's *fazenda*. Around us dogs wrestle, goats bleat, a rooster crows, and somewhere on the sprawling property is an eighty-four-year-old man who belonged to the same German school association as Waldomiro Lindberg.

Green gold made this place. Green gold is why Eduard came here in 1932 at the age of five, an orphan, brought from Germany by his sister. I don't know whether Eduard and his sister were economic or religious refugees. They certainly didn't come for adventure, though they found plenty once they arrived. It was all jungle back then except for the farm on which we are standing and one other, both several miles from the center of the Nova Dantzig colony.

The jungle is gone but the farm hasn't changed much, though the blue paint on the wood plank buildings is faded, washed gray in some places by rain and age. The biggest building in the complex is devoted to work, storing tractors and farming machinery.

Across from the big garage is the main house, small and meandering with a roof of clay tiles. Most of the tiles are as dark as the rust-colored soil, but some tiles are lighter, where the roof has been patched. The effect is that of flint corn.

In front of the house, laundry hangs on a line under a corrugated tin roof. In a place with a long rainy season, it seems wise to build a roof over the laundry line.

When we first arrive, a woman is standing inside the house in front of an open Dutch door, presumably Eduard's wife. She is visible only from the waist up, attired in black. She watches us get out of the car and look around, but she does not move from her spot.

I want to photograph this woman standing inside the faded blue house, but I remember the three women who threw fruit at me in Barbados years ago when I took pictures of them, possibly thinking my little black machine would rob their souls. Though I once worked as a lawyer for a TV network advising reporters and producers how to get footage of people up to the maximum limits of the law, in my personal life I don't want to steal anyone's soul. So on Eduard Schulz's *fazenda*, I raise my camera and point to it, asking the woman for her permission. She nods yes, then clasps her hands and continues standing behind the half-door while I take the shot, her face a model of enigmatic stillness.

Cesar has gone to find Eduard, taking Isabel with him. Roberta, Bruno, and I are on our own. We walk behind the house, finding a few small pigs in an old wooden pen next to three cabin-like buildings of similar size and shape. Their exterior walls are a beautiful palette of distressed paint colors. Two of the buildings have a brick base about a foot off the ground. The third building sits on cement blocks and bricks. The reason for these measures is rain. Around the base of the main house, which has wood extending all the way to the ground, there is a foot of rust stain from many years of high water mixed with red mud.

Two men are on ladders quietly working on one of the cabins. We only hear the sounds of animals, not the wild creatures that used to come out of the jungle and spook the pioneers, but domesticated pigs and goats. We walk to the left. About fifty feet ahead is a large wooden cross in the ground and beyond it, the dirt road by which we came and a huge green field bounded on the far side by a few trees and houses. I take a picture, trying to imagine the jungle of eighty years ago.

Near the cross is a wooden church, taller than any of the farm buildings and in better condition. It is painted ivory-yellow with brown trim, the entrance framed by four palm trees.

Walking back past the tangerine tree, we see a coffee bush bursting with clusters of little orange fruits. I realize that for all the cups of coffee I've drunk, I've never actually seen a coffee plant. It's a smaller bush than I expected. The fruits grow on tendrils mainly on the lower half of the bush.

Roberta spies a garden hose and we wash off our hands. The pace is slow here on the *fazenda* except for the constant dashes and tussles of the dogs. Two are pregnant. One is a puppy.

We walk around to the front of the house and find Isabel. Soon Cesar and an elderly man make their way from a different direction. This is Eduard Schulz, walking with his son on one side and Cesar on the other. As we are introduced, Eduard's smile reveals four remaining teeth on the bottom. He's trim with white eyebrows and hair, a pair of glasses over bright blue eyes.

Cesar explains that Eduard remembers Waldomiro's name and the name of Waldomiro's store, Casa Marumby. He remembers hearing the adults talking about going to the store in Rolândia. Apparently the store did have a physical address as well as a post office box. And Eduard's name is on the list of German school association members, so he and Waldomiro were obviously part of the same community. Eduard doesn't remember anything more than that, but he is sure that Waldomiro didn't remain in the area. Eduard's son tells us there is an agricultural pilot in Sertanópolis, about forty kilometers away, with the last name Lindberg. Perhaps he is a relation of Waldomiro, perhaps even the son of Waldomiro and Frieda. Cesar says he will call a friend of his who lives in Sertanópolis to inquire.

Eduard is as gracious as can be. We laugh at the dogs running around and he says the puppy is named Beethoven. I think of John McNaughton telling me about the Germans' chamber music concerts in the early days. Beethoven lives on in northern Paraná in the form of a puppy, his white and black coat streaked with red from back-scratches in the *terra vermelha*.

Roberta says to Eduard that he must have seen many changes in his seventy-nine years in the area. Yes, Eduard agrees, it has changed a lot.

"It has changed for the better."

Roberta asks how has it changed for the better, and Eduard says life was so hard when he first came. It is much easier today, much easier to survive now that the forest is gone and there are roads into town, food in the markets, and conveniences of modern life all around.

I could spend the rest of the day asking Eduard what it was like when the jungle encircled his land and the Germans played music in what Cesar called their "dancing backyards." I could ask were people really more afraid of the anteaters in the forest than anything else, as Cesar also said, but I don't ask Eduard any more questions. I'm enormously grateful to have met him, to have passed this Edenic hour on his *fazenda*, and I am sure I will always remember it. But Eduard has told us everything he knows about Waldomiro Lindberg.

chapter thirty-one

THE KINDNESS OF STRANGERS,
BRAZILIAN STYLE

WE'RE MOVING WEST, just like Waldomiro. Our next stop is Rolândia, the location of Waldomiro's house of machines, Casa Marumby.

Rolândia was also the next stop of the Northern Paraná Land Company as the company pushed west from Nova Dantzig. The Hotel Rolândia, the new colony's first structure, opened in 1934, two years after the settlement of Nova Dantzig. The name was based on the legend of Roland, a Middle Ages warrior who came to symbolize freedom and justice for the German peoples.

On the fifteen-kilometer drive, Cesar tells us that the Oktoberfest held in present-day Rolândia is the second largest in Brazil, even though its year-round population is only 57,000.

The sole occupant of the city's two-room German consulate, a young woman, seems wholly unprepared for our expedition party. She's trapped at her desk in the interior room, Cesar and the rest of us towering above her on the other side. Cesar is still a journalist through and through. I can tell his questions are going to go on for a while, and since I can't understand them anyway, I take advantage of the small restroom. The door is plywood; the appliances look old.

When I rejoin the group, Cesar is still asking questions. I am fortunate to have a Portuguese-speaking cross-examiner on my side. Despite his tenacity, Cesar does not seem to be getting very far. The woman is shaking her head and saying "*nao*" with some frequency. Every now and then Bruno tells me what Cesar is asking. Is there a directory of former businesses? Is there a listing of former residents? Does she know any elderly people who might remember Waldomiro and his store? These seem like relatively simple questions, and the woman keeps her answers short, but when the ball bounces back into Cesar's court it stays there dribbling for quite a while before he tosses it back. Finally, he gives up, taking a piece of paper from the woman with a couple of names written on it.

We descend the narrow staircase to the street and set off on foot.

The language barrier between Isabel and me is apparent in our silence. Helio wrote that Isabel would be glad to meet me but felt self-conscious about her lack of English. I assured him that wouldn't be a problem, thinking I would have a better grasp of Portuguese by now than I do. Back home, when I was driving around repeating the lessons of the language CDs, my capacity to create full sentences seemed much stronger than it does now, trying to speak about something other than being lost or whether the apartment for rent next to the large plaza has a terrace in front or in back.

It's odd, feeling warmth toward someone and not being able to communicate with her. Bruno is walking behind us speaking to Roberta. Nothing I want to say to Isabel is so important that I'm going to stop and interrupt them to ask for translation help.

Our destination is the Rolândia historical museum, housed in a large ground-floor room. Inside the door, the director greets Isabel like an old friend. Isabel has already been in touch with her about Waldomiro. During the introductions, the Rolândia director is especially pleased to meet Cesar. Though they head historical museums in towns only fifteen kilometers apart, they have never met before.

The reason we're here is that Waldomiro's name shows up in two books about the history of Rolândia. Isabel has made copies of the relevant pages for me. In a small book called *Rolândia—Terra De Pioneiros*

(1974), Valdomiro Lindberg is listed as one of the people who owned property in the "*gleba* Cafezal." *Gleba* roughly translates to "farming district." Is this the location of the 120 acres I might own?

A discussion ensues in Portuguese while I pull out my phone and look at the land record Rosangela sent as an e-mail attachment the day before. Sure enough, in the "*gleba*" column the abbreviation "Caf." is written three lines above Waldomiro's purchase, with ditto marks down to the line recording Waldomiro's purchase.

Bruno explains that, according to the director, Cafezal was an area settled primarily by Japanese immigrants, and the three names above Waldomiro's on the June 1932 land record are indeed Japanese. The consensus of the group is that Waldomiro probably did not live in the gleba Cafezal. They believe he likely bought the land as an investment. My already faint hopes of land ownership dwindle.

The director excuses herself to make a phone call in the back of the museum. We look at the old photos of Rolândia hanging on large easels, organized by decade, from jungle to small clearings to dirt roads to men with bushels of coffee beans to cars and stores and houses and weddings. All the while I'm looking for a glimpse of Waldomiro but I do not see him.

The director returns and says the author of the other Rolândia history book, Claudia Portellinha Schwengber, would be pleased to receive us at her house. Although Walter may have helped my father close down his emotions, Walter's ghost has done nothing but open doors for me in Brazil. I'm beginning to realize that John McNaughton isn't the only Brazilian to see a bit of Walter in himself. Many of the people of northern Paraná are descended from people like Walter who came from a foreign country and bought land in the 1930s. My walk back in time is theirs, too.

In the car, Cesar programs his GPS with the author's address. Somehow, we still manage to get lost. There's something confusing about the street numbers. It's late afternoon and I tell Cesar it's okay if he wants to stop searching for the home. If my energy is flagging, I'm conscious that the day must seem endless for Roberta and Bruno. But Cesar will not hear of it. He and Isabel continue talking animatedly, reprising what we've learned so far. Waldomiro may be my namesake, but Cesar and Isabel have adopted him. It's their search now, too. In fact, they have become the search leaders. They are like Mom and Dad in the front seat. Roberta, Bruno, and I are the children in the back along for the ride.

❧

Claudia and her husband step outside to meet us, full of smiles. She's wearing a floral blouse and cardigan. He's wearing a blue and white sweatshirt.

We all sit down at the large table in the dining room. Claudia gets out her book, *Aspectos Históricos de Rolândia*, and I lay my photos of Walter on the table.

It turns out that Claudia knows the name Waldomiro Lindberg because of the magazine ad for Casa Marumby. The ad is the reason Waldomiro appears in her book within a list of "*Relação de Pioneiros Alemães*." Poor Waldomiro, forever lumped together with Germans, but he was accustomed to that, living in the German section of New York City, and having been educated in Germany, at least according to Dad. Claudia's book devotes separate sections to Rolândia immigrants from Germany, Italy, Japan, Poland, Hungary, Switzerland, and other parts of Brazil, but there's no section for Danes, not even on the page entitled "*Relação dos Pioneiros das Diversas Etnias*."

Claudia has listed the names of German immigrants by the year of their arrival in Rolândia, and Waldomiro is in the 1938 group, but that's only because the Casa Marumby ad appeared in a 1938 magazine. Claudia echoes Eduard Schulz, telling us that the people she spoke with from the old days remembered Waldomiro Lindberg's name and the name of his store, but nothing more.

Claudia's book contains a map showing the ten "*Glebas de Rolândia*," and one of the districts on the eastern side is Cafezal. So it seems the land Waldomiro bought in 1932 wasn't located in Londrina or in Nova Dantzig. It was further west, between Nova Dantzig and what became Rolândia. This bolsters the theory that he did not live on the land in the Cafezal gleba. Otto Ulrich reported finding Waldomiro in Nova Dantzig in 1934, not Rolândia.

This raises a new question. Assuming Waldomiro lived in the house in Nova Dantzig where he and Ulrich were photographed, who owned that property? Had Waldomiro bought another parcel, or was he living on land he did not own, possibly sharing the house with Frieda or someone else? No one in the room can answer these questions. It's possible that they may never be answered, and I am beginning to think that is okay.

I bring up the 1939 legal protest listing Waldomiro's address as Rolândia. Since the trail goes cold after 1939 and no one remembers much about him, I have begun to suspect that Waldomiro was the person being protested against. The protest was lodged in São Paulo, and it makes more sense that an equipment supplier located in São Paulo would have filed a protest there than that Waldomiro would have traveled all the way to São Paulo to file a protest or found someone to represent him. There wasn't a huge amount of money at issue, only 351 milreis.

What I'm thinking is that Waldomiro may have ordered an item from a supplier in São Paulo and not paid for it, possibly because his own customer didn't pay him, but possibly for other reasons. Maybe Waldomiro stocked his store with products that didn't sell. Maybe the pioneers in northern Paraná didn't really want Underwood typewriters.

I put forth my theory that Waldomiro may have left Rolândia on the run from a debt, and Cesar surprises me with what he thinks happened next.

"He probably went to Mato Grosso. That was the next frontier."

Could it be? Could Waldomiro have wound up in the interior of Mato Grosso as his final destination? It's speculation, yes, but Waldomiro went somewhere, either alone or with Frieda. He certainly hadn't stuck around Londrina, Nova Dantzig, or Rolândia. It is as likely that he moved west with the sun as anything else, crossing the Paraná River once more toward a new frontier and a new dream.

In this case, my father's story might be accidentally true. Walter Lindberg may have died in the Amazon after all.

Claudia gives Cesar a few names of people who might know more about Rolândia in 1938 and 1939. I buy a copy of her book, and she inscribes it "*a amiga.*" To my friend.

Back in the parking lot at the Historical Museum in Cambé, it is surprisingly hard to say good-bye to Cesar and Isabel. We've spent five hours together investigating a story in the outside world that's been sitting inside my head for almost half a century. No one, not even my own parents, ever shared this interest as much as Cesar and Isabel. We hug and say farewell. I wonder if I will ever see them again.

The parking ticket on Bruno's windshield is a letdown. We jog up the street to the nearest store, a flower shop. Bruno asks the young woman behind the counter where traffic fines are paid and the woman points down the street, but she says the office is certainly closed as it's after 6 PM. Bruno asks if the ticket can be paid by mail. The woman examines the ticket. No, it must be paid in person. Bruno explains that he lives in Londrina. I feel a wave of guilt rush over me. Bruno is working on his thesis. He's already taken a day off to help me and he doesn't need to waste gas and a few hours to pay a parking ticket that he got doing me a favor.

The woman says something in Portuguese and Bruno's voice and body language relax. He says "*muito obrigado*" and takes out his wallet. It is remarkable what is unfolding. The shopkeeper has offered to pay the ticket for Bruno the next morning when the traffic office opens. She says she will let Bruno know after she's made the payment so that he won't worry. They exchange cellphone numbers and e-mail addresses.

As we walk back to Bruno's car, I am feeling sympathetic toward Walter and his decision to remain in Brazil. It's easy to feel like you belong in a place where people so willingly take on your burdens. For a man like Walter, who seems to have spent his life just passing through, the kindness of strangers may have been the only sort of kindness he knew.

chapter thirty-two

A THIN SKULL ON A BIG MAN

IT'S TIME FOR a drink, maybe two. When I hallucinated after the operation, I thought I was a balloon in the Macy's Thanksgiving Day Parade. I know I am not a balloon now, but I'm so full of information and emotions I need to deflate.

I am not James Joyce either, nor does Waldomiro have much in common with Leopold Bloom, but I feel as though I have just experienced my own Bloomsday, tracing a whole life in the course of a single day.

When Helio sent me his letter six months earlier, it seemed extraordinary that Waldomiro Lindberg's name appeared in a book. Now I've seen his name on a memorial and in official records. I've seen a photograph of him standing in a newly cleared section of forest and met a man who lived in his community and knew patrons of his business.

But what have we really learned? That is the subject we discuss over a bottle of champagne at one of Bruno's favorite restaurants, on the roof of a converted warehouse. Roberta, still in lawyer mode, is stuck on facts.

"We learned about the land purchase, the store, and the school association. What does that really tell us?" she asks.

I feel differently, I say. I feel as though I've read a biography of the man and talked to his shrink. I feel like I know Waldomiro now. He was an itinerant, a man who moved through life without forming attachments to people or places. Before 1924, he went from Denmark to Brazil and Brazil to New York. Between 1929 and 1939 he traveled from New York to Rio to São Paulo to Três Lagoas, Mato Grosso, Londrina, Nova Dantzig, and Rolândia, from which he departed sometime in or after 1939, possibly once again for Mato Grosso. He shows up in photos and lists and memorials, but no one remembers anything about him. He was aloof, a loner, the kind of guy you hear about in the lyrics of country music songs, the one who is always moving on.

Often such people have an exterior gleam, as Walter did, whether out of vanity, self-involvement, or the simple urge to absolve themselves of blame for why they are alone.

Somehow the evidence of Walter Lindberg's nomadism makes me feel better, I tell Roberta and Bruno. I feel less sad knowing that Dad and Grandma were just a stop on Walter's passage through life, some barnacles picked up by the man's anchor for the few years he dropped it in New York City. Based on what I've learned over the course of the day, it's not surprising that Walter left Dad and Grandma after five years. What's surprising is that he stayed with them that long.

The insult to my father feels less intentional in light of Walter's peripatetic ways. And yet, intention isn't all there is to a wrong. To assess the seriousness of an offense, the law looks at both the intention of the wrongdoer and the objective impact of his actions on the victim, and if the victim's injury is magnified because of some aspect of the victim that makes him more vulnerable, the wrongdoer, not the victim, is held accountable. This concept, called the "thin skull rule," seems to apply to Walter and my father.

As best we could determine—and I was aided by some excellent sleuths—Waldomiro lives on in no one's memories in Londrina, Cambé, or Rolândia; he left no lasting impression. Indeed, the only person he seems to have truly influenced, aside from me, was my father, the boy he abandoned, the vulnerable child he left behind, made sadder forever by Walter's presence in his life, his departure, and supposed death by violent means. Waldomiro was best remembered and revered by the one he had hurt the most.

"Why do you think you wanted to do this?" Roberta asks as a waitress fills our glasses from a second bottle of champagne.

Before I can answer, Roberta poses another question.

"Do you think your father would have wanted to know?"

This question is easier to answer.

"Not later in his life," I reply, "but when he was younger, when he could have come down here himself and confronted Walter."

"He should have made this trip," I continue. Then I start to cry.

"I'm making the trip he should have made" is what I say through my tears, and neither Bruno nor Roberta utters a word.

The answer seems right, true in that way that stops time for an instant, like lightening against a dark sky, but I still don't grasp all that it means.

English is being spoken at the next table. It's time to change the subject, return to the present, and eat our food. A young blond man at the next table, who looks like a California surfer, introduces himself. His name is Marc and he teaches English in Londrina. The two middle-aged Brazilian women with him are students. They've come out to dinner instead of sitting in a classroom, and what luck that they should be seated next to native English speakers. Tonight, the teacher has assistants. Marc is delighted, as are his students. The women turn their chairs to face us and we turn ours. Now we're a party of six.

chapter thirty-three

SMALL WORLD, BIG IDEAS

THE NEXT MORNING, Roberta's had her fill of private-eye work. She plans to visit an art gallery, which means that when the bearded man drives up to the Bourbon Hotel, I get into the car alone. This is not a big risk.

Klaus Nixdorf is a well-known business leader in Londrina, son of the land company's first agricultural director, Oswald Nixdorf, who founded the German community in Rolândia. Klaus is the author of the book that lists Waldomiro and Frieda Lindberg, and he's told me by e-mail that he was "born in the middle of the jungle" in 1934.

Right away Klaus looks familiar. A four-inch white beard is memorable, and I remember seeing Klaus and his beard outside the gate at the Londrina airport. He owns up to having decided to surprise Roberta and me, only he didn't bring a sign with our names on it because he figured he could easily pick two American women out of the crowd. I decide not to rub it in that we fooled him, walking right by. Maybe I look like a *brasileira* after all.

Instead, I apologize to Klaus for the mix-up and tell him how honored I am that a man of his stature took the time to meet us at the airport. It's another reason to like Brazil is what I say. I know I can't go wrong with that statement. Klaus has already written me that Brazil is "the best place on earth."

We drive north of the hotel to an area with nondescript four- and five-story buildings. Klaus parks underground and we take the small elevator to his office. It's one big room with several tables and desks.

Klaus sits behind the largest desk and I take a seat across from him. He tells me about a time during which Brazil wasn't "the best place on earth"—in 1942, when the government jailed his father and confiscated their family farm. Klaus was eight years old.

> They threw my mother in the street with four kids. We walked to Londrina, tried to find friends, but many people turned against the Germans then. My mother knew no Portuguese but there were four families who offered to help. Each agreed to take one child but instead my mother went to Curitiba. She sewed and we went into an orphanage. We almost starved to death. The food was very bad. There was flour made of corn and water. That was more or less our beginning.

So much for my notion of northern Paraná as an oasis for Germans during World War II. Klaus says he searched for a long time for the reasons why his father was jailed.

"Then a Jewish man offered me an explanation," he says. "We went to his house for dinner and he took me aside. 'I can tell you why your father was put in jail,' he said to me. 'Early in the war, Hitler sent four submarines to Brazil to start a base. The English destroyed the submarines. The president of Brazil was a good friend of Germany, but the Americans convinced him to work against the German people. Nelson Rockefeller was the head person dealing with the Brazilian president. Money was promised to Brazil but on the condition that Brazil put away the leaders of German, Italian, and Japanese organizations.'"

Klaus had no way of proving this allegation. Many years later, however, Klaus was asked to serve as the English translator when David Rockefeller, Nelson's brother and the head of Chase Manhattan Bank, visited northern Paraná. Klaus thought he might have a chance to ask David Rockefeller about the matter.

"I wanted to ask him . . . but I thought if I would talk about politics maybe David Rockefeller would say to the government, 'Don't give me any more people who would talk about politics,' so I did not ask him."

Klaus is perhaps a more reliable storyteller when it comes to his own actions and motivations. After the war, his family got its land back, but Klaus did not like being a poor farm boy. He dreamed of something bigger. He signed up for a Brazil-US farm exchange program and worked on farms in Wisconsin and Wyoming. After hitchhiking to Washington, DC, to resolve problems with his immigration status, he went on to study journalism, economics, and rural agriculture at the University of Wisconsin, playing the accordion in bars to earn money.

However, by January 1959 his dream had reversed itself and he longed to return to Brazil. "I put on the blackboard that I needed three passengers to drive to Brazil. Seventy-one people signed up, but after interviewing them there was only one left. One woman thought cannibals would eat her. None of the seventy-one knew how far away Brazil was. One guy came with me and we spent five months driving.

"We had all kinds of problems. We went to jail three times. Our documents were all wrong. We drove twenty-two thousand miles. The other man got very thin. We had no money for food."

Up was the only direction in which Klaus's life could head after that, and sure enough, his US education credentials impressed local authorities and he rose through the ranks to become secretary of agriculture for the state of Paraná. Then he became a businessman with multiple companies producing fertilizer, agricultural machinery, and seeds, and leasing taxis and airplanes. He says he divested his companies after adverse changes in the law, and now spends his time running a development bank trying to promote investment in regional projects.

To my surprise, he offers me a job. He hands me several brochures and asks me to be the company's representative in New York. He will pay me a commission on any investment I direct to Londrina. Of course I say yes. Klaus is not a man you want to say no to, and not just because he puts "Commandant" before his name (perhaps because he is a Rotarian, and perhaps not). It doesn't seem as though he has ever said no in his life.

"Brazilians are very good in ideas, and myself, too," Klaus says. "I have a statue over there, the seeder of constant ideas." He points at a statuette on a bookcase. "Why do we not get investors? We need not only good ideas, but good projects."

That is the role of Klaus's development bank, to put good ideas into project form and publicize the business opportunities that await investors in northern Paraná.

"Lisbon is as big as Londrina, but everyone has heard of Lisbon and no one has heard of Londrina. We have to tell people that we exist. We cannot be just like a chicken that doesn't say *clac-brah*. No one knows she laid an egg."

An employee walks in while we are speaking, a Swiss man. Klaus says he also has a representative in Miami. Klaus's big plan for the future is a bus tour all the way from Brazil to Canada to promote Londrina. After all, he drove the route once. He knows the way.

Klaus explains that his book grew out of his passion for Londrina.

"Brazilians are not much interested in history," he says. "It makes me very mad. When I was working on my book I had a hard time interviewing people."

Nonetheless, he managed to write a 575-page book laying out the history of Londrina, from the indigenous peoples who lived on the banks of the River Tibagi, some in a village led by a friar in the 1800s, to the first surveyor (Mábio Palhano, 1918), the first man with a scythe for cutting trees (Antonio Lourenco de la Veiga, 1926), the arrival of the British, and the building of the current city of factories, skyscrapers, and nearly 500,000 residents.

I ask him where he got the information about Frieda Lindberg, and he says all the names in the pioneer sections came from the register of people buying land from the *companhia*. This means I will have to go back to the Londrina Historical Museum and inquire again.

Klaus is sure his parents knew Waldomiro and he makes copies of the photos I have brought.

Klaus tells me that several leaders of the German community lived long lives and died recently, but for many years after the war, the German people in northern Paraná did not socialize with one another. For his parents' fiftieth wedding anniversary, in 1977, Klaus decided to assemble the families that his father had helped bring to Brazil from Germany from 1931 to 1939, both Jewish and non-Jewish.

"I said to my father 'give me a list of names.' There were twenty-two families on the first list. I had two drivers go to look and they found 220 families. Why did my father not know that all these people were still here? They were ashamed of what Hitler did. They had decided not to go to church or parties. I invited them all to a party for my parents and over one thousand people came."

Since that time, Klaus has made many gatherings possible through a social club he founded that meets once a month, with members from thirty-three nationalities who migrated to Londrina, Nova Dantzig, and Rolândia in the 1930s.

Though Klaus can talk wistfully about the past, he is unabashedly proud of the modern skyline that greets one today in Londrina. He holds up a color photo in his book showing a row of skyscrapers and says, "All of these buildings were created from 2004 to 2010 where there was nothing but vegetables."

I pay Klaus for a copy of the book as he tells me about a smaller development project he has in mind. He would like to install a "Hollywood-style walk around the lake" with the names of the Londrina pioneers inscribed in cement.

In Londrina, it seems, Waldomiro Lindberg's name may endure in multiple places long past any memory of the man himself. I think to myself that names may identify us, but how we live and how we love do it better. Still, I have to admit that the prospect of returning to Londrina some day and seeing Waldomiro Lindberg's name etched in a walkway has a certain appeal. Before I came to Brazil, I felt like I would kick Walter's headstone if I ever found it. Now I'm not so sure. I don't really know if I'd stomp on his name, or tip-toe.

chapter thirty-four

OF WRITERS AND PILOTS

THERE IS ANOTHER theory for why Klaus Nixdorf's father was jailed, and by that account I'm eating lunch with the jailor's grandson, a handsome man with dark-blond hair, great posture, and a wry smile.

Alan Thomas is the grandson of Arthur Thomas, the Scotsman who, on behalf of Lord Lovat, incorporated the Northern Paraná Land Company in Brazil and negotiated the transactions that gave the company title to three million acres. Arthur Thomas subsequently served as the company's general manager in Brazil for many years.

Academic writers have published articles critical of the land company as a hallmark of capitalist imperialism. In Sudan, where the company invested prior to beginning operations in Brazil, Lord Lovat and his fellow financiers, including the American Leigh Hunt as well as the Prince of Wales, are said to have enjoyed an unusually cozy relationship with the Sudanese government, which granted the company a monopolistic concession over a huge tract of land and guaranteed the securities offered to investors, all with the goal of ensuring a steady flow of cotton for Great Britain's textile mills.

Sudan proved to be good practice for Brazil, where the new Northern Paraná Land Company and its parent, Paraná Plantations Limited, requested and received very favorable treatment. The government helped the company protect its investment and "eliminate all doubts" about prior claims on the land through a two-pronged approach that involved purchase of a 415,000-acre concession from another land development company, destruction of those titles, and then purchase of the same land at "legal prices" from the government, followed by the purchase of hundreds of thousands of additional acres.*

The carefully planned transactions allowed the land company's advertisements to tout "ABSOLUTELY SECURE TITLES" as the number one reason why people should buy its land, followed by "FERTILITY AND HEALTHY CONDITIONS, GOOD ROADS, GOOD WATER."

To the governments of Brazil and Germany, if not to some political science professors, Arthur Thomas was a great man. He received commendations from both countries for his leadership in the colonization of northern Paraná.

Alan Thomas doesn't talk about the controversy surrounding the land company, nor does he tell me about his grandfather's commendations. They are reported in Klaus Nixdorf's book, and one has to give Klaus credit for writing so nicely about Arthur Thomas considering that, according to Alan, his grandfather and Klaus's father fell out around 1940. Alan tells me that Oswald Nixdorf allegedly owed Arthur Thomas money, and that is the other theory for why Klaus's father was jailed, having nothing to do with Nelson Rockefeller or World War II.

Alan tells this story with utmost neutrality. He radiates an "anything is possible" attitude as though he is neither confirming nor denying a word of what he says. He may have returned to Brazil after attending boarding school and university in England, but it seems he's got no

---

* See Bonnici, Thomas. "Postcolonial Historical Ambiguities and Environmental Tensions in Paraná, Brazil," *Revista Letras*, No. 70 (2006), quoting a deposition from banker Hermann Moraes Barros.

emotional investment in any particular spin here in his adopted country. He's not a booster like Klaus. He's more prone to understatement.

"I expected to stay in England," Alan says, "but I came to Brazil to visit. Well, the weather is nice and I stayed."

Ah, I say to myself, here is yet another person seduced by Brazil for reasons he cannot—or will not—specify.

Alan manages an English language school in Londrina. He has three children in the area, a sister in a town in the Amazon, and his father lives nearby in Londrina.

Alan is who I might be if Walter Lindberg had brought his family with him to Brazil rather than leaving them behind. Of course, if that had happened, I wouldn't be me—Dad would not have met Patricia Ryan in Virginia Beach, etc. But it is nonetheless uncanny to see how similarly our forebears' experiences in Brazil influenced both Alan and me. For me, the experience was condensed into a story. For Alan, it was the real deal. Alan's father grew up in northern Paraná and Alan is living the life of an expat, but in our heads there is not that much difference.

I hardly care about what's on my plate. Alan and I speak at length about explorers and explorer literature. We've read many of the same books and recommend new ones for each other.

Alan asks if I am familiar with the poetry of Elizabeth Bishop, and I am. She is an illustrious graduate of my alma mater, Vassar College, and back when Michael and I were together, I bought a copy of her *Questions of Travel* in a store on Cape Cod, drawn to her poems about Brazil. I've read an oral history about her by Fountain and Brazeau, so I know that Bishop had a Brazilian lover and lived in Rio for many years.

"Read her poems again," Alan advises. "Brazil is very fortunate to have had a poet of her stature write about it."

My talk with Alan is a testament to the power of my father's story, and the power of all stories to transport us to foreign places and other lives. Alan grew up in Brazil. His grandfather ran the land company. I grew up in Long Island, hearing a story about Brazil, and yet sitting here with Alan, it seems almost like we share the same background.

Indeed, I am the one writing about a man from two generations ago in Brazil, not Alan. He would like to write, he admits, but he says he would rather spend his time reading.

If and when Alan gets around to writing about his grandfather, there will be much to say. It is a rags-to-riches story with an international angle, back when the British Empire was synonymous with what would be called today the "global economy."

Arthur Hugh Miller Thomas grew up poor in Scotland, his father's death having left the family in penury. Journalism proved to be his ticket out of poverty, first a job in Dundee, and then a transfer to a paper in Singapore. He distinguished himself in World War II, befriending influential people during his service. From Singapore he went to the Sudan, where one of the directors of Sudan Plantations Syndicate was Lord Lovat, also a Scotsman. Thomas invested in a farm and became acquainted with Lord Lovat, who was favorably impressed and invited Thomas to represent his interests in Brazil.

According to Klaus Nixdorf's book, Arthur Thomas and the British investors initially came to Brazil to grow cotton, but cotton did not do well on the first farms purchased by the company in São Paulo state. The investors' interest then turned to northern Paraná mainly because of its valuable wood stocks, but also because of its fertile soil and the potential for coffee and other cash crops without the danger of frost.

Claude Levi-Strauss, who made anthropological forays to northern Paraná in the 1930s while teaching in São Paulo, wrote of "the miraculous soil, so rich that its mettle had to be broken, like that of a wild horse."

The British role in northern Paraná remains controversial, even beyond academic circles. There is a 1935 photograph in the first *Londrina Documenta* book showing a tennis court—"a tennis court in the middle of nowhere, a tennis court in the sertão" as described by a local photographer in today's Londrina. That was the British way, the writer asserts, "take your lifestyle with you wherever you go. Do not mix. . . . Do not interact with the natives."

The writer has more harsh words to say about the British: "Many worship the fact the Londrina was founded by Englishmen, as they are colonized culture, but they forget they bought and sold the land, then departed. . . . Who really built Londrina were, at first, Paulistas and [settlers from] Minas Gerais followed by migrants from all over Brazil and immigrants from the whole world."

Alan, on the other hand, is a Brit who departed but came back to Londrina. I wonder if Alan has resisted writing about his grandfather and Brazil because of the charged history he would have to confront. With so much ambivalence about his forebears, Alan may be wise to stay reticent and neutral. That's not the stance I've taken, I reflect as Alan walks me back to my hotel. His detachment has gotten to me, though. Alan is the one helper in Brazil I say good-bye to without taking a photograph. Somehow, I just can't bring myself to ask him to pose.

With a few minutes to myself before the next appointment, I open the Londrina map in the hotel lobby and notice in the "Touristics Attractions and Services" listings that there is a Parque Arthur Thomas. I find the park on the map. Avenida Europa and Avenida Paris run along its southern edge and then the name of the street on the western border catches my attention. Is this possible? The street along the western edge of Parque Arthur Thomas is called Rua Charles Lindenberg. It's misspelled, but it seems there is a Lindbergh street in Londrina after all. It's just not named after Waldomiro.

"Like the flier," I used to say when people asked for my name. I stopped giving that answer after I said "like the flier" to a young man and he asked if I meant the Philadelphia Flyer Eric Lindros.

Many younger people simply don't know about the famous pilot who flew in 1927 from Long Island's Roosevelt Field to Paris, the first solo flight across the Atlantic. For a time, Lindbergh was considered the most famous man in the world, and in 1932, when his son was kidnapped and found dead and Bruno Hauptmann was tried for the crime, writer H.L. Mencken called it "the biggest story since the Resurrection."

Standing in the Bourbon Hotel, I don't know how many people in Londrina are familiar with the story of Charles Lindbergh, aka Lindenberg, but he's got to be more famous in Brazil than the Lindberg who gave me my last name. Yet Walter Lindberg was a flier of sorts, always on the move, and in my family, like Charles Lindbergh is—or was—everywhere, Walter is best known for a one-way trip.

When I started analyzing my past, after the final break-up with

Michael, I was struck with how flight seemed to be the common theme of my heritage, all four blood grandparents leaving their homes, all arriving in New York City, a place for dreams and starting over: Dad's French Alsatian father deserting a German ship, his Hungarian mother sailing from Trieste, Mother's Irish father fleeing a poor life as a grocer's son in Philadelphia, and her German Alsatian mother leaving Rochester for New York after meeting her future husband in Miami Beach. And of course there was Walter, the one who left and never returned.

Maybe the name Lindberg, "like the flier," is the right name for us after all.

chapter thirty-five

A BALCONY ON THE RIVER

ALTHOUGH EVERSON, MY translator and driver for the afternoon, is handsome in a classic Brazilian way, dark-haired and brown-eyed, it's his voice that really distinguishes him. If the low register of a clarinet emitted words rather than notes, the words would sound like Everson's, deep and full, as if emerging from a tunnel of ebony wood.

Everson speaks English with ease, and his wife teaches English at Alan Thomas's school. That's how I came to meet Alan, after an introduction by e-mail to Everson by the woman who arranged for our ride from the airport.

"I've taken the liberty to mention your coming to Brazil to a friend of mine, who happens to be the grandson of Mr. Thomas (one of the settlers from Northern Paraná Land Co. who helped turn this city into what it is today), and he wishes to meet you during your stay," was how Everson phrased it in his message, quite elegantly I thought when I read it.

Now that I've got Everson's language skills and car at my disposal, our first stop is clear: return to the Londrina Historical Museum and look again for Frieda Lindberg.

The librarians welcome me back. Rosangela informs us that after my visit the day before she spoke to a woman who worked in the back office of the land company in the 1930s. Like the other old-timers, the woman remembers Waldomiro Lindberg's name, but nothing more. Her job revolved around documents, the woman told Rosangela; she didn't fraternize with the land agents. That could be the explanation, or the explanation could be that Waldomiro wasn't the sociable type with anyone.

Everson tells the librarians what Klaus Nixdorf said—that he obtained Frieda Lindberg's name from the land records, and Rosangela invites me to sit at the computer where I can scroll through a decade's worth of land-transaction ledgers. She and Ruth don't think they overlooked anything, but they start looking through their files nonetheless, willing to give the search another try on account of Klaus's authority.

Fortunately, the land transactions were recorded in very readable script. Still, I'm concerned that I will miss Frieda's name. I find the page Rosangela showed me the day before, from June 1932, showing Waldomiro Lindberg's purchase of the plot in the Cafezal *gleba*. I scroll through the records for 1933, 1934, and 1935. There's no Frieda, but the name Waldomiro Lindberg jumps out again at the bottom of the November 1935 ledger. Above his name is the word "*extornos*." The plot and transaction numbers, acreage and price are the same as the June 1932 entry: transaction 397, plot 116, 20 alqueires, 8,000,000 reis.

Everson takes a look and explains that "*extornos*" means an exchange. Three and a half years after he bought it, Waldomiro apparently surrendered the property to the land company. There goes my claim to land in Brazil.

At first blush, it does not seem like a good investment, buying land in 1932 and selling it for the same price in 1935, but given the company's practice of selling plots in exchange for a small down payment, with a deed to follow upon full payment, Waldomiro likely never paid the full cost of the land. Yet he had control over it for three years, able to profit from rental and/or farm income. Once could view the November 1935 "*extorno*" not so much as a sale back to the company, but as a release of Waldomiro's obligation to continue paying for the plot. Perhaps 1935 was when Waldomiro decided to open his store, and he needed his capital back.

I continue scrolling through the records until the very end without finding any mention of Frieda or any other reference to Waldomiro.

Isabel, who has driven to Londrina with a friend, surprises me in the museum library, where she hands me a CD made by Cesar that includes the photo of Waldomiro at the groundbreaking of the German school. Now, I have something tangible to show for the afternoon's efforts, and the chance to thank Isabel once more.

Isabel departs and Rosangela kindly accompanies Everson and me downstairs to the exhibits. The large room that used to be the train waiting area is devoted to coffee, charting the growth of the industry and displaying various implements used at different stages. Green gold fueled Londrina's growth for decades, making Londrina an important city in the international coffee trade, but Everson points out that the system of many small farms did not last. Large growers came to dominate the industry through consolidations and buyouts. Then frosts came in the late 1950s, and that proved to be a colossal setback from which the region's economy was slow to recover.

It all comes back to planet earth and the extent of alteration that natural systems will bear or accommodate. Humans could remove trees and plant coffee bushes, even place the coffee plants on the highest land to reduce the risk of frost, but humans would not be the ones to decide whether frost would come.

Even so, Londrina's coffee trade brought great wealth to some. It's to a former coffee plantation owner's grand house that Everson drives me from the museum. Bruno mentioned the house the night before and Everson knows just where it is. The *casa* on Avenida Celso Garcia Cid is a gorgeous mansion, straight out of *Gone with the Wind*, soft yellow plaster with white trim and a white balustrade framing the second floor balcony. The balcony runs the length of the house, supported by columns, and protects the entrance to the house from sun or rain. Metal lanterns, the sort one sees in the garden district of New Orleans, hang from the ceiling of the balcony.

The building is now a bank's office, but at least the architecture, a sliver of Londrina's past, has been preserved.

This mansion was not the sort of dwelling that workers from the countryside lived in when they came to Londrina, people like Everson's parents, who struggled in poor conditions. His father, a butcher, died when Everson was three, his mother when he was seventeen. After that, Everson left Londrina for six years, spending time in the real London and living on a kibbutz in Israel.

"You've got to get out of here to find out some things about life," he says.

He has been teaching English and providing translation services for the last sixteen years, ever since he returned to Londrina.

Everson has a fascination with words befitting his beautiful voice. Over the course of the afternoon he has pointed out words that are now archaic, such as the word "*machinas*" in Waldomiro's store ad. Today, a Brazilian would use the word "*maquinas*."

In the car he asks why my step-grandfather changed his name.

"Walter is very common in Brazil," Everson says. "W becomes V and you have Valdir. He didn't need to change his name."

Of course, I am not privy to the thought processes that caused Walter to emerge from his staged death in Três Lagoas with a new name. I can only infer that Walter wanted to make a strong statement about his new identity, a statement as strident as his one to Otto Ulrich that he would "never go back to New York."

Whether it is the result of Everson's soothing voice or the intensity of the last two days, I am exhausted. There isn't anything left I want to see in Londrina. What I want is to take Everson's voice home with me, so we return to the hotel lobby and I switch on my small tape recorder. I ask him to translate a couple of passages from the *Londrina Documenta* book.

We choose passages somewhat at random, somewhat based on how much we like the accompanying photos. Roberta joins us in our corner of the lobby with her journal, intent on adding more facts about how she spent her time, even though the art gallery she visited offered only a small collection, and there wasn't much else to do in Londrina for a regular tourist, someone not hunting for a ghost or an investment opportunity.

My head is spinning with facts, with what I know and don't know. I don't know if Walter and Frieda were married or if the Lindberg pilot in Sertanópolis would be my father's stepbrother. I'm not sure I care. I care about how pleasant it feels to relax on the sofa, look at photos, and hear Everson speak.

"I wondered what you'd be like," he admits.

"I'm not weird," I say.

"No, you're not."

One of the photos we look at by George Craig Smith shows a stretch of the Tibagi River visible through the posts of a simple wood balcony in present-day Jataizinho, fifteen kilometers from Londrina. The house belonged to the Maxwell Company. Northern Paraná was one of the places where instant coffee got its start.

The essay, written by a professor at the University of Londrina, speaks about memory and the past:

> The balcony takes us to a distant place, lost within ourselves in our memories and confused with our dreams. It could be a place alongside the Mediterranean, a Scheherazade dream, a lake on a farm in the State of São Paulo, a river in the Pantanal, a condominium beside a lake in the 21st century, but this is the house of the Maxwell Company in Jatahy, on the banks of the Tibagi River in the 1930s. It is not a dream, but it may have been, yes, a dream.

Obscured by modern development, the past in Londrina can seem like a dream. There's little objective evidence of Londrina's history, except for the occasional mansion, the train station, or the Casa do Pioneiro moved from its original location to the university grounds. Perhaps a culture that built itself by swiftly eradicating what came before it—the forest, the wildlife, the communities of people—moved easily into a subsequent stage of eradication, replacing the original city with newer structures.

As a person largely deprived of a past predating her own memory, I prefer cities that show their age. For me, it's not quite enough to know that a past exists. I want to see it with my own eyes in old buildings and grime.

We will be leaving Londrina the next morning, heading to a part of Brazil that remains forest, a protected section of the southern Amazon basin. I'll carry with me heavy books, the CD of old photos, and Everson's deep voice as the past's magnetism pulls me deeper into Brazil. I'll also be bringing my portable life support system—six prescription medicines—one of which must be kept cold, a challenging requirement in the jungle.

I'm so excited to be headed to the rainforest, I'm not even thinking about how far I will be from a hospital.

chapter thirty-six

MATO GROSSO

I DON'T NEED lichens to tell me where I am. Lichens grow on the south sides of trees in the Southern Hemisphere, but unlike Percy Fawcett or George Cherrie, I am not traveling by foot through parts unknown, in need of guideposts provided by nature. The interior I prowl is something other than virgin forest. So I will not need to cut into a water liana to find potable liquid, nor rub my skin with electric ants to make me smell like the forest and deter jaguars.

Nor need I fear attacks by the Nambikwara, as did the men who built and staffed Rondon's telegraph line between the Juruena and Madeira rivers. I'm not aware of the location of the closest indigenous settlement, or the last time a member of a native tribe was accused of murder.

All I really know upon arriving by truck at the Rio Teles Pires in the late afternoon is that the scene takes my breath away.

The river is wide here, perhaps not as wide as stretches of the Amazon or Madeira, but wide enough for the reflection of clouds, huge cumulous puffs mixed with broad, flat sheets. It is a simple but all-enveloping scene: the river, mirroring the clouds, the mouth of a narrower river across the way, trees growing out of the water along the near shore, illuminated with golden light on the western sides of their slanted trunks, bands of dense green foliage spreading across the horizon, an upside-down saucer of blue sky and above that, thick layers of white-hot light.

This is Mato Grosso, one of the world's most famously explored mysterious places, Fawcett's lost kingdom, fortune hunters' vault of gold, Roosevelt's lair of jaguars, Rondon's obstacle to a united Brazil, the Jesuits' purgatory of Indian souls awaiting salvation, Marshall Field's living museum of endemic birds and mammals—and quite possibly Waldomiro Lindberg's last frontier. This is Mato Grosso, where today men burn trees with impunity, turning mystery to smoke.

Alfredo takes our bags and Alesandro keeps the small motorboat still as the five of us step into it. Alfredo deposits my cold pack containing medicine into a cooler aboard the boat. Our driver will turn around and compress his spine for another two hours on the ditch-pocked dirt road that brought us to this small clearing. It was a long, bouncy ride from the northern Mato Grosso municipality of Alta Floresta, to which we flew from Londrina via Cuiabá. Thanks to the driver's good eyes, we saw a brown and white owl on the way, perched on one leg on a post not more than thirty feet from the road. Owls stand on one leg either to keep warm or rest. Given the heat, we had presumably found a tired owl.

On the outskirts of Alta Floresta our small truck came to a full stop, blocked by a hill of clay-colored dirt across the road. A Komatsu earth-moving machine was spreading the dirt and two men stood in the road with their backs to us watching the work. A large truck heading south was stopped on the other side, and it seemed like we might have to wait a long time until the two men turned around and the operator of the earthmover swung the shovel to the side. One of the men waved us forward, so over the mound of dirt we went.

It was a demonstration, before we even entered the forest, that the concept of order means something different here.

Alesandro starts the motor and the boat sends ripples into the reflection of clouds as we cross the Teles Pires to the mouth of the Rio

Cristalino, a third-tier tributary. A sign on the riverbank announces the area's protected status and a command, in Portuguese: no fishing, hunting, or camping.

The requests are almost quaint. It's not fishing, hunting, or camping that has besieged the great forest of Mato Grosso—over 200,000 square kilometers converted to farmland and grazing pastures since 1960, more than ten Manhattan Islands of trees cleared in one recent year alone. "No mining, logging, or burning" would be a more accurate statement of the threats to the reserve's integrity, not that forest pillagers are inclined to follow rules written on signs.

In 2005, a nun holding a Bible was shot dead in the state of Pará, just over the border to our north, where the Rio Cristalino has its source up in the São Joaquim mountains. The nun, Dorothy Stang, had lived in Brazil for thirty-five years. She worked with the rural poor opposing illegal deforestation, and she was killed in cold blood walking to a community meeting. It took several trials, but eventually two men were sentenced to prison terms. One admitted that the murder was revenge for the nun's claim that he had set illegal fires to clear land.

It would be nice to believe that things are different now, but in 2010 at least ten thousand forest fires were recorded in Mato Grosso; in May 2011 another leading critic of deforestation was gunned down in Pará along with his wife; and in November 2011, gunmen hired by ranching interests killed an outspoken indigenous chief in front of his son in a dispute over land in Mato Grosso do Sul, the state to the south carved out of the original Mato Grosso.

In the boat to the Cristalino Jungle Lodge, illegal fires and men who would shoot nuns and tribal chiefs seem far away. That is, of course, how Brazil's tourist industry wants it to be. A capped heron stands on a branch, dressed for a graduation ceremony with its pearly white body and blue cap. On another branch we spy a brown heron, its attention fixed on the possible location of its next meal. A drab water tyrant passes us without effort, flying low over the river.

The river curves now and then and unending stoles of green line the banks on both sides, above a meter of brown roots and leafless branches from when the river's water level was higher. Above, the green canopy is of fairly uniform height and color, but here and there a lone tree towers over the others, a recipient of some competitive advantage, at least for the time being.

Next to me, Roberta sits in an oversized life jacket that resembles the carapace of a tortoise, but she is smiling and I must be, too. It feels like the achievement of a goal just being on this river, in this place—and yet it is also a beginning. When I wrote a fictional treatment of the Walter story, the novel ended with the protagonist Isabel alone in a boat on an unnamed Amazonian tributary. I am living a sequel of my own making, picking up in real life where my imagination left off.

In the boat with us is a real Isabella, a twenty-five-year-old Brazilian from the state of São Paulo with flawless skin and golden brown dread-locks that hang below her waist. She is starting a six-month assignment as the translator at the lodge, so she, like us, sees the river with fresh eyes. She is wondering about her new home and colleagues, and I am wondering what it would be like to be her, on the verge of living in the jungle for half a year. She says she is nervous, but she laughs with the freedom of one who has never known unhappiness, or never been unable to shake it off.

There are no Brazilian guests on the boat, only foreigners, consistent with what Tatiana told us to expect. In addition to Roberta and me there are a man named Hans, a German diplomat stationed in Brasilia, and Brett, an American who lives on a farm outside Seattle. Brett notices things that we don't, such as how the cattle we viewed from the truck had fatty humps like Brahmin, animals that can tolerate heat. Indeed, Brazil has been enriching its cattle with Indian breeds for over one hundred years, a practice that is now officially banned, resulting in a black market for Indian bull semen.

Brett doesn't sell bull semen. He deals in sustainably harvested wood products, and he's taking a few days to look at wildlife after meeting with a potential supplier.

Bull semen would be of considerable interest to the exuberant men who filled the plane from Cuiabá to Alta Floresta, the latter being a place with four to five million cattle and just fifty-one thousand humans. Most of the men were wearing suits, a stark contrast with Roberta's and my hiking garb, and they all seemed to know one another. There was a lot of back-slapping in the aisle, a clubhouse atmosphere.

I found out after we landed that the men were headed to Alta Floresta for the annual bull fair. The fair is a major event, because with an estimated twenty-five million cattle in the state, a great bull is a valuable commodity. Many people know Mato Grosso as the leading soybean-producing state in Brazil, and soy is the reason why a highway is being paved east of Alta Floresta up through Pará to the Amazon port of Santarém, but the soil around Alta Floresta is too rocky for soy. Some crops grow, but cattle-ranching is the reason Alta Floresta was carved out of the rainforest in the 1970s, and cattle-ranching is what drives the local economy. The beef is exported primarily to Russia, Iran, and Eastern Europe.

I was a conservationist traveling incognito on a plane full of ranchers. What would they have said to me if I told them my employer's name? Mind your own business? Might they have been as hostile to me as the Nambikwara to Rondon's telegraph men?

But that's the thing. The fate of the Amazon *is* my business. I believe that the fate of the Amazon should be the business of all of us, because I have read about numerous studies showing that tropical deforestation contributes significantly to climate change, while standing tropical forests absorb carbon dioxide. Moreover, scientists say the Amazon is so vast that its moisture helps regulate the earth's climate, meaning that if the Amazon dries out because of too much burning and drought, as the Amazon Research Center and others believe is a distinct possibility, it's not just the Amazon region that will be affected. Over the last decade, few parts of the planet have been spared the devastating effects of prolonged drought. Major drought even happened in the Amazon in 2005 and 2010. What if that becomes the norm? What if it already is?

Throughout the Amazon, because of a moratorium on new soy areas, expanding pastureland has been the biggest reason for illegal deforestation. According to Brazil's environment minister, 710 square miles of forest were destroyed in the nine-month period ending April 2011, much of that occurring in Mato Grosso. In May 2012, the news was better in some places, but not in Mato Grosso. Although deforestation was down overall, a whopping 71 percent of illegal clearing took place in Mato Grosso, and Mato Grosso and Pará would again lead the list in rate of clearing between August 2012 and July 2013, a period during which the Brazilian government itself acknowledged that deforestation increased by 29 percent over the prior year.

Deforestation usually involves setting fires, which release huge amounts of carbon dioxide into the atmosphere. It has been estimated that if Mato Grosso were a country, it would be the fifth-highest emitter of greenhouse gases in the world.

On top of their role in regulating climate, forests help protect the quality and quantity of water supplies, not to mention providing special habitats for humans and vast categories of animals and plants.

When I was a girl, I thought the Amazon rainforest belonged to me because of a story, a story about the life and death of a man I never knew. As I arrive in the Amazon, I feel like the Amazon belongs to me because of science, the interconnectedness of all life, and my concern for the future of the planet that my son and billions of others will inhabit.

It occurs to me that those of us who accept the scientific theories about the importance of the Amazon rainforest to the planet are a little like Brazil's indigenous peoples of the past. We have no land titles, no deeds, no property rights in the conventional sense. Yet we feel our lives and our children's lives depend in part on the place, and we believe that gives us a natural right to care and demand responsible action by those on the ground in Brazil.

Otto Ulrich and Walter Lindberg thought they had the right to come to Brazil and remove its gold and gems. Eighty years later, I feel that I have the right—and duty—to ask the very opposite, that people leave important swaths of Brazil's land alone.

The boat makes a hard left and out of the forest juts a large wooden dock floating in the water, attached to land by a walkway. This is the entrance to the lodge, in a small cove. A welcoming party of hundreds of small brown butterflies greets us as we walk to the modest common areas. Stop for a moment and the butterflies land on hats, arms, bags. On the outside they are medium brown, but when one of them lands and opens its wings, bright purple bands are revealed, a minor but pleasant secret.

An estimated two thousand butterfly species have been found in the twenty-nine thousand acres of the Cristalino reserve, an area known mostly for its birds: 595 species, one-third of Brazil's cataloged total. The incredible biodiversity results from the convergence of several different habitats.

Initially, when planning my trip, I felt I had to see the area described by Ulrich, between the rivers Juruena and Ji-Paraná, farther west in Mato Grosso, where Ulrich said he found gold in 1926. That is where the maps would have taken Walter and Ulrich had the *Vestris* not sunk. The Juruena was also Rondon's base building the telegraph line, and the river where he and Roosevelt began "the difficult part" of their expedition.

Somehow the Juruena region seemed important at first, but it remains a challenging place, with few roads, no hotels, and "no law" according to a Brazilian guide based in Curitiba with whom I corresponded.

"I would think ten times before going there myself," this guide advised me, and that, along with my pituitary disorder and lack of experience surviving in the wild, was enough to give me pause. Maybe reaching the Juruena would have made for good reading, but not if I didn't live to tell the tale.

Another guide, based in the Pantanal, offered to take Roberta and me to the Rio Roosevelt, which is near the southern Juruena, but the price was high and the route involved stops in places of no particular interest to me.

My objective wasn't to find gold or retrace the famous expedition of Roosevelt and Rondon, much less the not-so-famous expedition of Otto Ulrich. It was Walter's story I was after, and there was no evidence Walter had ever headed to the Juruena.

I decided, like Brett and Hans, to look at birds and other wildlife at the Cristalino Jungle Lodge. The lodge's location in northern Mato Grosso, on the firing line of deforestation, appealed to me. The choice seemed prudent for a single parent with a health condition, and likely to please Roberta, as well as her worried sisters.

Yet the Amazon remains a place of secrets, and even the partially deforested Mato Grosso would have surprises in store.

chapter thirty-seven

HOWLERS

THE HOWLER MONKEYS are a cyclone of noise. From the moment we awoke at five, we could hear them across the forest, raspier than rain, a musical thunderstorm. Their sound was a long, rolled-out carpet we followed to their lofty throne, first by boat and then on foot. Finally, we stand in homage beneath them.

Only they've stopped howling. It's totally quiet.

Our guide, Brad Davis, whispers that there are probably six to eight monkeys up there in the tall trees. He spends some time off the trail trying to find a view through the canopy while we wait, standing as still as leaves, but eventually Brad gives up and we walk on.

The howling starts again now that we're gone, oscillating in note range and volume but stopping and starting in unison, a privilege of the alpha male to decide when. Brad plants the tripod he's carrying and focuses the scope on monkeys of a different sort, brown capuchins. One gnaws at the covering of a nut, wipes its nose, returns to the work of feeding itself. We hear sections of shell covers drop on the jungle floor.

We climb a 150-foot tower erected for people like us—birders, photographers, tourists, foreigners; the same people go by so many names. Our group includes three, in addition to Brad—Roberta, me, and a man with a bigger camera lens than mine. His wife is back in the lodge, tired after a sleepless night itching from insect bites.

We're above the canopy now, thick mist covering the jungle below. This is the bird zone, and it will last for hours as the mist evaporates, the trees grow distinct, and we become more accustomed to the hot sun and the sound of bees buzzing around our heads. Every so often the two-whistle blast of a screaming piha cuts through the forest. An Amazonian pygmy owl occasionally adds its aside.

Birders in the Amazon don't see much in the way of quantity. It's all about quality. A paradise tanager will fly in, lured by Brad's call or the app on his iPhone, and we'll look at its beautiful green head and blue belly magnified many times over in Brad's scope and take photos likely to be trashed for lack of clear focus, and then the tanager will scoot and we'll wait until blue-headed parrots show up for a flyby. Over the course of the morning we are graced with a ringed woodpecker, whose large head is orange, a beautiful blue dacnis with black stripes on its wings, and an opal-rumped tanager, which is in fact chiefly blue.

I feel for Roberta, who would rather be hiking. She is neither a birder nor a photographer, but she stands up from the small metal seat in the corner of the tower and comes to the scope when Brad locates white-whiskered spider monkeys through the eyepiece. He tells us these monkeys are endangered and found only in this part of the Amazon. Across the border in Pará, there's a tradition of hunting monkeys, but the heritage in Mato Grosso is more agricultural, so the monkeys have fared a little better here.

It's good to learn about some way in which Mato Grosso hasn't been destructive of nature, but Brad is only getting started. He's got much more to impart about the rainforest, information we'd never otherwise know. Two blue and orange macaws fly by and Brad tells us that in Peru, macaws are killed and eaten, their feathers used for lures. Deforestation actually helps macaws, according to Brad. There is less hunting where land has been deforested. Ranchers flood portions of their property and when the hardwoods rot, that creates cavities for macaws that monkeys, the macaws' main natural predators, can't get to.

Brad is Canadian, married to a Brazilian. He came to the lodge for an internship years ago and basically never left, like John McNaughton and Alan Thomas, only Brad is an expat who wears camouflage and carries a big scope.

I learn from Brad that I'm not really that far from the Juruena after all. There are in excess of 1,100 tributaries in the Amazon, a large body with over a thousand fingers, and the Juruena is just two fingers away. The Cristalino flows into the Teles Pires, and at its mouth the Teles Pires meets the Juruena. Both form the Tapajos, which flows north and meets the Amazon at Santarém.

We hike back to the boat after we can't stand the heat and bees any longer, stopping to admire the teepee-like roots of several palm trees and the myriad shapes of the vines called lianas. Before I left home, I read about research in Panama that lianas may be outcompeting trees in tropical rainforests, better able than trees to convert carbon dioxide into growth but less able than trees to sequester large quantities of carbon dioxide and help clean the air. Lianas can deprive trees of nutrients, literally choking them to death, but the lianas I see in the forest are things of beauty, corkscrews and braids, hoops and knotted ropes. I would much rather admire them than fret about them. This is, of course, how many people feel about environmental problems, especially climate change. We tend not to like topics that make us feel bad. We seek beauty and hope.

At the lodge we meet up with Brett, who spent the morning hiking with another group. I am so sweaty a swim in the river feels great before lunch. Isabella won't go in the water. She is afraid of caiman.

Roberta doesn't go into the river either. She sits on the ladder of the dock and gets her legs wet, while Brett and I are doing the crawl and backstroke. At home, swimming is my main exercise, usually in pools. What a thrill to be swimming in an Amazonian tributary with a handsome man in the sunshine after a morning of howler monkeys and spectacular birds. My fictional protagonist Isabel Norgaard never swam in the Rio Cristalino. I have bested her, and she was me.

After lunch comes siesta, a two-hour period when the lodge's generator is turned on to provide hot water and electricity. A German graduate student is working on his frog research in the screened-in common room under a ceiling fan. I join him with my laptop. Like Roberta, I think I should write chronologically, but I keep revising a passage about the feel of the mud on my sandaled feet walking to John McNaughton's office in São Paulo. How is it possible that was only four days ago?

In mid-afternoon we meet on the covered porch for our afternoon outing. It's pouring. Brad remarks, with nonchalance, that the end of the rainy season often brings the heaviest rains.

Roberta and I would like to hike anyway, but Brad says we can't go on our own—we're likely to get lost, lichens or not—so he agrees to join us.

We walk a couple of miles, to a giant strangler fig, a parasitic tree that's grown around another tree and overtaken it. For the most part, the forest canopy protects us from the rain. It's refreshing and lovely, and our lungs feel like they're hooked up to oxygen tanks, only the energizing air is coming from the trees.

It turns out that Brad owns 250 acres near the Juruena, property he bought on behalf of a Canadian company that was considering a carbon sequestration project. The project never went forward and now Brad may sell the land, but the likely buyers are loggers and miners because the property is extremely remote, a ten-hour drive from the nearest town.

Brad knows his birds and natural history, but he's got some hard-edged opinions about the Amazon. He's too polite to say what he really thinks of large conservation organizations with projects in the Amazon, such as the nonprofit for which I work, but he speaks his mind about indigenous peoples. He says some of them sell diamond-mining rights illegally, then call the government when they've had enough, force the mines to shut, impound the equipment, and sell it either to the same people who were mining before, or to others, repeating the cycle.

I don't like hearing this and the most accord-seeking proposition I can offer is that sometimes there are disputes within tribes—some members want to profit and other don't—but I get no "perhaps" from Brad. (Later, Roberta will remind me of what Tatiana said to us in São Paulo, that many Brazilians have low opinions of indigenous peoples, but that generalization may be as overly sweeping as the prejudice it attempts to explain.)

Brad says he is more concerned about the fate of the forest that Walter Lindberg helped to destroy—that is, the Atlantic Forest—than he is about the Amazon. There is only between 4 and 10 percent left of the Atlantic Forest, depending on the source of the estimate. One hears this complacence from many Brazilians—that the Amazon is still so vast, there's not much to worry about.

But what if the scientists are right who say that because of the 20 percent loss the Amazon has already sustained, what's left is getting close to a tipping point, after which dryness and fires will become rampant and tree deaths will spread like wind? Where will the beautiful birds go then, and the money-spending tourists, the settlers and the tribes? What will happen to the planet if the Amazon flips from a place where carbon gets stored to a net emitter of carbon dioxide?

I like and respect Brad and don't want to argue with him, but I believe that the time to prevent the Amazon from going the way of the Atlantic Forest is now. It takes a long time to change people's behavior. People need to be persuaded that economic development and forest conservation can coexist, and pilot projects have proved this, but it's a very different way of looking at land than as an infinite resource to be used for short-term human gain.

The municipality of Alta Floresta was all forest until 1973, when a man referred to as "the last colonist" decided to develop it and got permission from the government to clear 70 percent of the forest.

"Nothing resists work" is the motto of Alta Floresta, "*nada resiste ao trabalho,*" and it seems that isn't meant to describe the people there or the monkeys, but the land itself.

Remarkably, we are spending our time on land that has been preserved because of the last colonist's daughter. When I hear this from Brad, I know my choice of Cristalino was a good one. I am in Brazil both because of my father's contributions to my life, and because I grew up questioning his ways. So it has been with Vitória Da Riva Carvalho on a much larger scale, and it certainly hasn't been easy for her.

Initially, she established the first private reserve in northern Mato Grosso now nearly 30,000 acres. Then, in 2001, she and others persuaded the state to create a park adjacent to the reserve. Her goal is to link the park and reserve with several indigenous reserves and other parks, including the Juruena National Park, creating a great Southern Amazon Corridor.

What Brad doesn't tell us, though it is referenced in the brochure of the Cristalino Ecological Foundation, the lodge's sister organization, is how hard Carvalho has had to fight to maintain her achievements. In 2002, the same government body that created the park passed a bill to reduce the size of the park by almost half, allegedly at the behest of large landowners. In 2005, the head of the federal environmental agency in Mato Grosso and forty-six of his colleagues were arrested for taking bribes from illegal loggers, and at the beginning of 2006, a rancher from São Paulo was charged with deforesting 6,508 hectares of the Cristalino Park. At the end of 2006, another massive clearing was discovered. Even so, the Mato Grosso legislature again approved the reduction of the state park by thirty thousand hectares.

Carvalho has also had to deal with landless peasants called *sem terras*, often armed, who do the bidding of loggers and ranchers, invading and destroying habitat.

We were taught to think of explorers as heroes in grade school, from Columbus to Daniel Boone to Lewis and Clark, but now, as an adult and conservationist, I know that exploration has often been a precursor of development, radically altering the very wilderness that bestowed upon the explorers their supposed greatness. Roosevelt's *Through the Brazilian Wilderness* is full of statements about the development potential of the fine places he is passing through admiring the birds and other wildlife.

In contrast to questionable male wilderness heroes of old, operating in the same man's world that killed all of the children and most of the women aboard the *Vestris*, I am glad my tourist dollars are supporting a brave woman like Vitória Carvalho, who is pushing back against land grabs by profiteers, even against her own father.

chapter thirty-eight

A PLATFORM WITH THE LOCALS

THE NEXT MORNING, the forest looks different. It's as though my eyes are adjusting, the way it takes a little while to see in the dark. From today's bird-watching perch I don't just see a forest, I see individual trees. No longer is the panoramic green made of thick brushstrokes. It's the work of an infinite number of small brushes, some dipped in colors other than green, such as the brown of dead branches, the dark red of certain bark.

The heat and humidity remain the same, however—unforgiving.

Even though there's some shade over today's wooden lookout, on a ridge overlooking a dip in the forest, I'm hot and itchy with sweat. The bees are annoying. I'm thinking about the river and another swim. Not many birds are flying in.

Later, Brad leads us along the ridge, past purple and red flowers growing on the edges of rocky clearings, under a yellow-headed vulture circling in the blue sky, into the habitat of poisonous frogs where Brad catches one with a yellow stripe as we make our way down wet rocks to the boat.

Finally, we're back at the lodge, where our swim is liquid gold. Veins swollen from heat recede and my head clears. Several of the lodge's employees are in the water and this gives Roberta confidence, so she swims, though she doesn't put her head in the water. She and I tread water next to the platform where Nira, a staff member of the Cristalino Ecological Foundation, is resting. It's Saturday, Nira's day off, so she's ridden in the truck up from Alta Floresta with two new lodge guests.

Nira loves her job with the foundation, which works to preserve the Cristalino reserve, educate adjacent residents about the forest's importance, promote sustainable, diversified farming, and develop financial mechanisms to compensate people who protect areas important for water production such as river banks and land around springs and on hilltops. It seems the new city of Alta Floresta is already experiencing adverse impacts on its water supply from having destroyed most of the surrounding forest, leaving fewer tree roots to absorb pollutants, regulate flow, and prevent silt from running off into the river—the very same problems plaguing the water supply of São Paulo as a result of so much clearing of the Atlantic Forest.

I notice Isabella standing on the shore on the other side of the dock. She stands there for a while, and then walks away. I ask her about it at lunch, and she says she was going to tell us that a caiman had been spotted along the shore, but when she saw all of us in the water, she decided against yelling "caiman!"

The bigger excitement on Saturday is the giant anaconda wrapped around a tree up the river. We saw it on the way back from the trailhead, and now everyone is taking a boat ride to see it, including the newly arrived couple from Amsterdam. I'm happy I catch it slithering *Harry Potter*–style and get a photo of its head about to enter the water.

On a hike we hear the beautiful song of a musician wren. The sound is like that of a soft piccolo, the second note dropping nearly an octave from the first, followed by several haunting notes in between. The local story about the wren is that two women fell in love with the same man. The man chose the younger of the two and the older woman asked her god to turn her into something the man would never be able to forget.

"I never understood how you could forgive your father," Roberta says to me when we're back in our room, as though the wren story has prompted her to speak about lost love. Roberta knew Michael and me when we lived together in Washington, back when I expected to spend my life with him. She knew how upset I was six weeks earlier after hearing of Michael's death, just a few weeks after I had visited him. By then, the cancer had spread to his brain.

Roberta also knew my father—he liked her very much—and it surprises me that I've never heard this harsh judgment from her until now.

I tell her about my theory that Walter's abandonment made Dad irrationally afraid of further abandonment—by me. Of course, I didn't know about Walter's abandonment when Dad's stroke caused my anger to evaporate, when Dad turned sweet and grateful, and the only feelings I knew toward him were love, admiration, and, yes, occasional frustration and pity.

I feel defensive so I resort to what I do well, making an argument to Roberta based on facts, but what facts can fill this divide of twenty-plus years? She wants a rational explanation for why I forgave my father, and that, truly, I cannot explain.

I step into the outdoor shower surrounded by jungle plants and I wonder. Have I been the wren singing for over two decades ever since the break-up with Michael? Why didn't I get up and leave the dinner table that horrible night? The question still haunts me. Now there is a new question: Was I wrong to forgive my father?

In the middle of the night, I awake with a dry mouth. I drink some water, concerned that I may be dehydrated, and realize I've been dreaming that we were supposed to wear garments to symbolize affection and concern for the rainforest but my garment wasn't right. It didn't cover the area from my waist to my thigh. Part of me is exposed, my most private part. I need to buy something flat and brown, like a giant butterfly wing.

With obvious religious word play, the store where I head is Lord & Taylor, and inside the store are a modern church and a baseball diamond, whose owners proudly say it is the only indoor baseball diamond in the rainforest. My dreaming brain has punned on my father's story: not a search for diamonds in the Amazon, but a baseball diamond.

Outside the building with the church and the baseball field, a man built like Brad falls into a wide, seemingly bottomless pipe extending deep into the ground. I dangle my leg for him to grab while I ask my good friend Alice—my son's godmother—to hold me steady.

Brad climbs out and I walk into a large hardware department in which renovations are underway.

I'm not sure I'll tell Brad that, in my dreamlife, he needs me to save him.

The following morning, a Sunday, Roberta and I walk with Alfredo through the pagans' church, the forest, with Isabella translating Alfredo's Portuguese. He shows us miracles: trees whose roots make a tea that pulverizes kidney stones, another tree that produces a natural sunscreen, discovered just six months ago, plus a leaf that extends a person's life after a snake bite and another leaf that oozes a natural anesthetic.

There are sculptures in the forest, six-inch-high cones made on the forest floor by the Amazon cicadas. The cicadas spend years underground feeding off of tree roots and building the cones for shelter from the inside of the earth up through the ground. Finally the insects emerge and sing for a short life of fifteen days.

"Others sing to live. It sings to die," says Alfredo, and this makes me think of the story I've been pursuing, so many years underground, all through my father's life and much of mine. On this seventeen-day trip the story has been out in the open, released from its shelter inside me, and truth has been singing. I wonder whether the story of Walter Lindberg will be dead to me by the time I return home. Is that the outcome I should be hoping for, replacing an old story with new ones?

I feel like something is changing inside me, like the renovations in my dream, but I don't know what it is.

At lunch, Roberta and I sit with the couple from Amsterdam, one of whom works for Greenpeace. In Amsterdam, she tells us, it is easy to raise money to help protect rainforests. They are nice people, eager to talk, but I don't feel like talking, not even about rainforest preservation. Roberta gets up to grab a beer from the refrigerator and sits back down, preparing for more conversation before siesta time. I don't feel like drinking either. I'm thinking about the sunshine on the dock. I'm thinking about a swim.

I leave the table to change into a bathing suit and carry my damp clothes to the dock. It's so humid my passport and the photo books have curled up like jellyrolls.

Fortunately, no one else is on the dock so I can hang my underwear and shorts over the backs of the chairs as though I own the place. For some reason, getting my clothes dry is really important to me now, and the dock is the sunniest spot around. The sky is bright blue and there isn't a cloud in sight.

I lie down on a wood recliner and glance over to see that my clothes now have appliqués of brown butterflies. I've only been here three days, but a layer of butterflies on my clothing looks entirely normal, as normal as it feels not to wear jewelry or makeup or use any of the skin and hair products I've brought along. It is surprising how fast the adaptation occurs, becoming a little more like a wild creature in wild surroundings. I've worn the same pair of dry pants the last few afternoons and the same T-shirt to several meals.

Our every need is being taken care of at the lodge: food, guides, activities. Our only responsibility is to take care of our bodies, but that is a full-time job with the heat, humidity, insects, and sudden downpours. How much more daunting would life have been in Waldomiro's day, the pioneers living in simple wood houses without electricity, hauling water from the Cambé River, cooking over carefully tended fires?

I decide to swim, feeling comfortable enough to go into the river alone. I climb down the ladder from the dock, and I'm breast-high in the water when I see the head and two eyes on the water's surface about a yard away. I do the backstroke fast. There's no one to ask if it's a caiman or a turtle. I'll practice caution.

There are disadvantages to being alone.

I sure get cooled off later in the day when the sunshine gives way to rain while Roberta and I are kayaking down the river. Today, the weather fooled even Brad, sun turning to rain around 4 PM, with so little notice that Brad let us leave our rain jackets behind when we got into the kayak.

Roberta and I laugh all the way down the river as the rain falls harder and harder because what else is there to do? A person can't fight the jungle and win. Work with it, accept it, and defend against it, but put away the hubris to think it can be overcome.

The rain pellets us for six or seven kilometers. Then it tapers off and the sky begins to brighten. As we approach the lodge we are greeted by a rainbow above the green canopies on either side of us, spanning the two sides of the river. My shoes are on the dock where I left them, covered in butterflies and perfectly dry. The rain was ours alone.

Sunday evening before dinner, I sit with Isabella and two other lodge employees—Maria and Eliana—who, on account of our language barrier, attempt to show me the rules of a Brazilian card game. After dinner, with Isabella's help, I thank Maria for letting me join the card game, and she looks at me as though I have just paid her a high compliment. Alfredo asks if I will come back next year, and a big part of me wishes that I don't have to leave at all.

Before bed, as we pack, I realize I haven't thought about my dog in several days, which, as any dog owner knows, is a long time. I've barely thought about my son. He and I have had no ability to communicate since Londrina. Then it hits me what I've really learned these last few days in the Amazon. Here, I've learned how far away there is.

"There" is New York, my primary home for half a century, and yet after just three days of living next to the Rio Cristalino, it is New York that seems foreign. In New York, bats do not zip past me on the way from the dining room to the bathroom. Macaws do not let out guttural cries to warn of imminent rain. Caiman do not line the riverbanks and giant anaconda do not sun themselves around trees.

It would be difficult for me to live here, next to a river in a rainforest. My desmopressin acetate pills pulverize from moisture when I touch them, and I am drinking whole pitchers of water to try to compensate. Yet with each day, the pull of the place has strengthened, like a snake tightening its hold on its prey a little bit at a time. It occurs to me that Walter may not have rejected Dad and Grandma so much as he became embraced by a wholly new kind of place that would not release him. After discovering the truth about his abandonment, I had assumed that there was some per-ceived defect with Dad and Grandma that sent Walter away, and kept him from returning. Then, after I learned of Walter's nomadism, his departure and failure to return seemed attributable to his character and habit more than anything having to do with Dad and Grandma. After three days in the rainforest, I am beginning to see things differently yet again.

Despite all the physical challenges, I like how I feel here, the strange-ness, how the challenges and novelties make me live from moment to moment, not in the past, not in the future. I have traveled often but never have I become so fully absorbed in another place, and if this is happening to me after such a short time, with all the love that I feel for my son (and dog), in living conditions much more comfortable than the Atlantic Forest was eighty years ago, how much more would this suction have been felt by Walter? I have learned that he was a man weak at forming attachments to people. If my strong bond to my son feels like it's barely enough to free me from the hold of the snake, how can I expect Walter to have broken free and returned to my father?

I am sad to be packing and leaving, but with the fold of a shirt I realize that I no longer begrudge Walter for choosing to stay on in the frontier of Brazil rather than return to New York. I feel like I can finally see things his way.

I realize that my anger at Walter Lindberg is gone. I say good-night to Roberta and sleep very well.

The next morning, the whole forest appears to be burning. White smoke covers the trees, but it's not smoke. It is mist, thick mist revealing only the tops of the darkest, most densely packed trees, which look like enor-mous heads of broccoli, their stalks wrapped in white.

Birds start to call and the mist seems alive, moving and changing shape before our eyes, gradually floating to the west, the work of count-less ghosts flying off to their day beds as the sun's rays clip their back-sides. Eventually, the pretend smoke vanishes and the forest comes fully into view. There was no fire, at least not today.

There was no visible sunrise, either, due to clouds, but that's okay with Roberta and me. We have only a few hours left in the Amazon. We arose early and climbed another tower with Brad and Isabella to watch the day begin from above the forest. No matter how the place presents itself this morning, we are grateful.

Some of the morning's birds are familiar, the blue dacnis, the olive tanager, but the best sighting comes only moments before we prepare to descend the tower. Brad hears the call and then catches the bird in the scope. It is a goshawk, a bird Brad has been waiting eight years to see, one of only four birds he hasn't seen since beginning his love affair with Brazil.

Sometimes that's how a quest ends, without notice or fanfare, as simple as a bird flying through the sky and you hear it and then see it because you were standing in the right place at the right time with a mind open to possibility.

As the boat pulls away from the dock, I feel this way about all the people at the lodge—Isabella, Alfredo, Alesandro, Eliana. Our time together was brief, in human terms no longer than a bird's flight from one perch to another, but I will never forget this place deep in the forest where my anger at Walter Lindberg took wing.

chapter thirty-nine

AND THEN WE GO ON

OTTO ULRICH JOURNEYED through territory in Mato Grosso that was, as he put it, "partly swampy and partly jungle." We are doing the same, though approaching the swamp from a different direction.

The largest freshwater wetland in the world, the Pantanal expands in size the night we arrive, in a torrential downpour. Roberta and I are traveling south on the unpaved Transpantaneira Highway splattered with water and lined with ridges that shift location every few meters. Seeking the smoothest terrain, our driver veers back and forth across the road, spending much time on the wrong side.

The rain is so loud outside our room that I use earplugs to sleep. When I remove the plugs in the morning, liquid pours out of my left ear. I don't dwell on what this might mean. There's a sunrise happening and I've got to get outside with my camera. The capybaras nestled with their young are just waking up. The sky is a flag with stripes of neon both pink and orange, a jamboree background for the huge wood stork standing on the branch of a dead tree with nothing else around but soggy ground glistening in the early light.

The birds are big here and easy to see because of the open landscape. We promised Brad we would stay loyal to the birds of the Amazon, but it is impossible not to be seduced by the large, strange creatures in the Pantanal, the roseate spoonbill whose beak could scoop ice cream, the rufescent tiger heron with a white zig-zag stripe like lightening down its brown chest, the jabiru with its long white neck, red midriff, and black bottom, pure elegance as it struts and spreads its wings to take off. The Wright brothers might have gotten a jump on flying from watching this bird.

When Ulrich made his way through the Pantanal on his way to find riches, did he stop to admire the birds and take in the beauty of the landscape? Before I left New York, I found a 1938 article about the rituals of various Brazilian indigenous tribes and the natural intoxicants and stimulants they used. The author was none other than Otto Ulrich. I should not forget that he was a writer as well as a gold-seeker, with his rare Guarani dictionary that sank to the bottom of the ocean along with his maps, so maybe he did notice a bird or two when he was here.

Ulrich was hardly alone seeking a better life in Brazil in the late 1920s and 1930s. People from dozens of countries sought the same. Many stayed, helping to make Brazil what it is today, a place of multiple ethnic traditions and the seventh-largest economy in the world.

Our guide, Aynore Soares—lean, tawny, with cropped black hair on his scalp and face—has ancestors spanning the globe, from Spain, the Netherlands, Portugal, and the Middle East.

During our morning walk, he tells me he has been shot at three times, twice while working on a covert mission involving diamond and gun smuggling for Brazilian intelligence and once as a bodyguard for a wealthy man under threat of assassination. This comes up when Aynore stretches his left arm and massages his shoulder and I ask him what's wrong. The shoulder is where Aynore says the bullet passed through— better than hitting his client, whom he had shoved out of the way.

When Aynore announces the presence of tapir tracks in the palm grove and draws his knife, I anticipate human-to-tapir combat.

Instead, he takes a few steps and cuts a stray palm frond that is blocking the trail. I tell him my incorrect supposition and we laugh at my ignorance. Soon we come upon a band of marmosets in the trees. My neck is sore when I look up, and I know it's not a bullet wound. I wonder if I have a case of warbler neck from looking at birds, or if my soreness could be caused by the bumps that have developed at the base of my scalp, which I assume to be a collection of insect bites aggravated by camera and binocular straps.

We exit the palm grove into the hot sunshine. I feel glad for Aynore's strength. Around him, I wouldn't dream of complaining, so I don't ask him to walk more slowly because I'm feeling faint. I keep up.

After the first weekend trip I took with Michael and his friends, his best friend from college pronounced me "a trooper." I had slipped down a hill and made light of it while limping in the dark. The moniker was meant as a high compliment, but it felt familiar. Before Michael, I had taken many a road trip with my college boyfriend and his friends from home, a fun-loving group, to put it mildly. The time I requested a bathroom stop on the way back from New Orleans, it meant a pull-over on the highway with a jokester tossing me a roll of toilet paper. I laughed, too.

I was raised to have a certain go-along, no-complaining attitude, which morphed into adult behavior that made it easy to act like one of the guys, even as I considered myself a feminist. I had learned early that I could be a better companion to my father, and be taken to more fun places by him, if I was strong like he was and never whined, a little soldier in pigtails. I could allow my mother the quiet time she wanted for her household tasks if I kept myself busy, asking little more of her than to drive me places to get sewing supplies, take music lessons, or see a friend. I sensed her anxiety early and readily accepted responsibility for rectifying it, such as the time she drove us to Kennedy Airport to pick up my father from a business trip and I asked to use the restroom. She put a quarter into one of the meters the doors had back then, but the stall turned out to be a changing room with no toilet. Mother grew visibly upset. She had to use another dime to get me access to a toilet, and for months after that when I had an extra quarter from earnings or allowance, I would stick the quarter into the change purse in her pocketbook as if it were my penance.

It took me years to realize that Mother's anxiety had nothing to do with the expenditure of thirty-five cents and everything to do with the experience of driving in the dark to an airport on her own, and worrying that we would be late to meet my father. The responsibility I felt for her mental and emotional state matured so that as a high school student, I understood that I could be relied upon to help lift my mother out of depression only if I was stable and self-sufficient myself. Lest I have any doubts about what was expected, Dad spoke explicitly to me about it. I was fifteen, home from school for a visit. Dad pulled the car into the garage and happened to mention before I ran inside to hug our dog that I ought to pay attention to remaining sane. Little did he or I know how I would violate that request years later after the tumor came out. I never knew if he remembered our conversation in the car, because, of course, we never spoke about it again.

My body had tested the limits of its presumed self-sufficiency long before my cells aberrantly made a tumor. Toward the end of second grade, my skin started to peel off, mainly on my hands, but also in other places. The illness came on suddenly, first a headache outside on the patio and the next thing I knew I was confined to my bed on the second floor of the house, unable to move my left leg at all. I would awake each morning with eyes glued shut from excretions during the night, and I would hop down the hall on the good leg to the bathroom and splash water on my face to rinse the dried pus from my eyelashes. Eyes open, I hopped back to bed and waited for my mother to bring breakfast on a tray. This continued for a month.

I don't recall taking any medicine, though perhaps there were pills or liquids dispensed that I have since forgotten about. I do recall the black-and-white television placed in front of my bed so that I could watch Rangers games to take my mind off the pain and unpleasantness, the Rangers being one of the teams my father and I liked.

During the day, the pediatrician would sometimes stand next to my mother on the other side of the room, over by the closet, and the two of them would whisper. The doctor wanted to bring me to a hospital. My mother refused. As Mother later told me, if her daughter was going to die, she preferred for that to happen at home.

I didn't die. Apparently, there was more than a little of my grand-mother and father in me and I did not succumb to whatever virus or bacteria had infiltrated my system, just as they had survived the influ-enza outbreak when so many others died.

I did, however, grow up to be a mother, and that's when I realized that rioters could have claimed the streets, I could have been fired from my job, and we could have been down to eating food brought by Meals on Wheels before I would have let my seven-year-old child hop down a hallway on one leg with his eyes glued shut to splash water on his own face. I would have stood outside his room listening for sounds of his stirring. I would have placed a chair outside his door and read the news-paper, waiting for some noise. At the very least, I would have given him a bell and insisted he use it, bringing a basin full of water when he did.

That was me for my son. For myself, there was still enough of the girl inside who had hopped blind on one leg for a month that when I felt dizzy walking five kilometers in the sun in Brazil next to Aynore, I just kept putting one foot in front of the other and tried to make him laugh. At least both of my legs worked.

Aynore and I have one thing in common: photography. Aynore takes even more shots than I do, unusual for a guide. This morning he is particularly pleased with one of his photos of a rufous-tailed jacamar standing on a twig. He thinks he might be able to sell it to a magazine.

He looks at another of his shots and shakes his head. "My father says that photographers are frustrated people," he says.

"Your father is not a photographer?" I ask.

"Oh, yes, he is a photographer." We share another laugh.

Aynore says that the word for "taking" a picture in Portuguese means "remove," and this makes me think again of the women who threw papayas at me in Barbados.

The act is so reflexive, seeing something beautiful or unusual and bringing the camera to the eye, a tic. Am I a frustrated person, like Aynore's father? Perhaps both exploration and photography draw the restless, people who want more.

Aynore is the type of person who belongs in a region like the Juruena with "no law," not me. In fact, Aynore has camped out along the Juruena River with his father, an expedition guide, and his younger brother. It was "very wild," and they heard jaguars in the distance, but Aynore wasn't afraid.

"We knew what we were doing," he says.

I nod, knowing how much that would not have been true for me.

Roosevelt did me a favor before my trip, asserting in *Through the Brazilian Wilderness* that there are two types of people, those who are good at exploring and those who are good at writing about exploring. Of course, Roosevelt hoped he was the rare person who could be both—the "true wilderness wanderer . . . a man of action as well as of observation"—but walking as a follower in the hot sun of the Pantanal, I readily accept that I don't have Aynore's fearlessness and survival skills.

I may be a trooper, and compared to Michael I may have been a risk-taker, but I'm no daredevil. I only tried that once.

Senior spring of high school, shortly before graduation, my best friend and I got into the back seat of a black two-door Falcon after visiting friends at a boys' school about twenty miles from our own. We had stayed too long talking, laughing, and listening to the Allman Brothers. The evening dorm check at our school would be taking place within the hour.

No one we knew was headed east, so we stuck out our thumbs. The first ride took us part way, dropping us off at a quiet intersection, where the Falcon swerved around the corner and stopped in front of us. The tall young man in the passenger seat got out, pushed his seat forward and motioned for us to get in. We were late. There seemed to be no other option.

As I slid to the far side of the back seat my shin bumped against something hard. It was a case of beer. The driver and his passenger asked me to pass them each a bottle. I did as told.

When we reached the rotary and drove half way around, the Falcon did not take the exit for Route 2 east toward our school. The driver continued around the rotary and headed west in the direction from which we had just come.

"What are you doing?" I asked.

"You'll find out," the passenger replied.

Impulsively, I hurled myself toward the space between the front bucket seats, as though I could perform a James Bond feat and wrest the steering wheel from the driver's hands without getting us all killed. The passenger pushed me back and made a fist with his hand. I could smell the beer on his fingers.

"Try that again and I'll bash your face in," he seethed.

I retreated to my corner of the back seat.

"Where are we going?" asked my friend, filling the silence with her soothing voice.

"To a lake," replied the driver. "We were there last weekend. The rocks cut us. We're going to show them."

My friend proceeded to tell the men that we liked nature, too. We had spent the previous weekend with my friend's older sister in Maine. My friend told the driver and passenger about how beautiful it was up there, how we climbed a mountain, sat on top, and watched birds fly.

She kept on talking as the driver turned north on Interstate 495, no trace of fear in her voice. I stayed quiet, wondering what would happen if I smashed a beer bottle on one of the heads in front of me.

The car took an exit off the highway. There were no streetlights. It was a long, straight road and I assumed the lake waited at the end. Suddenly the glare of a gas station appeared on the left and the driver flipped on the car's overhead light to check the fuel gauge, there being no dashboard lights. He told the passenger they needed gas and turned into the station, a low-budget operation, with only a few pumps and a glass structure with no door, not much bigger than a telephone booth.

I kicked my friend several times, knowing this was our chance but having no idea how to take advantage of it. My friend said she needed to go to the bathroom. The passenger said he did, too. He got out and we pushed his seat forward and scampered out the door. It felt amazing to stand but there was no time to rejoice. The passenger walked to the far end of the dark pavement and I hurried to the driver of the only other car in the station. I told her we had been kidnapped and asked her to take us to safety and she replied that she did not want to get involved. She drove away. Then I went to the teenage attendant, now the only other person at the station, and asked for a dime. There was a pay phone inside the glass structure. As I heard a man say "police," the hand of the passenger grabbed the receiver and hung it up.

There was a stalemate, the passenger and I standing behind the car, my friend standing outside the driver's door, speaking through the rolled down window to the driver, who had remained in the car.

"Come on," the driver said finally to his friend. "Get in. They don't want to play anymore."

The passenger obliged. As the car drove away, I wrote down the license plate number with a pen I'd grabbed inside the glass structure. I still have the pen.

We called the police, who came and got us. We telephoned an official at our school, who agreed to drive up and meet us at the police station. When we walked in, the two men were already there, seated against a wall. They had been apprehended because of the car description and plate number. They glared at us as we walked by.

The officer who spoke to my friend and me in the little room at the end of the hallway told us there were no charges to press. The officer said what did we expect, a couple of girls hitchhiking at night, and did we have any idea how many dead female bodies they found along Route 2 on the way to Cambridge.

We really didn't.

My friend called her parents from a phone on the wall. I heard her say, "No, you don't have to. It's late. I'll call you tomorrow. Don't worry. We're fine now." Her parents had asked if they should fly up from Philadelphia at once.

I reached my father on Long Island, awakening him. I told him what had happened. He asked a few questions, which I answered.

"I hope you learned your lesson," he said, and then hung up the phone.

It wasn't clear to me which lesson he meant.

My friend became a therapist. I went on to practice law. That's how I know that it is a federal crime to take people across state lines against their will. We could have pressed charges had we wanted to, had we not wanted to get the hell out of Merrimack, New Hampshire, graduate with our classmates, and go to college in the fall as if nothing had ever happened.

I never stopped marveling at my friend's good instincts that night, and in the Pantanal, when the gruff taker of bullets Aynore Soares laughs at something I say, I know I am putting into practice the lesson my friend taught me—how to use communication to cut through differences and make oneself seem real. It can even save your life.

There's a small swimming pool at the Araras Eco Lodge and it feels great to get cooled off. I am hoping the chlorine in the water will help the bumps on my neck, which seem to have grown.

The temperature is comfortable under the thatched roof where I sit with Roberta during siesta time writing and reviewing the morning's photographs. It's especially nice when a breeze blows through. An owl calls *hoo-hoo* from high up in the mango tree, a hummingbird explores a nearby vine, and male birds advertise their availability for mating despite the heat. Like us they seek protection from the sun, calling for females from the leafiest trees.

Of all the sounds in this part of Brazil, the one I like best comes from a bird whose species name I don't even know. The call resembles two notes blown from a wooden flute, always the same two notes in pitch and length, cycling between several measures of rest. The flute is an instrument I never learned to play, and therefore I am all audience for its sound. I feel no desire to compare or compete, no urge to question how the sound might otherwise be.

This is probably a good attitude for a newcomer in Brazil.

The end of the rainy season is a slow time in the Pantanal just as it was at the Cristalino. Roberta and I have the hotel to ourselves except for one other guest, who keeps to himself.

There is a big map on the outside wall of the lodge where I like to linger, recalling the times I inspected a map of Brazil on my kitchen table, wondering if I would ever set foot on Brazilian soil. About sixty miles northwest of the lodge is Cáceres on the Paraguay River. Back when the town was called São Luís de Cáceres, it was the last civilized outpost that Roosevelt, Fawcett, and Ulrich passed through. Roosevelt described it as being "on the outermost fringe of the settled region of the state of Mato Grosso, the last town we should see before reaching the villages of the Amazon."

But Roosevelt's party spent time even closer to our location. Before reaching Cáceres, the group took a detour off the Paraguay River to ascend the Rio Cuiabá and the Rio São Laurencio, on the banks of which the men stayed at "the great São João *fazenda*, the ranch of Senhor João da Costa Marques." American and Brazilian flags were hoisted and "the band played the national anthems of the two countries."

From Roosevelt's perspective, the purpose of the detour was to hunt, see the birds of the Pantanal, and gather specimens for natural history collections, all of which amounted to wasted time as far as Rondon was concerned. Rondon felt disconcerted about being taken away from his telegraph and nation-building activities and assigned to guide Roosevelt, which diverted him for eight months from work he regarded as vastly more important.*

As best as I can determine, the ranch where Roosevelt stayed was as close as thirty miles from our lodge, and who knows how much closer he came on horseback. We are seeing the same features, a "whole country [of] marsh, varied by stretches of higher ground; and, although these stretches [rise] only three or four feet above the marsh, they [are] covered with thick jungle, largely palmetto scrub, or else with open palm forest."

Almost one hundred years since Roosevelt's visit, the idea of shooting a jaguar or tapir, as he did, is repugnant. It would also be exceedingly difficult. So few jaguar remain, it would be astonishing even to hear, much less see, one.

But a great deal of what Roosevelt described about the Pantanal still applies:

---

* See Diacon, Todd A. *Stringing Together a Nation, Candido Mariano Da Silva Rondon and the Construction of a Modern Brazil, 1906-1930.* Durham, North Carolina: Duke University Press, 2004.

The birds were tame, even those striking and beautiful birds which under man's persecution are so apt to become scarce and shy. The huge jabiru storks, stalking through the water with stately dignity, sometimes refused to fly until we were only a hundred yards off; one of them flew over our heads at a distance of thirty or forty yards. The screamers, crying curu-curu, and the ibises, wailing dolefully, came even closer. The wonderful hyacinth macaws, in twos and threes, accompanied us at times for several hundred yards, hovering over our heads and uttering their rasping screams. In one wood we came on the black howler monkey. The place smelt almost like a menagerie.

Some fault Roosevelt for not seeing the conflict between his admiration for wildlife and calls for conservation on the one hand, and his shooting of game on the other. He made a distinction between "the mere big-game butcher" and "the big-game hunter who is a good observer, a good field naturalist [who] can do work which the closest naturalist cannot do." Roosevelt put himself in the latter category, stating at one point, "I shot a capybara representing a color-phase the naturalists wished," and describing in detail the evolutionary history and habits of other animals he killed. For the animals that were his prey, the end result was the same whether the animals were killed for science or sport. For countless other creatures, and for humans—who depend on well-functioning natural systems whether or not they spend time outdoors—Roosevelt brought better outcomes, instigating passage of the Wilderness Act, supporting stewardship of federal parks, campaigning against the killing of birds for hat feathers, setting aside many thousands of acres of federal land—in short, doing more than any other US president to advance protection of natural lands and species diversity.

Like Otto Ulrich and Walter Lindberg, Roosevelt was not one-dimensional. By today's standards, we may judge him as full of contradictions. Even though he foresaw some of the species extinctions that have occurred since his death, his was a wildlife world of plenty compared to ours. It didn't seem strange to him to come to Brazil and kill big game for the pleasure he got from it or for the value of hanging specimens in a museum in New York City, just as it didn't seem wrong to men like Ulrich and Walter to come to Brazil and plunder its gold.

On my twelfth day in Brazil, I find myself less quick to judge these men. They were products of different times, when both the finite character of many natural resources and the interrelationship of life on the planet were less well understood.

On my twelfth day in Brazil, I find myself less quick to judge these
Aynore and I mount our horses in the late afternoon, when the blue and yellow macaws fly to their nesting box in the mandeve tree, the swamp turns from green to amber, and the jabirus and tiger herons leave the shade. Roberta is not interested in riding. The way I felt on today's long morning walk to a ranch and back, I didn't think I would be either, but a swim and some rest have given me new energy.

"Attention to caiman and wasps," Aynore says as we pause outside the old barn while my horse, Chicara, flings her tail and shakes her head in ceaseless battle against mosquitoes.

Aynore's job is to protect me, and I trust him. Of course I will follow his instruction to give the caiman with their shark-like teeth a wide berth as we ride by. So far I've only seen caiman inert in the Pantanal, sunning themselves near the edges of ponds or lying on mud flats with watercress-like weeds on their backs—but I know they can move fast.

As for wasp stings that might cause Chicara to shy or buck, all I can do is try to stay in the saddle even though I'm not wearing leather chaps like Aynore, who looks like a classic *panteneiro* cowboy this afternoon. I take the opportunity to press my thighs and knees into the Pantanal saddle, remarkably comfortable for me, if not Chicara. These horses are a special breed, accustomed to hard work, the peculiarities of the Pantanal, and the rigorous requirements of *panteneiros* who spend whole days in the saddle.

We set off toward the gate, a plume of Deet trailing behind me, my umbrage at the chemical having been surrendered to reality. "Long pants, closed shoes, insect repellant" are Aynore's usual instructions, and he doesn't mean the all-natural product I bought at a health-food store back home, which now sits on a shelf inside the lodge. I like a polka-dot pattern, but not on the backs of my hands.

We haven't even gotten through the gate when Aynore's horse refuses and gives a few small bucks. He doesn't like Aynore getting close to the post to remove the chain. Aynore sinks his spurs into the horse's sides. The gate opens and Chicara and I pass through, giving Aynore's horse almost as much room as I intend to give the caiman.

Six or seven large cattle make way for us to pass, we negotiate a second gate, and after a turn we come into the vastness of the Pantanal, a vastness one cannot see from the road. The light is golden. There is no man-made element in sight, no noise except the birds and cicadas, and the occasional suction of Chicara's hooves lifting out of the mud as my hips roll front to back.

This is the way to see the Pantanal, I say to Aynore, who resists conversation. As he's told me previously, attributing the quote to his father, "This is not fru-fru. We find the animals. We tell you the toucan eats eggs, fruit, and baby birds, and then we go on."

I'm seeing his point as mud turns to water, and I realize that we are not going to be walking around bodies of water; we will be walking through a very large body of water, the swamp itself. This becomes apparent when Aynore's horse halts and jumps back, creating a splash in Chicara's face. In the Pantanal, the horses spot the caimans before the humans do, and that is what has just happened. There is a caiman swimming across the water in front of us. We stop and wait for it to disappear into the reeds on our right.

This is definitely not a fru-fru experience. I've ridden horses all my life, eastern and western, on trails, over jumps, and through ponds and streams, but I've never been on top of a horse that was working so hard, each step a struggle to extract a hoof from the swampy bottom with no ability to see what's on the ground below four feet of dirty water. The water gets deeper, up to the stirrups, and then my feet go under, which is fine. I won't need these old shoes in Rio.

We come, finally, to dry land, where monkeys are playing in a tree and we hear an agouti. The sun's rays are low. It doesn't seem as though Aynore intends to go back the way we came. I see the barn in the distance and relax, which is premature on my part. Aynore's horse, ever vigilant, bolts when it sees a caiman lying on the ground across the trail just outside the gate to the barn.

Aynore tells me to stay close to the fence, and I do exactly what he says.

When I get off Chicara, I feel elated. Riding, for me, has always been about conquering fear, and after this ride, I've earned the good feeling that comes with a successful reach to the other side of anxiety. At dinner, we are finally joined by Brazilians on their way to see wildlife. There's a spot by a river where the chances of seeing a jaguar are said to be better than anywhere else, and the two women will be heading there the next day.

Roberta and I are leaving for Rio in the morning, but I don't feel envy for the Brazilian women. We have seen so very much natural beauty, and even though we haven't shot any game, we have taken a lot in our own way, not just photographs. Brad told us that animals in the wild know humans are adept at finding things, such as good spots to rest, nests, and water, so they follow our tracks to find the same things, sometimes at the cost of animal life. Even a walk in the woods has its consequences. It's hard to be human and not take in some way. Enough, is how I feel this evening, time to get back to a city, where the taking is more limited to our own species.

Besides, I am not sure I could endure another day of walking with Aynore in the sun or paddling a canoe or looking out for caiman. The neck bumps and ear discharge are getting worse. I am thirsty all the time, and hot. I've begun to take the antibiotics I brought with me, though I am not letting on that I'm a bit worried about what's ailing me. I don't want to ruin Roberta's trip with a health issue. Carrying a pitcher of water to our room in the dark after dinner, I don't even flinch at the snake that glides across my path.

chapter forty

RIO

ROBERTA AND I say nothing in the back of the taxi to Lapa, but we are thinking the same thoughts. Will I be hospitalized? Will we have to change our plane reservations? Will I recover?

I had been looking forward to texting my son from Playa Ipanema, but when the time finally came and I could smell the sea, there was no joy to communicate, no inside joke to share. The white beach, blue water, and green island hills looked like someone else's pretty picture. My body was there, walking on a sidewalk along the sand with Roberta, yet the scene seemed as remote as a distant landscape viewed through the window of a speeding train. Away from the coast for over two weeks, I should have longed to take my shoes off, feel the warm sand and the cool sea on my feet, but such pleasures only belonged to others.

I was so far from being the girl from Ipanema that it was ludicrous even to think of the song my son had learned so well. I was the sick person in Ipanema, the boils on my neck having turned to welts, pus draining continuously from my left ear, dizziness, fatigue, muscle aches, no appetite, and head throbbing so badly that I could hardly feel the sun's rays.

Denial was my real companion, not Roberta, but when Roberta said she was hungry I went along. Sitting down seemed like a good idea. As we waited for lunch at an outdoor table a few blocks from the beach, my hand went once again to the back of my head where I felt a new lump much larger than the others. I hadn't wanted to disturb the trip, hadn't wanted to confront that the boils might be more than a bad reaction to mosquito bites or nylon straps. I hoped that swallowing antibiotics for a day would make my symptoms go away but clearly that hadn't happened. Finally, I said something to my friend and she said, "You've got to see a doctor."

She was right, of course. So, after a phone call to our hotel for advice, we hailed a taxi and asked the driver to take us to the Hospital Espanhol. Time is a snail, and so is the car, stuck in Rio's Friday afternoon traffic.

I feel badly because Rio was supposed to be Roberta's part of the trip. I feel worse thinking of my son's worries. I dismissed his superstitious warning that the same fate that befell my father could happen to him— losing a parent in Brazil. Now I can't help but let in this possibility. What if I have a tropical disease that keeps me from returning home, perhaps even kills me? I am the same age as Percy Fawcett when he disappeared. Must I fail, too?

It's too depressing inside the hospital waiting room, so Roberta waits outside on the sidewalk, not far from the tall guard wearing a dark suit, the best-dressed person around. I see Roberta's backside every time the door opens and someone walks in or out.

It's taking so long just to tell someone my symptoms that I call the hotel again and the manager gives me the name and number of a doctor the hotel uses in emergencies. I call the doctor and she's willing to meet me at a different hospital, but then finally the double doors open and a man approaches me, introducing himself in English.

Roberta joins us and we walk through the doors to the patient area. I tell the doctor about the ooze from my ear that started the day after we left the Amazon.

"Were you swimming?"

"Yes. I have these, too." I pull up my hair and show him the boils.

"Ahh. Does it hurt very badly?"

"Terribly. My whole head. Do you know what it is?"

"Yes. I've seen it before."

"Can you cure it?"

"Yes," he says, a little slowly for my New York ears. "It can be cured."

Tears flood my eyes. Roberta lets out a sigh.

Before I am given the cure, I have to pay, which I gladly do. My insurance card is worthless, but a visit to the emergency room in Rio costs only 400 reals, about $200.

The doctor is quite sure that parasites entered the ear during one of my wonderful swims in the Rio Cristalino and that they have left me with an infection. I have probably had a fever, which accounts for the fatigue, light-headedness, and extreme thirst that began in the Amazon. The doctor doesn't know the type of parasite, but he leaves me with the definite impression that the infection and boils are related, the parasites inside my head somehow causing the growths on my skin.

Continue with the antibiotics, the doctor says, as he writes prescriptions for three more medicines. He hands me his card and I see that his name is Vinicius, the same name as the poet who wrote the lyrics to "The Girl from Ipanema."

Dr. Andre Vinicius Novaes takes care to describe how often I should use each medicine and even gives me his cellphone number, which I use an hour later because one of the drugs isn't available at four *drogarias*. We go back to the hospital and get a prescription for a substitute. Finally, as the sun is setting, we have the drugs and a taxi to take us back to the hotel. I put one of the prescribed painkillers under my tongue.

By the time the car climbs the hill to the Santa Teresa section of Rio, the baseball bat has stopped hitting my head.

At the hotel, I fall into a deep sleep and dream of being shuttled from one place to another, needing to be hidden at times, it being unclear from whom I must hide. People put me on a trailer that's like a stretcher. I sink blissfully into the embrace of a man who wraps his arms around me from underneath.

It's impossible to say who he is. His face is indistinct. He could be any or all of the dead men with me on this trip—Walter, my father, Michael—or love itself, pulling me into the warm earth.

※

The next morning I wake up early, before Roberta. I am so relieved, and full of gratitude to the hotel and Dr. Vinicius for helping me. My head and body still ache—not as badly as the day before, but badly enough that I take another of the strong Brazilian painkillers and curl up on the sofa in our anteroom, closing the door so my good friend can keep sleeping.

I feel humbled by my body's fragility, the invisible ease with which the Amazon got to me, even as I reveled in its lushness.

I find that I am uninterested in Walter Lindberg.

The morning before, I had been a different person: While Roberta visited an art museum in downtown Rio, I searched fruitlessly for Walter and Otto Ulrich in the database and archives of the Bibloteca Nacional, my dizziness so bad that my eyes could hardly focus on the records. The Bibloteca Nacional is where Percy Fawcett found the Portuguese explorer's diary that first gave him the idea of a lost city of gold in the jungle. If I thought I would find anything remotely similar, I was guilty of fantasy. Walter Lindberg and Otto Ulrich were not great *exploradores* worthy of mention in Brazil's history of itself. Not even the name of Lord Lovat—chief investor in the Northern Paraná Land Company—could be found in the library's records.

After the library, while Roberta visited a modern art museum, I wandered through the Museu Historico Nacional and along the port, looking at the small fishing boats and the old ferry terminal, imagining Walter Lindberg's Rio.

Not today. The trip to the emergency room left me changed utterly. Like Emmy Kern so many years ago, I am no longer interested in facts about Walter Lindberg. Today, elated to know I have a future, I choose the living over the dead. I want to experience Rio with my friend, who has loyally given me over two weeks of her time.

"Are you sure?" Roberta asks when I announce that I don't want to go to Botafogo to look through the archives of the Museu do Indio for old photos of Rondon's expeditions.

I am certain.

On the way out of Mama Ruisa, a lovely small hotel converted from a mansion, we meet the owner, Jean Michel Ruis, a Frenchman who came to Brazil six years ago.

"Why did you stay?" I ask.

"I still don't know."

The answer sounds so familiar.

Our first stop is the huge flea market held every Saturday beside the port. Roberta likes flea markets and that means today I like them, too. It's amazing what people think to sell, crumpled Volkswagen car catalogs, coasters from the wedding of Prince Charles and Princess Di. I follow Roberta from stall to stall, buy a CD of Tom Jobin's songs for Justin, and snap pictures of the old tower from the 1500s that used to mark the boundary of Rio, reflected in the mirrored exterior of a modern office building. The shot's layers of then and now are a testament to Brazil's transformation.

We walk through an arch into a section of old Rio that's been preserved, full of clubs and restaurants cleaning up from the night before, getting ready for a new day. School children walk through. Look up, their teacher says, see the stucco bell towers, the walls of porcelain tile, the old bells hanging across the alleys. Look back in time, but keep moving.

It's a beautiful day, no day to be indoors, and we take advantage of one of life's rare chances for a do-over. We arrive by subway, and because it is Saturday, Ipanema Beach has been transformed from the serene place it was the day before to a celebratory one, packed with women of all sizes in bikinis and men laughing and holding children. The air smells of suntan lotion and I can't wait to put my toes in the ocean, but first I ask Roberta to take a photo with my cellphone.

I wave with my right hand as she snaps the shutter and then I text the photo to Justin with a note: "Today I am the girl from Ipanema." I know it's corny, but sometimes so is love.

In the evening, we eat a traditional Brasilian cod dinner at a small restaurant. We talk about Roberta's mother and how Roberta's grieving is going. She gives me a guarded answer—she won't really know until after she gets home. We laugh about her sisters making me promise I'd take good care of Roberta on our trip. I did that well, didn't I, intercepting the parasites in the river before they got to her? Somehow, she knew not to put her head in the water, but such restraint never occurred to me. A lifetime of desire went into that river. The head followed the heart.

Who knows what would have happened, Roberta says, had Walter never left New York. It's an aspect of the story that, like so many others, we can never know, and yet I feel as though I have answered all the questions I wanted to, including the one she posed during our first dinner in Brazil: What had I hoped to find out?

Only two weeks earlier, I believed that knowing why Walter left my father and grandmother could only come in the form of someone presenting the information to me, such as a person who had known Walter in Brazil. I assumed that the answer could only take the form of a factoid out there in the world, waiting to be found. Instead, the answer was something only I could supply from within myself. I had to inch my way toward it, feeling it, drawing inferences from all the available information, including so many people who remembered nothing at all about the object of my search.

The question may be complex, but the answer is simple. Walter Lindberg left because he couldn't stay, and he would never go back to New York because he had found a paradise that enveloped him.

I believe John McNaughton's theory that Walter meant to say good-bye amicably when he staged his death and had word of that sent up to Grandma, and he went on to live a life that felt more right to him than being the head of a household in New York City.

His flight, Roberta points out, may actually have served my father's best interests, for had Walter stayed, he wasn't ever going to turn into the admirable father figure in real life my father yearned for, a figure whom, missed out on twice, Dad invented. A loving, absent stepfather killed by cannibals or betrayed by partners was probably better than a deadbeat one cheating on your mother or moving out and disappearing in New York. She's a good lawyer, my friend. Maybe I should give Grandma a little more credit, too. Maybe Grandma knew what her son could take and what he could not.

Rio Scenarium is three floors of excellence in human bonding, energy, and self-expression. Bands play samba and bossa nova on the ground floor, men and womendancing all around them, boxed in by spectators and people eyeing the vast room for an empty table or chair. Another band plays in the back room on the second floor. Tonight it's mandolin, guitar, and drums. Everyone comes to this former warehouse and antiques store in Lapa to listen to music and dance, the young and the middle-aged, the black and the white, tourists and Brazilians.

Upstairs, Roberta and I stand behind a circle of five young women who are dancing the samba. The circle grows larger as more women join until there are at least ten. Each woman takes a turn in the middle of the circle except for one, who declines when her friend tries to pull her in.

Some of the women wear skirts and others wear pants. Some are short and some are tall. One's arms go up, one's arms reach out. One swings her hips wide, another merely sways. But for all the differences among these women, their feet agree. Their feet are in perpetual motion, whether in high heels or flats. They are tap-tapping on the balls of their feet, back-front-together, back-front-together. I think of Bruno telling us that Brazilians use over four thousand words for Americans' 1,500, and this seems true of dance steps, as well. The ratio may be even higher, five movements for every one of ours.

I think also of Brad, speaking about Brazilian diversity and his life as an expat on our last morning in the Amazon. For all the different ethnic traditions in Brazil, Brad observed, you'll find rice and beans on nearly every table every day at lunch and dinner. There's nothing comparable in Canada. In the United States, Thanksgiving turkey may be the closest we come.

In Rio Scenarium, the samba step seems like rice and beans. For all the thousands of variations of being human from the ankles up, the feet here agree on a national step. There appears to be a basic agreement to be Brazilian, on the dance floor, at the dining table. I'm no history scholar, but it seems that Brazil's brand of assimilation was not to request that people leave their identities and traditions at the border. You can stay different, Brazil seems to have said, just give us your feet and a section of your plate.

Tonight, I give Brazil my feet. I stand in the crowded room, glad it is so dark no one can see me try to imitate the young women. I am tired. My head hurts and my throat aches. I feel as if I might faint, but I can't help but try the national step.

My father was a good dancer, a little flat-footed with his size 13 feet, but smooth in his movements and attentive to his partner. How my father learned to dance is a fact I'll never know, and tonight I'm okay with that.

Who knows, maybe I have inherited the ability to dance the samba through some sort of DNA modification effected by the story. When I take replacement hormones, they work because receptors inside my body bind to the drugs' properties. Why shouldn't a story do the same thing, prime our brains and bodies to bind with the real thing when it comes our way?

My feet are moving better now. It's starting to feel right. Push back and tap, push front and tap, stay light and quick, add hips. Yes, I'm with the rhythm now. It's so fun, I wish Roberta would try, but she refuses. She tells me she has no confidence in her dancing, and this revelation is in itself something. The music at Rio Scenarium may not move my friend to dance, but it has made her admit to a feeling that helps me understand her better.

Me, I feel like I have always known this step, and maybe I have.

chapter forty-one

ON A SILVER TRAY

"HOW IS BRAZIL?" is the question in a friend's e-mail the next morning.

Brazil is like no place I've ever been. One of the hotel's employees has brought me coffee on a silver tray a half-hour before breakfast officially begins. He's learned that I rise early. When I heard footsteps coming down the hall, I thought, "Could it be?" And then there came a cheerful "*Ola*" and the sound of the heavy wooden door to the anteroom sliding open. I couldn't thank him enough.

Mother once declared that she would be "nothing" without her rules, but in Brazil, I've seen rules bent to powerful effect, including a doctor who gives out his cellphone number to a new patient, and now an employee willing to veer from hotel policy. All of this bending of rules doesn't create "nothing." It creates warmth. It makes me feel cared for.

Neuroscientists have found that when pianists think about playing the piano, the same neurons in their brains are activated as when they actually perform. The same phenomenon might even occur watching a sport that one plays. For a tennis player, some scientists say, observing Roger Federer in a match engages the same parts of the brain as when one is on the court hitting (or missing) forehands and backhands oneself.

Is this what happens in the purest empathy? Do we literally feel the wounds to our loved ones as though they are wounds to ourselves? That is what I believe as I reply to my friend: "I have boils on my neck and scalp, but inside I no longer feel so wounded for my father."

Whatever the source of the original wound, it feels like a thing of the past as I take my coffee to the balcony of Mama Ruisa and look out at clay-colored roofs and the beauty of Rio de Janeiro in the early light, the harbor and hills in the distance. In my job at The Nature Conservancy, my colleagues and I worry about coastal development being in harm's way as sea levels rise throughout the world, but all my eyes can see now is that Rio's coastal development is a work of art.

What a troupe of people have helped me, I'm thinking—from John the expat lawyer to his accountant Valdir, the accountant's aunt Isabel, her son-in-law Helio, the graduate student Bruno, former journalist Cesar, the commandant Klaus Nixdorf, the Brit Alan Thomas, the vocalist Everson, all the good people at the jungle lodge, even gruff Aynore holding out his camera time and time again to share a photo. All of them came to me like Brazilians to a soccer ball. I hardly had to work for it. They were strangers who knew only that I had traveled a long way seeking answers about my past in a country where I did not speak the language and did not know the way. That was enough for them to want to help me.

I feel more cared for by this band of strangers than I ever did by my family.

This realization is what practically makes me drop my coffee. This is what pushes me to kick past the goal posts into the net, only I'm suddenly in a daze and I don't know if I have scored in my team's goal or the opponent's goal because what I so belatedly grasp is that I haven't been trying to close a wound out of empathy for my father. I have been trying to close *my own wound*. I *am* my father insofar as Walter Lindberg is concerned. I am the abandoned child. That's how I feel.

I probe this idea. How could it be so? My parents had always been present physically, sometimes to an unwelcome extent. Then I comprehend: Theirs was a different sort of absence than Walter's, harder to label and pound the walls about, but it was an absence nonetheless, and I had never named it before: emotional abandonment. Right or wrong, I could see that I had been feeling it for a very long time.

On Thanksgiving Day, almost twenty-five years earlier, I feared my parents were going to eat me. With my mind spinning out of control after the operation, I lay under the coffee table in my parents' den as they ate turkey from plastic platters that my father had picked up at his club. I could smell the food, but I thought it was a ruse. I thought mine was the true flesh they intended to carve, and I wondered how much longer I had to live.

It was a chilling memory, one of many that had stayed with me from that delusional time, like the hallucination in which I believed a camera was televising live from inside me to the Thanksgiving Day Parade audience. For nearly a quarter of a century, I had thought the turkey incident simply showed how well my parents could pretend that things were normal when plainly they were not.

Now, suddenly, in the early light of Rio, the true meaning of my hallucinations stood revealed. A part of me really did feel that my parents had eaten me alive, and that they had interfered with my most private behaviors. Nor could I dismiss these as old thoughts, washed away by the passage of time, my father's stroke, the birth of my child, Mother's death, Michael's death, and everything else that had happened since I'd sat at the picnic table by the beach, wondering where my life had gone wrong. My dream a few days earlier in the Amazon bore uncanny similarity to the camera hallucination. Roberta had made her comment about my father, I'd thought about Michael, and I had dreamed of being unclothed and exposed from my waist to my thighs—no camera this time, but the same idea. It seemed my mind was repeating itself, calling out for me to pay attention. Now, finally, perhaps I could do that.

When I'd said to Roberta and Bruno through tears in Londrina that I was making the trip to Brazil that my father should have made, there was much more to it than that. I could see now that in the guise of searching for Walter Lindberg, I had been seeking a means to understand and accept my own parents' actions toward me. That had been the true reason I needed to go to Brazil, not to find more facts, but to locate my wound and heal. No wonder I could never give a satisfactory answer to Justin. I didn't understand it myself until this moment.

I'm still the only person on the balcony, which adjoins a large common room, as big as a ballet studio. It is a pleasure to gaze around the room without being disturbed, to appreciate the aesthetic of the designer who decided to leave so much space around the modern furniture and let the wood floor go without rugs. Despite all the empty space, the room does not feel cold. Black-and-white photos on the walls, lead-framed windows, colorful chairs, and well-placed flowers give it warmth, and yet there is space in this room to breathe, to think, to be oneself.

My father had been intrusive in a terrible way the night he attacked Michael verbally, but with the blinders off it takes me little time to see that the sense of being eaten alive has deeper origins and includes my mother's conduct.

Each of my parents wanted me to be a different person who suited his or her ideal child and companion—like many parents, perhaps. For Mother, I could provide the cultural companionship Dad could not. I always knew how to behave with her. I knew what she liked to talk about, and what she liked to do—museums, meals in restaurants, a little shopping as long as she did not feel rushed—and yet it rarely seemed to work the other way. If I expressed sadness about something, this was referred to as my being overly emotional. On a trip we took to Ireland, when the still undiagnosed tumor had grown so large I had recently been prescribed distance glasses, Mother commented that I never seemed to complain. Why would I? I had learned long ago to keep my true thoughts to myself around her. Something as simple as a request to cease giving me presents that consisted of pink clothing would not be honored, much less my choice of boyfriend, so why would I cheapen words by uttering that which would be ignored? I would speak of things out there in the world, as she wished—of art, and food, and beautiful scenery—and in restaurants I would send back her coffee if it wasn't as hot as she liked, just as I would let her take three hours in the kitchen later in her life to make her dinner and wash the dishes because those were the things that mattered to Mother at that point, and I had been raised to take good care of her.

I knew how important I was in satisfying each of my parents' needs and learned to act accordingly, one way for Mother, one way for Dad, and when we went out as a threesome to a restaurant, I was the ball that bounced between them, keeping the conversation moving.

With Michael, the masks I wore for my parents came off, and I was conscious of feeling with him like a complete person, living on a spectrum of womanhood and selfhood of a breadth I'd never known. In one moment I could listen to Michael analyze a heady topic, from Nietzsche to the failings of the modern press, which usually pushed me to think and debate more clearly, and in the next moment I could be called "sweetheart"—and that felt like the person I had been training for all my life, trying to be my best in all ways, worldly and domestic, masculine and feminine, not having to choose, but being everything I could be at once, and honestly.

That was what my parents' interference and lack of emotional support had robbed me of—not just Michael, but my fully realized, independent self. My parents were so accustomed to seeing the masks I wore for them, they could not understand that a real person lay underneath, longing to fuse her separate selves, and that Michael had been the one to help me do it.

I had mourned my father's death and my mother's, and I was still mourning Michael's, but I had never really mourned for myself, for the girl who hopped on one leg and the teenager who heard her father hang up the phone after she'd been kidnapped. That was all just life, the cards that were dealt, but in Brazil, the deck was shuffled differently. In that way, Roberta was correct. There was a bigger wound than I realized, and when I arrived in Brazil, I was still suffering from it.

I thought that after his stroke, I forgave my father for his interference with Michael, but I see now that Roberta was wrong in that respect. I hadn't fully forgiven him—until now. There was so much more I hadn't even realized I needed to forgive him for, and Mother, too—a life-long carving up of me into his share and hers. Both of my parents would have died for what I meant to them, but rarely had I felt them connecting with and supporting what I meant to me.

It was Aunt Connie who gave me the warmest, most instantaneous support when I announced that I was pregnant. I'd gone up to her apartment in Westchester, which was full of inherited knick-knacks and worn Persian rugs. My cousin Susan was there, too. I was nervous on account of anonymous donor sperm not being the usual way people in our family begot children. I needn't have worried. Aunt Connie's mother had been a vaudeville star, and a bit of the rebel lived on in the daughter.

"Finally," Aunt Connie said in her dramatic way, like she was thanking the heavens for a miracle, "you're doing something completely for yourself!"

The wording didn't sound quite right—I was sensitive to the notion that parents owned their children—so I asked Aunt Connie what she meant. She described visiting our house when I was young and having the sense that my life was a set of tasks prescribed by my parents.

"I would see you sitting at the piano to please your mother and I would think to myself, 'Let this child go outside and play.'"

For Aunt Connie, it seemed that my getting pregnant was a way of going outside and playing. I believed that I had gone outside and played a lot in my life—at boarding school, at college, with my boyfriends, with work colleagues, and on vacations with friends—but Aunt Connie hadn't witnessed all of that, so it was intriguing that this concept of me as a pawn or extension of my parents was what jumped into her mind when she heard that I was going to have a baby. Maybe all that playing on my part had been my own form of running away, trying to put some separateness between my parents and me that wasn't really there at its core.

Doors are starting to open in the hotel, so I take my coffee back to the anteroom, glad to hear Roberta breathing deeply, still asleep. I want to be alone as all of these thoughts come together. It is just like in the Amazon dream: Renovations are in progress.

I hadn't ever analyzed the evidence the way a lawyer might if trying to prove a case, but sitting a few feet away from a slumbering litigator, I have to admit that there are many pieces of evidence Aunt Connie might have used to prove her case. For example, there was the matter of my choice of musical instruments. I had played the piano and clarinet since childhood, and though I loved both instruments, I was far better at the clarinet. My high school teacher encouraged me to consider a symphony career, but my parents preferred the piano, the instrument Mother played, and her mother, too. I gave a recital on piano and clarinet in the spring of my senior year, for which I'd prepared all year, but

when the time came to start college, Dad agreed to pay for me to continue lessons on piano, but not clarinet.

Of course my proficiency on an instrument was up to me, not anyone
else, and there were plenty of reasons besides lack of continuing instruction why I didn't go on to play clarinet in a philharmonic orchestra. Yet
Dad's decision had been upsetting, and his rationale peculiar.

"You can't play the clarinet alone," was Dad's pronouncement on the
matter, and his words now seemed fraught with meaning. Why should
the solo capacity of an instrument have been the litmus test? I wanted to
play with other people. I always had. Was that truly what Dad wanted for
me? A life alone, like Rapunzel in the tower? Was that the real reason he
had railed against Michael, to try to keep me alone and available to him?

If so, I could now allow myself to feel that it had been a lot to ask,
too much, expecting a daughter to make up for the loss of two fathers, a
dead brother, a deceitful mother, and a withdrawn wife.

Mother sometimes said that there was no point in giving me advice,
since I was going to do what I wanted to anyway, as though having my
own opinions about my life was a fundamental breach of the parent-child
contract. For Mother, raised mostly by servants rather than parents, not
doing what one was told was a violation of the rules. I hated her obsequi-
ousness toward rules, and yet I had become a lawyer. I suppose I wanted
to contain rules, rather than risk letting them contain me—but in Brazil
rules seemed fluid. Sometimes they were horribly flouted, as when defor-
esters shoot a nun, and sometimes they were bent out of generosity, as
when a stranger offers to pay a man's parking ticket to save him the trip.

"We did the best we could" were Mother's last coherent words to me,
the night before she died. It was her absolution for all of our wrongs, all
of our ineptitude as a family. It was—like her piano playing, her non-
interference with the Walter Lindberg story, and all her other gestures,
such as being first in line at the mental ward each day—a quiet testament to love. Love was never easy in our family, and it was never loud.

I had known since Mother's disclosures to me in Washington that
her upbringing had damaged her. The discovery that Dad had been
mistreated was more recent. What was brand new was recognition of
the cavernous wound that had lain within me, and yet Aunt Connie
was right that the boundaries between my parents and me were always

blurred, the roles always a bit unclear. In the end, that's probably why I failed to leave the table the night of the attack on Michael. Complete separateness from my father just wasn't in my repertoire then, nor was it after the revelations in the State Department documents. I was my own emotionally abandoned child, but after learning about Walter's physical abandonment, I easily took on my father's wounds, and so I plunged into research and headed to Brazil thinking it was a factual investigation I was up to, some sort of crusade for or competition with my father, but really I was being driven by a gaping, longstanding, even desperate need to understand and forgive those closest to me.

Remarkably, this is what happened. It was my wound which I no longer felt, my wound for which I had rung the bell in Londrina, wishing the dead could hear me. It was my wound which Brazil had helped to close.

◆

Fortunately, I was not alone in Rio as these thoughts came to me. There would be no strange eyes staring at me as I descended the ladder and set off for a fresh swim, only the eyes of my friend, who was now awake.

"Hey M," Roberta called from her bed. "How are you feeling?"

"Pretty good," I answered. "I'm looking forward to being with you today."

It was true. With Michael and my parents gone, no more masks, no more struggles, I wondered whether I could synthesize all of the strands of my past, who I truly was, and what I'd only pretended to be as a service to others, into one coherent whole.

At least I could try.

◆

"Now I *am* worried about you," Roberta says. She's got her iPhone up pointing at the view from high up in Santa Teresa in the Parque das Ruinas, but my camera is still in its bag on my belt. It's not that I'm having a relapse. It's that I've just said to myself I can't take this photo. It's too beautiful to capture. I'm going to look with my eyes.

We walk back inside the structure, an old palace that, having burned, was ceded to artists who added glass corners and an elegant spire of metal stairs.

I am thinking about what Aynore said about photographers being frustrated people, and how they "remove" a photo in Portuguese.

We head up the stairs to the next level. The view is even more spectacular. I have the initial urge to raise my camera and am surprised by an even stronger counter-urge.

I stop walking, and let Roberta go on. I grab the rail. In the amount of time it would take to press the shutter, I have suddenly understood my drive to photograph, to document. It is an urge to prevent loss. The compulsion to "take" the shot, to "remove" the scene comes both from the recognition that the scene matters and the anticipatory disappointment that what matters about it cannot be preserved.

Yet the idea that if I take the photo I will never have to lose the scene is a delusion, because the act of taking a photograph interferes with appreciation of the moment. It causes the very loss, depriving the beholder of the experience of beholding, which it is trying to prevent.

I had thought it was only Mother who viewed the world as if through a lens of loss, but I now see how I have inherited that perspective, too.

The fact is, I can't close my eyes and visualize a scene, not even a candle or a sheep. There is only black. So now I comprehend what not taking a picture means. It means a big loss of detail and no substitute for a visual memory. Mother said I hated to leave places as a girl, and perhaps this is why. I knew I wouldn't have visual memories to take with me. What I seem to do instead is convert visual memories into words, so I can still know that the lianas formed circles and braids on the banks of the Cristalino, even though I can't picture them unless I look at a photograph.

What if I accept this about my brain, keep the camera turned off, allow myself to experience the moment, and then try to hold onto the feeling of the experience? What would that be like?

There's a 290-degree view of Rio from the top of the structure. We walk along the viewing platform. There's a spot where I could put the sun at my back and take a good shot, but I don't. I find the will not to raise the camera, the will to accept what lies before me as impermanent, because that's what life is, a series of beautiful, impermanent moments never to be repeated, except in the movies. Life *is* loss. Do I choose to love the life part or the loss part?

My eyes tear up. I actually have no urge to raise my camera. I may not be able to summon the actual scene, but I know I will always remember the feeling. A part of me will always be standing here, for here I have come to the end of my search for that place of more. I don't know everything, but I know enough. The parts unknown can stay that way. In the Park of Ruins, I find a wholeness that tells me I am free to leave Brazil.

I have several books to bring back to Long Island and many photographs, but one thing I won't be taking with me is Walter Lindberg. He deserves to stay in Brazil, the only place where he ever returned in his relentless pursuit of dreams, always looking to the future, not the past. I'm going to leave him in the country he chose, partly in the jungle and partly in Londrina, where he can be Waldomiro, the brave pioneer, until the end of time—or at least until the concrete totems crumble and the land company's records turn to dust.

chapter forty-two

HOME

THE WOMAN SEATED to my left holds up her iPhone and says to her companion, "I love my phone." Moments later, the woman on my right, holding a different device, mutters that she hates her new phone, but then she says it's cool how it auto-syncs with her Google calendar.

I have been back in the United States for three days, but fortunately all is not hardware and software in my native country. Robert Pinsky, a former poet laureate, is minutes away from talking about my search for Walter Lindberg.

Pinsky won't mention Walter by name. In fact, Pinsky's never heard of the man. Pinsky doesn't know me, or my son, who isn't even one of the graduating seniors to whom Pinsky's talk is directed here in Concord, Massachusetts. Justin is seated in the back of the tent with the other sophomores, and I'm just another audience member, seated between two adults I don't know.

Nonetheless, Pinsky helps explain the last year and a half of my life.

The human body doesn't compare to large cats or bears or almost any animal in its natural ability to survive, Pinsky observes in a deep and commanding voice. I can certainly agree with that statement, still taking antibiotics as a result of a simple swim in a river.

We lack claws for cutting and thick fur for protection, but humans have something that no other animal has: We "cooperate with the past."

"The practice of communicating information about the past is what has made humans thrive."

More poetically, Pinsky says, in effect, that because our teeth are weak "we tell stories across generations."

Some of us do, I say to myself, but not all of us. Roberta's mother told so many stories "they gave me my sense of my place in the world," Roberta said in her eulogy.

Not mine. My mother had difficulty talking about the past in story form. She provided fragments, things that served as symbols, such as Neil's Atmos clock, and the lesson that the past was best left a secret. Dad had one whopper of a story in him, and it sank into me like a barbed fishhook.

Pinsky's remarks seem to justify every minute of pain and every hour I thrashed alone swimming through a sea of documents, following the line that would take me back across time, forging my own dialogue with the past because we didn't engage in that dialogue as a family. This desire of mine wasn't strange, Pinsky is saying. It was human.

One of the best clues left for me was one of the last to be found. I thought I'd opened every drawer, sifted through every box after Mother's death, and then one day I realized I hadn't ever gone through the contents of the organ bench that had come with Mother into my house.

It was Marion Kondolf Ryan's Hammond organ, purchased in 1936, and inside the bench were Marion's organ lesson plans from the 1940s, even some of Uncle John's old violin music. I didn't find the Damon Runyon column about my grandfather John Ryan, but I did find a newspaper dated February 19, 1943, the *Daily News Record*, a fashion trade journal containing a half-page feature about Marion along with a photograph. In that article I learned more about my grandmother than I ever did from Mother.

For one thing, I learned that Dad's mother wasn't the only grandmother of mine who kept secrets.

Marion had taken over the John W. Ryan English Shops after her husband's death in 1939, and, according to the article, "few outside the organization know that it is merchandised and has been built up by a woman. Mrs. Ryan, with a pleased expression, admits that she connives at this small deception by signing a large 'Marion' in business correspondence and letting others believe, if they wish, that this name, which is also a man's, does, in this case, belong to a man."

I couldn't be too harsh about this practice. I'd done the same thing as a reporter, using initials in my byline. There was a connection between my grandmother and me that went deeper than a common name or fitting into the same flapper dresses. We both had hid our womanhood in our work lives.

The article went on to praise Marion's business acumen, describing how other retailers followed her lead when it came to new lines of merchandise. The profile closed with reference to Marion as "one of New York's smartest and most efficient business women."

I had to try to laugh. How perverse it all was—to realize I'd grown up hearing praises for the man who left, but never heard the story about the woman who stayed, took over the family business, became a quiet leader in a male-dominated field, and allowed her children to keep living in the grand style to which they were accustomed.

Before my trip, my cousin John wrote to me, "It's a shame our parents couldn't talk about the past. What a cruel deficit to give to a child."

I agree, minus the word "cruel." If my search taught me anything, it's that Mother and Dad never withheld the past out of spite. For different reasons, their upbringings had forced them both to shed their pasts. They had done the best they could, as Mother put it the night before she died. That was a lot better than Walter had ever done insofar as family was concerned.

My parents improved upon Walter's record. They showed loyalty, perhaps their strongest joint value, and not a bad one by any means. They stuck around. They gave me a great deal, and yet, incapable of sharing their pasts with each other, incapable of weaving the strands from their different pasts into a new set of clothes for our family, they gave me a rag bin instead of a family lore. It was a deficit, for sure.

Fortunately, some of the rag fibers were of excellent quality, and with some effort, beautiful garments could be stitched after all. Thanks to Grandma, I do know how to sew.

There are many colors in these new garments I've attempted to make for my son and me: the rich green of coffee plants and palm trees and the Irish countryside that Grandfather Ryan eschewed. There's the red of northern Paraná's soil, the black and white of the piano keys through which my mother's heart spoke to me. There is the color of sand, from beaches up and down the Atlantic Coast, where it seems all of my fore-bears felt pleasures of at least a fleeting sort. There are patches of blue like the ocean crossed separately by a Hungarian and a Frenchman to give me my father, Elsa and Melville leaving their pasts for something they thought would be better. There must have been times when they thought they had found it.

As a result of my search for Walter, I will never look at my parents and my life with them in quite the same way. I've come to understand them better, perhaps better than they understood themselves, and to know myself.

And yet, the success of my search was only partially related to the factual information it uncovered. Discovery of Walter's abandonment was only capable of causing me such distress because of my own feelings of being abandoned, so factual knowledge alone could never have closed the wound. I had to feel my way to recovery, and what better place for an experiential cure than Brazil, a deeply sensual place where people think and feel differently? The pull of Brazil, its mysteries, its generosity in people and natural abundance, may be the truest part of the Walter story. Brazil never disappointed. If anything, it exceeded my expecta-tions. From my first encounter with John McNaughton in São Paulo, Brazilian ways opened me to a different sort of learning, to knowledge not borne solely from factual accuracy and completeness, but also from how one interprets information at hand and appreciates how intricately each piece of it is webbed within larger contexts.

We all create myths out of our parents, not only those who leave for foreign lands. The perspective of a child is inherently self-centered and narrow. We don't even have memories from the period in our lives when most of us spent the greatest amount of time with our parents, infancy and early childhood. We change over time, as do they, and the memories we do have can be imperfect. Our parents had lives before us, and they have lives away from us—at their jobs, with their friends, in their volunteer work. If they survive and grow old, the relationship changes again, as I saw after my father's stroke.

Dad had only a few years with Walter, and the myth he clung to in place of a father was romantic, strong, and violent. I had to go to Brazil, step into and out of Walter's shoes, to see the myth of the explorer dead and betrayed in the jungle for what it was: camouflage for a damaged man. Now, Walter's incessant movement from place to place looks a lot more like running away than any of my blood grandparents' journeys across sea or land. At least Marion, John, Elsa, and Melville stopped when they got to New York. The hero of my father's story kept on going, always.

I had to be cared for and guided by people who were themselves descendants of pioneers from throughout the world, wanderers and searchers, and I had to get an infection and stand in an emergency room in Rio to feel the difference between Walter and me. The boy waiting for me back home was someone I wanted to see as much as I wanted to go on living.

I finally get to hug my son after Pinsky's talk. Justin has no idea why there are tears in my eyes, no idea about my trip to the emergency room, and my fears that I might not return. I'll try to keep it that way, which seems like a justifiable white lie. Besides, no parent wants to hear "I told you so" from a fifteen-year-old.

We'll lavish attention on our dog on the trip home to Long Island and stop at a McDonalds, one where people won't be dancing the bossa nova. We will have a great summer, even though he's a teenager, because I am so grateful for him and for the capacity to love him as I do. At the height of the summer heat, the boils will return to my scalp several times along with the pain. I'll be on more rounds of antibiotics and will lose a small patch of hair above the forehead. Others probably won't notice, but at times it will be all that I see when I look in the mirror, proof, like the scar on my thigh, of the journey I undertook.

At least I will find out from my doctor at home that the infections were not quite as dramatic as the Brazilian doctor led me to believe. According to Dr. Blake Kerr, there were two infections, one in the ear, one on the scalp. It wasn't the internal infection that caused the boils, as I'd thought.

Sadly, Dr. Kerr will say the ear infection probably arose from refuse in the river. The doctor can't say whether my pituitary condition predisposed me to getting ill. Maybe the lesson is that there's no pristine place left in the world and that wilderness is a human construct. Still, I'll be happy at the end of the summer to hear that a Brazilian judge halted construction of the Belo Monte dam across the Xingu River, and unhappy to hear a week later that a different Brazilian authority allowed construction to proceed. The battle over the Amazon will continue, perhaps until there is as little left of it as of the forest whose decimation Walter pioneered, but all of us should hope the story plays out differently.

Secrets and half-truths are ways in which humans attempt to obliterate the past in service of what they perceive to be their current needs, and deforestation can be a version of the same thing as its participants— who are really all of us—use up natural resources in the name of progress without sufficient regard to long-term impacts such as warming temperatures, drought, and degradation of water supplies.

Yet there is hope: Miners and treasure hunters are not the only ones who believe there is gold in the Amazon. "Forest gold" is what Nature Conservancy scientists call the carbon sequestration value of trees in the rainforest, and these biologists turned gold seekers have installed equipment in various parts of the Amazon to measure the amount of carbon stored. The biologists hope that the measurements will lead to tangible results, saving the parts of the forest that do the most good for the planet. There are also numerous organizations working with local people in Brazil, restoring natural lands along rivers and teaching more productive farming techniques to attain greater yields from existing farmland rather than clear additional acres of forest.

"There will be development," says the head of The Nature Conservancy's Atlantic Forest program. "The question is where."

It's too soon to say whether an actual, enforced end to rampant clearing is likely to come from the efforts of scientists, economists, and local advocates such as the last colonist's daughter. There is excellent work being done in communities, in pilot projects with farmers and ranchers, trying to show that Brazil can continue to lift its citizens out of poverty and protect natural resources at the same time. We should all hope that Brazil's leaders pay serious attention to these efforts. It's not just the past that deserves human cooperation. Nature deserves it, too. Otherwise, there won't be much of a future for many a species, humans included.

Reasons for optimism exist if one looks hard enough. For one thing, forests can regenerate. Nature has proved resilient, from Brazil to the Adirondacks, and this is true for the immaterial parts of humans. As I learned through my search for the truth underlying my father's story, children can grow up and raise their children differently from how they themselves were raised. Secrets can be bared, truth spoken, and people, like forests, can heal.

In the months after my trip, I will mostly honor my promise to leave Waldomiro alone, down in Brazil, but I will be too curious about the source of the name of his store. It's a bit of an addiction, this information-gathering thing. I will discover that Marumby was the name of one of the oldest railroads in Brazil, opened in 1885, a 110-kilometer route that connected agricultural parts of Paraná to the harbor of Paranaguá. It is also the name of a state park said to have one of the most beautiful natural landscapes of Paraná, including Olimpi Peak, a favored destination for hikers and climbers.

In naming his store in Rolândia, perhaps Walter was referencing his own past, one which may have included work on the Marumby line. "Marumby" does sound like "Mamore," and Otto Ulrich could have confused the two in his testimony about Walter's work experience. At any rate, it is not a Rosebud I will chase.

Nor will I use my camera as much. I will sit and watch more, even though I know I won't have a vivid recollection of the scene. A photograph is another kind of fact, and it's not always important to have that sort of record of experience. Michael used to say that my ability to discern meaning in symbols was one of my strengths, but if true, it is only one that I honed through lifelong observation of my parents turning experience into things, wearing gifts instead of saying "I love you," polishing things rather than connecting with the people who offered them. I resolve to polish less myself and connect more.

When I am tempted to complain about anything, I will remember how I felt standing at the edge of the Rio Teles Pires or the top of the Park of Ruins, and how it felt to glide under a gift from the heavens, when a rainbow emerged at the end of our kayak ride on the Rio Cristalino. I will remember the care my friend Roberta showed for me in Ipanema, and wonder when Klaus Nixdorf's bus from Londrina will pass through New York. I will wonder which team he supported in the 2014 World Cup final—Brazil or Germany—and then I'll just send him an e-mail and ask him, because he is my friend now. I will look at photographs of Eduard Schulz's *fazenda* on occasion, because otherwise I would think I had been dreaming about the color of the soil, and I will think about my other friends Isabel and Cesar, safeguarding the past in northern Paraná.

And when I am driving near my home and hear a radio interview with a psychologist asserting that the mentally ill might be healed if the content of their delusions could be unpacked, I will pull off to the side of the road, listen carefully, and wonder whether the speaker is onto something. Some of my post-operative delusions, though short-lived, were my mind's way of telling me truths I didn't want to admit. It took a trip to Brazil almost twenty-five years after the delusions for me to see the truth embedded in them.

I resisted. I put those seemingly crazy thoughts into the Indonesian basket along with the pretty childhood memories of trips to the World's

Fair, and I created my own story, that of the dutiful daughter with the doting father, to cover up my feelings of being treated unfairly by those closest to me. But the cover wouldn't hold, chomping dog or not.

I'd been sniffing at the Walter story for a long time, and maybe I had a dog's nose for the truth that lay underneath. I really started digging only a matter of weeks after the final break-up with Michael, well before I had any objective evidence that under the story's fine surface lay a huge breach, an encapsulation of our family history—betrayal: Mother raised by servants, not permitted to eat with her parents except on holidays, locked in a bedroom to protect her from a violent father; Dad abandoned and lied to, left to make his own way in the world based on his brain and good looks.

This was the curse I had broken when I said no to Michael, that I didn't want to try to conceive a child with him if he wasn't sure about his desire to be a father or his will to navigate with a baby on board the schism between our families.

Over the years, I had doubted myself. I didn't wish for a different child than the one I had, but I did wonder why, after all we had been through, I'd let the child issue be the one to undo Michael and me. Men are notorious for having pre-parent jitters, and Michael had gone on to be a stellar father. I would joke sometimes that I had been insufficiently entrepreneurial, but I could see now why his apprehension mattered so much to me, why I preferred trying to give a child twice my love than half the love of a reluctant couple—because I came from a long line of people who hadn't been emotionally tended to by both of their parents. Deep inside, I trusted myself to do a better job of parenting on my own than Elsa and Walter together, Marion and John, Patricia and Jean, or Marian and Michael once he started expressing misgivings. I'd been the one to hop blind down the hall on one leg, already knowing at age seven that I shouldn't bother calling out for help. Dad was at work. Mother was downstairs washing the breakfast dishes. The only help that was available was in my other leg.

I understood now that I had taken a position with Michael based on what I knew and what I felt. I hadn't gotten up from the table when Dad assaulted Michael, I hadn't whined after my father hung up the phone rather than offer to fly to Massachusetts after my kidnapping, but I had walked away from the possibility of diminished love toward the next generation. That didn't make me a hero or a fool—but it did make me a person with at least one very clear boundary: I wouldn't inflict the sort of emotional barrenness I had known on another.

There was consistency in me and it went way back. Following Walter Lindberg to Brazil had revealed it. Approaching family differently, trying to support my child emotionally in ways that I had not been supported, as well as fostering and respecting his independence, was absolutely my highest priority and always had been. That's why, as much as I missed him, I had encouraged him to attend high school away from home, in a place where he could live within a large community of caring people, rather than in an isolated hamlet in a house of two.

So when Justin tells me that he's thinking of speaking about our family during his senior presentation to the entire school, I smile and know that everything I went through was worth it. We have by now discovered a second half-brother from the same donor father, all three boys born within a three-month period, so "family" has become a novel adventure. Still, Justin tells me he that he intends to turn to the tried and not-so-true for his first line: "Until I was thirteen, I thought my great-grandfather died in the Amazon."

My father's story is my son's story now, to do with what he wants. It's not just a story about the man who gave us our last name, a man most likely Danish who died sometime after 1939, maybe in Mato Grosso, maybe not. It is also a story about my son and his mother, about using what is given to you and following your intuition to discover what you must—to heal, to change, and to love.

In grade school, as I lay with my left leg paralyzed and my skin molting, my father returned one afternoon from a business trip. He sat on the bed wearing a dark suit and handed me a sheet of small stickers with birds on them. The names of the birds were printed underneath the color pictures. My father read the names out loud. Together we looked at the pictures. I liked the Baltimore oriole by far the best. Its chest plumage was bright orange, and the wings were black with white streaks. I thought the oriole was the most beautiful living thing I had ever seen.

Many years later, when my own child was in grade school, I went into New York City to have my left hip replaced. Experts say it is usually an injury for which one has been compensating for quite some time, combined with an active life, which wears down the cartilage and requires a joint replacement in middle life.

The operation took place on a November day, the same month as the pituitary operation, but this time all went according to plan. I recovered at home, where my mother cooked meals for me and my son did his homework lying in my bed. My colleagues at the nature organization set up a wireless connection so that I could work from home when I felt up to it.

A month or so later, free of hip pain, I returned to the office, a converted old farmhouse whose grounds are dotted with large, stately trees. In the back are two enormous copper beeches at least a century old, where red-tailed hawks sometimes perch, their sharp eyes looking for rodents in the field below.

To enter the front door of the building, one must pass by a huge crab apple tree, said to be the largest on Long Island where, every spring, a Baltimore oriole returns from afar to build her nest.

ACKNOWLEDGEMENTS

To all who helped convert my jumble of thoughts and urges into something tangible, you have my deepest gratitude. In particular, for their willingness to brainstorm or read chapters and offer editorial advice, I thank John Lacy Clark, Jennifer Clarke, Marcy Friedman, Bruce Horwith, Laurie Smith Parker, Allen Peacock, Regina Scott, Elisabeth Seldes, Cathy Suter, Patricia Vanderleun, and Lena Walstam. Many friends offered encouragement and assistance of one sort or another, among them Jo-Ann Armao, Monica Banks, Cathy Bostron, Paul D'Andrea, Michael Denslow, Scott Fain, Gail Freeman, Marla Meg Gordon, Jan Guszynski, Emily Herrick, Alice Jump, Dan Kornstein, Mary Landergan, Marina Dunn Nelson, Randy Parsons, Susan Taylor, and Nikki Wood. My colleagues at The Nature Conservancy, Lucy Cutler and Nancy Kelley, kindly allowed me to work part-time while writing. Sergio Lob, Andrea DeBroka, Renata Lob, and Duncan Littlejohn provided invaluable introductions to my generous helpers in Brazil. Elizabeth Parker introduced me to Counterpoint, where editor Nicole Antonio proved a pleasure to work with. I am truly fortunate to have a friend like Roberta Steele, who accompanied me on the trip of a lifetime. For his brilliant assistance, I thank David Lamb, a gifted editor. For everything, I thank my son, Justin Melville Lindberg, an extraordinary young man by any name.

Marian Lindberg's father as a boy, early 1920s, when he was known as Melville Jean DePay, with his mother, Elsa Roth DePay, in New York City. (Photographer unknown)

Walter Lindberg on a ship
or pier on New York Harbor,
either November 1928 or
March 1929. (Photographer
unknown)

Tres Lagoas. July 1929

This photo of Walter Lindberg in Brazil was sent to his wife and stepson one month before
Walter's alleged murder.

Mez: *de Junho* de 1932.

VENDA Nº	LOTE Nº	GLEBA	NOME	NACIONALIDADE	AREA	AREA TOTAL	PREÇO POR ALQUEIRE	JUROS	VALOR DA VENDA	OBSERVAÇÕES
396			Transporte			5047,96				2.848.722*400
1	372	216 baf.	Guiiti Hamada	Japon.	80-	✓	450°	Inc.	18 500 000	
1	373	214 —	Hirose Takeshi	—	15-	✓	450°	.	6 750 000	
1	374	222 —	Hashimoto Kuniyoshi	—	10-	✓	400°	10%	4 000 000	a/v.
29	375	99 Jac.	Gustav Kruger	Allemã	5	✓	400°	10%	2 000 000	
1	376	201 baf.	Katayama Citaro	Japon.	10	✓	450°	Inc.	4 500 000	
1	377	25 cam.	Hiromichi Ichioka	—	15	✓	450°	.	6 750 000	
3	378	27 ~	Kanemasa Honda	—	20	✓	450°	.	9 000 000	
2	379	13 bag.	Francisco Chojnowski	Poloney	50		500°	n/ha	25 000 000	a/v.
3	380	10? bond.	Gustav Budernik	Allemã	1		1.250°	.	1 250 000	a/v.
24	381	18 B yr.	Salvador Carrocini	Brasil.	15		500°	10%	7 500 000	
4	382	16	Dr. Amedeo Boggio Merlo	Ital.	1	✓	400°	n/ha	400 000	a/v.
8	383	15 bag.	Gines Lopes Lopes e outros	Hesp.	50	✓	550°	Inc.	27 500 000	
6	384	164 —	Pedro Mattarazzi	Ital.	5	✓	600°	10%	3 000 000	
6	385	166B —	Oreste Sanfilice	Bras.	10	✓	600°	10%	6 000 000	
6	386	162 —	Andrè Lorenzino	Ital.	5		600°	10%	3 000 000	
6	387	163 —	Francisco Feltrim	Bras.	5	✓	600°	10%	3 000 000	
7	388	313 Jac.	Tomikiti Yokoyama	Japon.	60		600°	10%	36 000 000	
7	389	51? baf.	Antonia de Jesus Gomes	Port.	5	✓	450°	Inc.	2 250 000	/
8	390	10 bond.	Adelinas João	—	1		1.250°	n/ha	1 250 000	
8	391	107? cam.	Francisco Chaves	Aust.	8	✓	600°	10%	4 800 000	
10	392	56? bond.	João Goncalves	Port.	8	✓	1.250°	10%	8 750 000	
18	393	50 —	Dr. R. Raggulaeff	Russo	3		800°	n/ha	2 400 000	
28	394	221 baf.	Shimada Biuiti	Japon.	10	✓	450°	Inc.	4 500 000	
33	395	210	Morimoto Thosabro	—	20	✓	450°	.	9 000 000	
33	396	209 .	Kojima Yonosuke	—	30	✓	450°	.	13 500 000	
25	397	114	Waldomiro Lindberg, João Sorreiram e outros	Dinam. Brasil.	80 10-		400° 400°	10%	48 000 000 4 000 000	
22	398	2 R.V.	Masaioshi Endo	Japon.	10	✓	450°	Inc.	4 500 000	
32	399	4 .	Kutuoshi Asso	.	10	✓	450°	.	4 500 000	
424			segue		437-	5047,96			221 600 000	2.248.722*400

Clearing trees to build homes and create farmland in northern Paraná, 1936.(Courtesy of Cambé Historical Museum)

The new settlement of Nova Dantzig (also spelled Nova Danzig) in northern Paraná, 1937. (Courtesy Cambé Historical Museum)

The author's father and grandmother in or near New York City, late 1930s.

TOP: Bruno Sanchez and Roberta Steele in Londrina, Paraná, pointing to Walter Lindberg's Brazilian name on the Pioneer's Memorial, 2012. (Photo by Marian Lindberg)

Marian Lindberg ringing the old church bell in Londrina. (Photo by Roberta Steele)

Isabel dos Santos in Cambé, formerly Nova Dantzig, 2012 (Photo by Marian Lindberg)

Cesar Cortez, director of the Cambé Historical Museum. (Photo by Marian Lindberg)

BELOW: Members of the German community in Nova Dantzig pose where a portion of the Atlantic Forest has been cleared for construction of a school, 1935. (Courtesy Cambé Historical Museum)

Mitgliederliste

Mitgl. Nr.	Name	Mitgl. Nr.	Name
1	Erich Anger	40	Erika Wiedmann Nilson
2	Arthur Axt	38	Antonia Sarwade
3	Richard Graefe	36	Hubert Timmary
4	Johann Grossmann	35	Erwin Fröhlich
6	Alberto Koch	43	Robert Zier
7	Gaston Kuck	44	Oscar Zier
8	Richard Noske	45	Hermann Rascher
9	Carlos Sarwade	46	Waldomiro Lindberg
10	Johannes Schindler	49	Dora Axt
11	Martha Tkotz	50	Margarita Anger
13	Rudolf Neudan	51	Rita Tkotz
21	Werner Haase	52	Ronald Tkotz
22	Otto Garthner	53	Fritz v. Ulaszewicz
24	Raimar Ulaszewicz	54	Cassiano Schönherr
25	Otto Stern sen.	55	Annie Ulaszewicz geb. Arendt
27	Jorge Philipp	56	Olga v. Ulaszewicz
28	Eduard Schulz	57	Erna Schönherr
29	Max R. Mosimann	58	Charlotte Kuck
30	Peter Haase	61	Hellmut Hameike
31	Richard Nilson	62	Peter Tkotz
37	Hanni Schindler	63	Wilhelm Braunschweig

Summa: 42 Mitglieder

Neu Danzig d. 24 Februar 1935

Erich Anger

1. Scharführer

The list of supporters of the German School. Waldomiro Lindberg is at #46. Eduard Schulz is #28. (Courtesy of Cambé Historical Museum)

Eduardo Schulz on his *fazenda*. (Photo by Marian Lindberg)

Aynore Soares after riding through the Pantanal, 2012. (Photo by Marian Lindberg)